Spying on America

Also from Westphalia Press
westphaliapress.org

Spying on America

Leon G Turrou's
The Nazi Spy Conspiracy in America

Introduced and Edited by Paul Rich

WESTPHALIA PRESS
An imprint of the Policy Studies Organization

Spying on America
Leon G. Turrou's
The Nazi Spy Conspiracy in America

Westphalia Press
An imprint of Policy Studies Organization
dgutierrezs@ipsonet.org

For information:
Westphalia Press
1527 New Hampshire Ave., N.W.
Washington, D.C. 20036

ISBN-13: 978-1-935907-17-6
ISBN-10: 1935907174

Cover design by Taillefer Long at Illuminated Stories: illuminatedstories.com

Updated material and comments on this edition can be found at the Westphalia Press website: westphaliapress.org

This edition is dedicated to
Alain Bauer, a grand master of
intelligence and security studies.

INTRODUCTION TO THIS EDITION

AN EARLY WHISTLE BLOWER

With the advent of the Internet, debates over American espionage and civil rights have become frequent, but this is not the first time that there has been public debate about the role of the American government in thwarting foreign powers.

Those for whom the name Leon G. Turrou seems somewhat familiar are likely to be inveterate film buffs who on some late night Saturday program have seen the 1939 film *Confessions of a Nazi Spy*, which starred Edward G. Robinson and George Sanders. Hollywood took many liberties with Turrou's book, and it is worth recalling what actually happened in the late 1930s.

In January 1938, a postman in Dundee, Scotland, thought he saw peculiar behavior on the part of a woman hairdresser and the Military Intelligence Department of the British War Office became involved in monitoring her. The British authorities alerted their American colleagues to what seemed to be a ring of American spies. Turrou, an FBI agent, was put on the case.

The head of the FBI, J. Edgar Hoover, didn't want his agency involved because he felt it was a complex and muddled situation. But the Bureau reluctantly did take responsibility. Turrou's interviews, including those with Dr. Ignatz Greibl, head of the ring, tipped the agents to the investigation and some fled. Even worse, Turrou talked freely to the New York press. He was denounced for his openness, which allegedly was more for fame and money than to expose the situation.

This was a high or arguably low point in a remarkable life. Leon George Turrou was born in 1895 in Kobryn, Poland. His father had died before his birth and his mother soon after. He was adopted by a rich businessman and went to schools in Berlin and London, moving to America at the age of eighteen. There he became a translator for the *New York Times*.

In 1916, Turrou joined the French Army, was wounded, and while recovering met his future wife. In 1923, Turrou returned to America and worked as a postal inspector. In 1928, Hoover hired him and while an agent he was in a shootout with the gangster Pretty Boy Floyd, part of the Lindbergh baby kidnapping investigation, and agent in the case of the crash of the USS Akron (ZRS-4). When he became involved with the Nazi spies, Hoover became angry over the leaks to reporters, heard that Turrou planned a book, and fired him.

During World War Two, Turrou was an intelligence officer on the staff of General Dwight Eisenhower. He was decorated with the Bronze Star for his courage.

After the war he worked for the billionaire J. Paul Getty and lived mostly in Paris. He was involved in negotiations with the Vietnamese in the mysterious affair of the missing pilot Captain Robert Tucci. He died in Paris at the age of 91 in 1986.

Leon Turrou is arguably an original whistleblower and his revelations about government security got him into deep trouble. He was not the only one to tangle with Hoover, and his subsequent career suggests a more substantial motive than fame or money.

Paul Rich
Garfield House, Washington

H

THE NAZI SPY CONSPIRACY
IN AMERICA

LEON G. TURROU

THE NAZI SPY CONSPIRACY
IN AMERICA

By

LEON G. TURROU

With Fourteen Illustrations from Photographs

ILLUSTRATIONS

CHAPTER ONE

ON June 1, 1937, Dr Ignatz T. Griebl, widely known New York surgeon and obstetrician, sailed for Germany on the s.s. *Europa*, of the North German Lloyd Line, with a handsome woman who was down on the passenger list as Mrs Katherina Moog Busch, of New York.

They received most unusual attention on board, particularly from a crop-haired, blond man named Karl Schluter, carried on the ship's manifest as a steward. They were closeted with him in his cabin, F21, almost daily, and no officer interfered or even looked askance. For Schluter was no ordinary steward. He was *Ortsgruppenführer* of the *Europa*, which meant that he was supreme arbiter of matters political and pertaining to the National Socialist Party on board the ship. He was also a dangerous Nazi spy organizer and 'contact' man.

At Bremerhaven Dr Griebl and the woman were met by Kapitan-Leutnant Dr Erich Pfeiffer, an erect, autocratic man with a cold blue eye. The crowd on the pier had not recognized him or even known he existed. If it had, there would have been a good deal of whispering and gaping. For he is head of the Bremen office of the *Marine Nachrichten Stelle*, which is the Nazi Naval Intelligence Bureau, in charge of all Nazi spy activities in North and South America.

A nod from him, and they were through the Customs. He led them, with a solicitude strikingly unlike his appearance, to the Berlin express, on which they found a compartment reserved for them. He told them reservations had been made for them at the Adlon, Unter den Linden, in Berlin, one of Europe's most luxurious hotels.

7

THE NAZI SPY CONSPIRACY IN AMERICA

"I have much to discuss with you, Herr Doktor, concerning matters in the United States," he said. "But that must wait, for the others are anxious to see you at once."

An hour after they reached their rooms at the Adlon there came a knock on the door, and in walked a haughty, aristocratic man with blue eyes and blond hair, followed by a fat, bald man with small, sly eyes. Griebl recognized them at once, for Schluter had talked often of them, with pride as well as awe. He had seen and actually talked to them upon a memorable occasion. They were Kapitan-Leutnants Udo von Bonin and Hermann Menzel, chiefs of the *Marine Nachrichten Stelle*, with the entire world as their province.

Yet even they were not so high as the pudgy Dr Griebl went that day. They led him to the German War Ministry Building, 72 Tierpitzufer Strasse, and into the secretive, heavily guarded offices of the *Nationale Geheim Abwehr*, which is the Nazi Secret Defence Service, a euphemism for world-wide spy operations.

There Griebl was ushered into the presence of the powerful Colonel Busch, supreme chief of all the far-flung Nazi spy system, confidant of Adolf Hitler, answerable only to *Der Führer* himself. Under him are co-ordinated all Nazi spy activities; under him are the experts who weigh and fit together the bits of information gathered up by the Nazi spy drag-net. It is he who decides what secrets must be secured at any cost.

"I have summoned you here, Dr Griebl," said Colonel Busch, "because I wish to thank you personally for your work in the United States. You have served the Leader and the Fatherland well. I am sure you will continue, and even increase, your efforts."

He paused, weighing his man.

"We do not ask you to do this solely out of your patriotism, which is unquestioned," he continued. "For your aid in certain matters which will be explained to you later, we offer you a fine home in Bavaria. We offer you the rank and pay of a Captain in the German Air Defence. That pay will be accumulated for you until, through desire or necessity, you come back to live in Germany."

Dr Griebl took it coolly. His eyes glittered behind the tortoise-shell glasses, but his voice was composed as he quietly explained how flattered and honoured he was by the kind words of the great Colonel Busch, and how grateful he was that his efforts were considered of some value.

"But I have a request to make of you, a favour," he added. Kapitan-Leutnants von Bonin and Menzel stiffened at his audacity, but he went on. "There is a property in Giessen that I desire," he said. "It belongs to a Jew, Berliner. Perhaps a little pressure. . . ."

Colonel Busch listened as he told the details. Then he nodded. "It shall be done," he said. "Several aspects of the matter are a trifle . . . well, bluntly, illegal. But in view of your services to the Party, I am sure they can be overlooked."

Griebl and Mrs Katherina Moog Busch—who preferred the name of Miss Kate Moog—lunched at the Adlon that day. The next day they met again for lunch, this time on the Hotel Eden roof-garden. Von Bonin and Menzel had recovered completely from their disapproval of Dr Griebl's audacity, and become quite attentive, particularly to the beautiful Miss Moog. At this second luncheon Menzel said little, eyes sliding from person to person, but von Bonin was suddenly quite talkative.

"You have been in Washington, Fräulein?" he said in a chatty tone.

"Oh, yes, often," she told him.

"And you know many people there?"

"Oh, quite a few," she said.

"And, of course, some very important personages there?"

"Well," she smiled, "some."

9

He looked directly into her eyes. " Come, now, Fräulein," he snapped. "This is no time for modesty. Some of the highest officials and the most powerful leaders of your country are your friends, *nein*?"

Her eyes, long-lashed, widened in amazement. Menzel, seemingly intent on his soup, watched her closely.

"And certain Senators and important officers of the Army and Navy are also your friends?" von Bonin continued. "Is that not true, Fräulein?"

She gasped, "But how . . .?"

He leaned forward. "There is nothing, Fräulein, we do not know about you. We know all about your connexions. You can be very useful to us—as useful, in your way, as Dr Griebl."

She glanced towards the man she loved, but he kept his eyes on his plate.

"I?" she breathed. "I can be useful to you?"

"Yes."

"But . . . how?"

"Your Army and Navy do not pay their officers well. They are very poorly paid, in fact. Many of them are in debt. We have ways of determining who those are. The loan offices in Washington have a sort of rating-bureau, so there can be no duplication by borrowers. We have access to those files."

He paused, as if expecting her to register enlightenment. But she shook her head. "I still don't see how. . . ."

"You don't, eh?" he demanded. His fingers drummed on the table, while Menzel kept watching her out of the corners of his eyes.

"You are a beautiful woman," von Bonin resumed suddenly, throwing the compliment at her as if it were an accusation. "You have powerful friends—well, acquaintances, as you insist—in Washington. If you opened a fine house or apartment in Washington, and surrounded yourself with pretty *mädchen*, and much good food and fine liquor. . . ."

Her eyes remained intent, but bewildered. Impatience crept into the haughty officer's voice.

"You still do not see?" he snapped.

She shook her head.

"*Ach!* Don't you see that if you invite these officials, and with them these underpaid Army and Navy officers, to your establishment, you can introduce them to our secret operatives? Young officers in debt, disillusioned; bitter older officers with families and heavy expense . . . pretty girls . . . good food . . . good drink . . . and our agents to tell them how they can make money?"

"Oh!" breathed Miss Moog. "Oh!"

Abruptly he shrugged his shoulders, as if dropping the subject. "It is really Kapitan-Leutnant Pfeiffer's matter. He will speak with you further on the subject in Bremen. I mentioned it only so that you would have time to think of it."

He caught a faint signal from Menzel.

"And about money," he started anew. "I nearly forgot. The German Government will of course pay for the flat or house, and for the expense of operating it. We cannot guarantee you a salary in the beginning, but you will live handsomely, and there will be two or three trips a year to Germany with expenses paid. Later on we may be able to make even better arrangements."

Then he let her glimpse the blackjack behind the cajolery.

"Besides," he said, "there is a house you own in Germany, *nein?* At present virtually the entire income goes to the Government. And—who can tell? It might be found necessary to appropriate the entire income, or even to confiscate the property. On the other hand, it might be that we could arrange it entirely differently. . . ."

Kapitan-Leutnant von Bonin nodded towards Dr Griebl.

THE NAZI SPY CONSPIRACY IN AMERICA

"The Herr Doktor," he continued, "can testify how well we repay loyalty and services to *Der Führer* and the Fatherland."

He did not demand that she should give an answer immediately. Both he and Menzel telephoned her, separately, several times during the remainder of her and Dr Griebl's stay in Berlin, but whether because they were smitten by her charms, or because they wanted to deal with her directly without Dr Griebl's knowledge, remains a mystery. She did not see them again.

Two weeks later Dr Griebl and Kapitan-Leutnant Pfeiffer met again, in the lobby of the Hotel Columbus, in Bremen. They met at seven o'clock in the evening, and Miss Moog was to join them at eight o'clock for dinner. Meanwhile the men found a quiet corner in the bar and sat down to talk. At first they merely exchanged amenities and compliments, sparring and feeling each other out. But as the glasses were emptied, and refilled, and emptied again, the weakness appeared in the frigid armour of the gruff, autocratic Pfeiffer. He had a passion for boasting of the accomplishments of the Nazi spy ring he directed. Not foolishly or dangerously, but with a tested, trusted man like Dr Griebl he could not resist.

"There are many things I could tell you, Herr Doktor," he said pompously, but with a gleam in his eye, "which would amaze even you. For, after all, Griebl, though you are the trusted head of our espionage base in New York—I might even say our most important espionage director in America —we are not foolish enough to allow any one man to know too much. Even you might be apprehended and forced to talk."

Griebl shrugged. "That is possible," he said calmly, "but highly improbable. They are fools in the United States. They do not think of espionage. Besides, I am above suspicion. I am not only a reputable, prominent physician, you must remember, but also an officer of the United States Army Reserve."

Pfeiffer nodded his head. "I know," he said. "That is fine. You are a clever man, Doktor Griebl. But as I said before, there is much you do not know. You must realize, Griebl, this is a far more elaborate, a far vaster matter than anyone besides the leaders here in Germany comprehend. I'll wager you do not know one-quarter of our operations in Washington. I'll wager you cannot name one-tenth of our agents in the United States. You know some of the members of three or four of our cells in America—that is all. *Gott im Himmel*, Griebl, you are not the only sly one! There are men whom you know well, working with you openly in the un-concealed Nazi organizations in America, whom even you do not suspect of being your fellow-espionage agents—just as they do not suspect you!"

Griebl raised his eyebrows. "So?" he said. "That is interesting."

"That is nothing!" snapped Pfeiffer. "The things I could tell you! I'll wager you do not know that we now have a base in Seattle, also. And that through that base we sell many of the secrets of the United States defence to the Japanese!"

Griebl showed amazement.

"To the Japanese?" he murmured, wonderingly.

"That's right!" declared Pfeiffer, obviously enjoying the effect of his disclosures. "The Japanese consider the United States a potential enemy. They fear the Pacific Fleet. They are always most anxious for naval and military secrets of the United States. But because of their appearance, they are marked, and find it impossible to do real espionage in America themselves. So they must operate through others—and when we uncover anything of value to Japan, we sell it to them!"

A boy came through paging Dr Griebl, with the message that Miss Moog had arrived. They joined her, and through dinner, because the place was so public and so many waiters hovered over them, the talk was light and far from spy matters. The dinner was long, with wines and liqueurs, and when it was over Pfeiffer had unbent so far that he gallantly offered to show them the town. He took them to the Astoria Café, the most pretentious night-club in Bremen, and found a table which commanded a fine view, yet allowed them to talk, under the flow of the music and gay voices, without being overheard.

There they drank champagne and talked. Until three o'clock in the morning, while the music sang of romance and honour and love, and dancers swayed by, they talked of the Nazi spy ring in America, and of the Nazi conspiracy against the national defence of the United States.

They talked of Schluter, and the sly, dangerous Theodor Schütz. They talked of the red-headed Jenni Hofmann, and how, from a lead in America, she hired a Nazi spy in Czechoslovakia. They talked of grim, dour Otto Herrmann Voss, who stole aviation secrets, and of Werner Gudenberg, whom no one could suspect. They spoke of Günther Rumrich, the former U.S. Army sergeant, and of the perilous assignments sent him by Nazi spy headquarters. They talked of Karl Eitel and of the secretive Schmidt, who was the paymaster. They recalled the dangerous, brilliant spy, Wilhelm Lonkowski, whom Griebl helped flee the country when American authorities stumbled on his trail.

They talked of the Nazi spy base set up in New York, and of the base in Montreal, Canada, headquarters for all Canada and part of New England. They discussed the spy base at Newport News, and the sub-bases at Boston, Buffalo, Bristol, Philadelphia, San Diego, Bath, Me., and elsewhere. They chuckled over the fact that there was a Nazi spy contact in the offices of one of the most important naval designers in America.

They talked of Antonie Strassmann—Astra, the famous German aviatrix, now living in New York, who, Pfeiffer

14

declared, had betrayed the Nazi Government and now must be punished. They talked of the *Geheime Staats Polizei*, the unit of the *Gestapo*—the dreaded, brutal Nazi secret police— which was now operating in the United States, and of Karl Friedrich Wilhelm Herrmann, its swaggering chief in New York.

And Pfeiffer began again to tell of things which made Griebl again prick up his ears. Of how he got the plans of the new anti-aircraft gun developed under great secrecy at Fort Monmouth, N.J., before they even reached Washington for final approval. Of how he got the details of an important confidential talk in Washington. Of how he knew that the talk was on the weaknesses of U.S. war vessels, and on proposed drastic changes in their design.

"Griebl," he said, "within a comparatively few hours I knew the details so thoroughly that I could draw you the proposed new design!"

He paused, studying the effect on the faces of the American doctor and the beautiful woman across the small table. The orchestra was playing a Viennese waltz, but it did not soften his mood. Instead, suddenly, his manner grew hard and autocratic again, and he leaned forward stiffly, his eyes harsh.

"You do not know how far we have gone. No one knows, no one dreams. Our destiny, under Adolf Hitler, is boundless! Listen.

"In every strategic point in your United States we have an operative. In every armament factory in America we have a spy. In every shipyard we have an agent—in every key position. Your country cannot plan a warship, design a fighting 'plane, develop a new instrument or device, that we do not know of at once!

"But that is not enough!" He hammered the table with his fist. "It is not enough! We must have more information! We want the blueprints of the aircraft carriers *Yorktown* and *Enterprise*. We want the mobilization plans for the Eastern seaboard of the United States. We want the West Coast plans, the Mexican border fortifications, the Canadian border. We want the weaknesses of the new bombing 'planes you are building, and the fortifications and defences of New York Harbour. You understand me, Griebl?"

The pudgy American nodded. The woman stared at them both; then her wide glance swept to the dancers.

That was the night of June 23, 1937. I now know what happened that night from Dr Griebl and Miss Moog, and from investigations which verified their stories. But at the time no one in the United States Government knew that a Nazi spy ring was in existence in America. No one suspected it, not even the Federal Bureau of Investigation, or G-2, the United States Military Intelligence. The idea would have seemed too preposterous. Why should Nazi Germany conspire against the U.S. national defence?

It was not until seven months later that we got an inkling—and then only an inkling.

CHAPTER II

SHORTLY before midnight of January 28, 1938, the trans-Atlantic cables began clicking a confidential code message from London to the General Staff, War Department, Washington, D.C. It was very late the next afternoon before the completed message lay before Lieutenant-Colonel C. M. Busbee, of the General Staff, and the United States Government had its first real indication that a desperate Nazi spy plot was afoot.

But the information and the warning in the cable pointed to a conspiracy so vast, so melodramatic, and so fantastic that the General Staff at first felt it must be a hoax. They shot fast queries over the cables, and back came full verification of authenticity. The information came from M.I.5, the British Military Intelligence, through an American attaché in England. The attaché had seen the evidence. He knew the details of how it was secured. There was no doubting it.

Colonel Busbee got no sleep that night. At dawn he was arranging to fly to New York. By 9 A.M. he was closeted with Major Joseph N. Dalton, Assistant Chief of Staff of G-2, the United States Military Intelligence, at the headquarters of the Second Corps Area, Governors Island, New York.

Major Dalton is one of the ablest intelligence officers in the world. But he is one man. He has two assistants for the entire Second Corps Area. His assistants are capable men, too, but he and his assistants, swamped with desk-work, cannot police an entire corps area against spies. Major Dalton called a taxi and brought Colonel Busbee to the New York headquarters of the Federal Bureau of Investigation, on the sixth floor of the United States Court House, in Foley Square. At 2 P.M. on Sunday, January 30, 1938, the Nazi spy case was thrown into the lap of the F.B.I.

All there was to go on was what M.I.5 had stumbled across, and been shocked by, hardened as intelligence officers are to spy desperation. The British have a real intelligence service; America has virtually none. The American nation is not at all 'spy-conscious,' or on guard against spies; the British are very much so. They have to be, situated as they are in a section of the world seething with hatreds, and vulnerable as they are, geographically, to surprise attack.

Even the postmen are on the alert there. It was a Scottish postman, in Dundee, who first lifted the cover off the gigantic Nazi spy ring in the United States.

There lived at No. 1 Kinloch Street, Dundee, a middle-aged hairdresser named Mrs Jessie Jordan. As far as anyone knew, the only relatives she had were in England and in Germany. Yet the postman noticed that she received a great number of letters from the United States, France, Holland, Canada, and South America.

He began to wonder. He communicated his wonderment to his superiors. They in turn notified M.I.5. Shrewd, bespectacled Colonel Hinchley Cooke, chief of the counter-espionage division of the British War Office, took up the trail.

The British officials have a decided advantage over their American counterparts in cases of this sort. Under a rarely invoked law, their intelligence agents may secretly open the mail of citizens and examine it, if the national defence is threatened.

Colonel Cooke soon learned enough to warrant this drastic step. He found Mrs Jordan had been married to a German, killed in action with the German Army in the World War. He found she made frequent, mysterious trips to Germany, and went to the offices of high Nazi officials there. He found that she had been seen loitering round British fortifications, sketching. He issued the orders to examine her mail.

And he discovered that the innocent-appearing address, No. 1 Kinloch Street, Dundee, was a mail relay-station for a vast, international Nazi spy ring. Nazi spies over half the world, writing for instructions from Nazi headquarters, sent their mail to that address. The envelopes were addressed to Mrs Jessie Jordan, the hairdresser, but the letters inside were written to a mysterious "N. Spielman," at Bremen, Germany, who apparently was a powerful Nazi spy chief.

For what she did, Mrs Jessie Jordan was sentenced to four years' imprisonment. But among the intercepted letters were several from America. In them a Nazi spy in the United States, who signed himself "Crown," submitted for the final approval of "N. Spielman" progress reports of his activities against the United States. These letters M.I.5 delivered to the American attaché, who cabled them to the General Staff, which turned them over to the F.B.I.

The three major points revealed by these letters were as follows:

1. The Nazi Government was so anxious to secure the secret plans for the defence of the East Coast of the United States that its spies had worked out a plan to seize them by force. They were to lure Colonel Henry W. T. Eglin, Commanding Officer of Fort Totten, N.Y., to a hotel room, with the secret orders in his possession, and there overpower him and seize the papers.

2. Nazi spies were plotting to steal the confidential codes and maps of the United States Army Air Corps.

3. Copies of White House stationery were to be prepared by experts in Germany. President Roosevelt's signature was to be forged on them in a spectacular effort to secure the complete blueprints of the newest American aircraft carriers, the *Enterprise* and *Yorktown*.

It was almost too fantastic to believe. If it had not come from such unimpeachable sources, there is a chance that it might have been filed away in a pigeon-hole. There was no conceivable motive. Germany and the United States were supposed to be quite friendly nations. The Nazi Ambassador, Hans Dieckhoff, was being cordially received in Washington. Germany's citizens in America had utmost liberty; the Government even permitted uniformed Nazi Storm Troopers to drill, and accorded them police protection against anti-Nazis. It was utterly preposterous and unbelievable—yet there it was.

The first step we had to take was to protect Colonel Eglin and the secret coast-defence plans. We warned him, and sent agents to guard him. We knew some details of how they intended to lure him to a hotel room with the plans from the intercepted letters; the complete story I learned later from spies we captured.

The scene was to be a room in the McAlpin Hotel, Broadway and 34th Street, New York City, rented by one of the spies. At first officials toyed with the idea of having a woman lure Colonel Eglin to the hotel, but there were two flaws in that plan. One was that they could not decide how they could get him to bring the secret orders to a rendezvous with a woman, and the other was that they found that he was not the type of man who could be lured to a hotel room by a woman.

The staff work of these Nazi spies was most thorough. One of them, who was working on the plot, but who never saw Colonel Eglin, was able months later to give me a perfect description of him. He told me Colonel Eglin was five feet, eleven inches, but seemed even taller because of his military bearing; that he weighed 170 pounds and was obviously in perfect trim; that he was fifty years old; had very alert, intelligent, and slightly prominent eyes; pointed, dark moustache which seemed waxed, and dark hair strikingly streaked with white.

The second and final plan was to entice him to the hotel room by faked military orders. One of the spies, a former non-commissioned officer in the United States Army, familiar with the correct military terminology, typed out the following order:

> A secret emergency staff meeting is scheduled to be held at the McAlpin Hotel, New York, N.Y., on [left blank, apparently to be filled in when the date was definitely decided]. Your attendance is requested, and you are called upon to observe the following details:
>
> 1. You will not divulge the nature or circumstance of the meeting to anyone.
>
> 2. You will appear in civilian clothes and arrive and leave unattended.
>
> 3. You will time your departure so as to arrive at the Hotel McAlpin at 12.20 P.M.
>
> 4. You will seat yourself in the main lobby of the hotel and will await being paged as Mr Thomas W. Conway. After identifying yourself as such you will be escorted to the meeting-rooms.
>
> 5. You will bring with you all mobilization and coast-defence plans in your possession, also pertinent maps and charts and a notebook for entries at the meeting.
>
> 6. It is repeated that the utmost discretion is expected of you in regard to this meeting, as no one is to be informed except those directly concerned.
>
> 7. You will acknowledge receipt of this memorandum by repeating the same to the officer 'phoning you this message.
>
> Signed:
>
> MALIN CRAIG
> MAJOR GENERAL
> UNITED STATES ARMY
> CHIEF OF STAFF

A spy was to telephone that message to Colonel Eglin at Fort Totten. The same spy, a man with the bearing of a soldier and experience in the United States Army, was to approach Colonel Eglin after he answered to the name of Thomas W. Conway. Then he was to lead the Colonel, with the secret papers in his possession, to the trap.

There two other Nazi spies, disguised as window-cleaners, were to be waiting. They were to overpower him and seize the papers. They were not to kill him "unless absolutely necessary."

They were to leave their window-cleaners' disguises behind, together with a copy of the *Daily Worker*, New York Communist newspaper. This was to show the police later that the deed was the work of Communists.

It sounded, it must be admitted, like a silly, a most preposterous plot. It sounded as if it couldn't work; as if it were impossible that Colonel Eglin could thus be lured to a hotel room with the mobilization plans. But as Colonel Busbee and Major Dalton and the F.B.I. operatives thought it over, it became apparent that it was possible that it might have worked. After all, America is at peace, and totally lacking in spy-consciousness. The very brazen preposterousness of the plot was in its favour. How could a sane, intelligent man, though he might be puzzled by the oddness of the meeting-place, suspect that the spies of any nation would be going to desperate lengths to secure the defence plans? The message sounded like a genuine military order, and Colonel Eglin's soldierly training was to obey orders. . . .

"The matter," wrote the spy "Crown" to his chief in Germany, "will probably stir up a little dirt. But I believe that it will work out all right.

"The arrangements have been made with extreme care, every little detail has been reckoned with, and so it remains to be seen how the affair will work out."

That plot was never carried out, but the possibility that it might have worked was heightened in our minds later, when, deep in the spy investigation, I discovered how, by a trick just as seemingly childish and simple, a Nazi spy secured confidential information from an Army post in America.

The spy had been ordered by his headquarters in Germany to obtain the exact figures on the strength of the Army in the Second Corps Area, the names of the commanding officers, and other data.

A telephone call did the trick.

The spy got Fort Hamilton, N.Y., on the 'phone and brusquely commanded to be connected with the Sick and Wounded Clerk at the Station Hospital there.

"This is Major Milton," the spy snapped. "I am about to deliver a lecture before a group of physicians in Brooklyn. I require the statistical reports on venereal diseases in the Second Corps."

He didn't give a hoot about the venereal disease figures. But the reports are so drawn that, in addition to those figures, they give the exact man-power of the army in this area and the names of all officers, and just where they are stationed, together with other incidental data.

"I am at 86th Street and Fourth Avenue, Brooklyn," the spy continued in the same military tones. "I am in civilian dress. You will send those reports to me at once, by special courier, in a taxi."

"Yes, sir," the Army clerk replied eagerly. "The Major shall have them as soon as possible. A man will start at once."

"I want them in twenty minutes!" snapped the spy, and hung up.

Within twenty minutes a taxi went racing up to the corner and a soldier leaped out, holding an official envelope. The spy stepped forward. "From Fort Hamilton?"

"Yes, sir," replied the soldier, saluting smartly. "Here it is, sir." And he handed over the envelope. It was as easy as that. The spy paid the taxi-driver, but not for a ride back to the Fort. The soldier was left to get back the best he could, but he went off cheerfully, conscious of having pleased the brusque Major Milton.

There is a Major Milton stationed at the United States Army Building, 39 Whitehall Street, New York City, but, of course, he was unaware that his name was being used.

Colonel Eglin promised to be careful when we informed him of the plot against him, and he was. But he was inclined to laugh at the matter, convinced he would not have been fooled by such an order.

We were amazed to learn that the spies were right in picking Colonel Eglin as an officer with access to such important secret plans. Fort Totten is the headquarters of the 62nd Coast Artillery, an anti-aircraft unit which had a short time before figured prominently in General Headquarters Air Force manœuvres, but it is not customary for officers of the rank of Colonel Eglin to have custody of such plans. But Colonel Eglin is a more important member of the U.S.A. Army high command than his rank indicates. How the Nazi spies knew this we still do not know. We did find out, however, that because he had represented the Army in several missions in Europe, he was considered in diplomatic circles in several European capitals to be a very high officer of the Army.

The two other Nazi spy plots mentioned in the letters to "N. Spielman" were harder to block. It seemed, in fact, impossible.

No details were given in the letters of the plot to steal the confidential codes and maps of our Air Corps. Copies had to be, of necessity, in a number of places and in the hands of quite a number of Army officers. Colonel Busbee and Major Dalton issued a warning to all Army posts—but there was no telling where the spies might strike, or how deeply they had wormed their way.

As to the plot to forge President Roosevelt's signature and to fake White House stationery, all we had to go on was the marvellously accurate printing-specifications contained in the spy's letter to "N. Spielman." The letter referred to plans for obtaining the blueprints of the aircraft carriers *Yorktown* and *Enterprise*, but gave no details. We could not broadcast warning too widely, for we did not want to startle the spies into flight. We wanted to keep the trail warm, slight as it was. The letter also indicated that the faked stationery was to be used for other spy coups—but there was no hint as to their nature.

There was the problem as it lay in the lap of the F.B.I. There we were, suddenly aware that a most fantastic and apparently dangerous and desperate Nazi spy conspiracy against our country was under way with all hell liable to pop loose any moment—and not a single clue to the identity of any of the Nazi spies.

All we had was the name—"Crown"—typed as a signature to the typewritten letters to the mysterious "N. Spielman." It was, obviously, a pseudonym. Who was this dangerous Nazi spy who called himself "Crown"? What did he look like? Which of the 9,000,000 people in the New York metropolitan area was he?

Where could we begin? Our trap was set in case they got after Colonel Eglin, but we had little faith that that would happen. We felt they must know that their plan had gone wrong.

At first there seemed one possible clue to the identity of "Crown," a slim clue, but one to work on. His letters to "N. Spielman" indicated that he was a former pilot in the United States Army Air Corps, and that he had recently applied for reinstatement.

"When it came to fill out the space as to the choice of station," the treacherous Nazi spy here wrote to his master in Germany, "I named the following in the order given:

"Mitchel Field, Long Island, N.Y.
"Barksdale Field, Louisiana.
"Albrook Field, Canal Zone.

"I named Mitchel Field as choice Number One because it is the Headquarters of the Eastern Division of the G.H.Q. A.F. I have comrades out there, and can do some good work there, such as code-books, maps, etc.

"I am awaiting your instructions. . . ."

And so the F.B.I. checked up on every former Army pilot who recently had applied for re-enlistment. We followed them, we checked their movements, we used every possible means of investigation. But in vain. We got no trace of "Crown" that way.

Every moment we expected the telephone to ring and bring word of a spectacular spy coup. It was a harassing, nerve-racking period.

We knew "Crown" lived in New York. He was apparently a man of some education. We knew he had served in the United States Army as an officer or as a clerk in the office of an Army executive. He was apparently familiar with photography, and knew how to make precision measurement. He was daring, carried himself like a soldier, and had imagination.

He had recently moved from one flat to another, was married, and probably had at least one child; his German was fluent and academic; his English was very good; he used a typewriter with facility, but with the 'hunt-and-pick' system; he owed a lot of money; and he was a liar.

How did the F.B.I. know so much about him, if we had not the slightest clue to who he was or where to find him? Partly from careful study of the letters which the British Military Intelligence had intercepted, and partly by deduction.

That he lived in New York and had moved recently was plainly stated in the letters. The rest was for the most part deduction. That he was married and had at least one child was indicated by the fact that he bothered to mention that his new flat was "larger and brighter, and on the ground floor," which sounded like a family man. The language of the letters indicated education and a good mind. Close examination of the typing revealed that it was done swiftly but with uneven pressure, as the typing of a man much used to the machine, but who had never learned the professional touch system.

That he was fluent in academic English and German was indicated by references to translations. That he had served in the Army was proved by the perfect military tone of the faked orders he drew up to lure Colonel Eglin to a hotel room.

That he was daring and had imagination was plain from the dangerous schemes he undertook, and that he carried himself like a soldier was probable, because he was to be the spy who was to approach Colonel Eglin.

That he owed a lot of money was indicated by the way he referred to money in his letters to "N. Spielman." He had a way of referring to it back-handedly, like a man in need of money but ashamed to come out with it because he had no legitimate excuse.

That he was a liar was proved by his reference to himself as a former United States Army pilot now seeking re-enlistment. Our check-up in that direction was too thorough for us to have made a mistake. So "Crown" was, for reasons of his own, lying to his chief, "N. Spielman."

That he was familiar with photography and knew how to make exact, minute measurements was shown by the specifications he sent for the manufacture of fake White House stationery in Germany.

He had clipped from the *New York Times* of December 14, 1937, a reproduction of President Roosevelt's memorandum to Secretary of State Hull on the sinking of the United States gunboat *Panay* by the Japanese.

This he enclosed in the letter to spy headquarters at Bremen, with the following marvellously exact instructions:

(1) Quality and size of reproductions of White House letter-sheets to be same as this letter.

(2) Imperative that no watermarks can be detected on letter-sheets.

(3) Envelopes 105 × 240 mm.; same quality as letter-sheets.
Specifications for printing

(1) The words "THE WHITE HOUSE" to be exactly same as per enclosed clipping. Begin 14 cm. from the right-hand margin and 45 mm. from the top. To arrive at precisely the exact size of type, enlarge enclosed photographed document so that enlarged typewriter letters correspond with the typewriter letters of this letter. This will give the correct proportion.

(2) Similar heading on envelopes, in upper left-hand corner. First letter, 'T,' to be placed 7 mm. from left margin and 15 mm. from the top.

(3) Quantity of each: 50.

(4) To be sent by special messenger.

That letter was mailed January 19, 1938, from New York via the Dundee spy relay-station. Undoubtedly expert engravers and printers in spy headquarters in Germany were already at work on them. Soon they would arrive here by 'special messenger' and be handed over to "Crown." Soon the coup might be executed. And here we were knowing so much and yet without a single real clue.

Who was the 'special messenger,' and how did he get to "Crown"? Evidently he plied regularly between "N. Spielman" and "Crown," for when "Crown" wrote that he had moved, he added that he had "already sent you my address" by this messenger.

"Crown" had not slipped up even on that point. Whoever

he was, he was too sly to give any clue through the mails as to his identity or residence. There was, of course, no return address on his letters. The postmarks showed only that they were mailed from Bronx Central Annex, N.Y., which was no real clue. The original letters had been sent on to "N. Spielman" after M.I.5 copied them; so even the slim chance of finger-prints was out.

We guessed that the messenger travelled on German ships which docked at Piers 84 and 86 in New York, but that was not much help. So did thousands of other people. How could we tell which was the Nazi messenger who knew the spy "Crown"?

Then into F.B.I. headquarters, waving a letter, burst the agent who had been assigned to act as liaison with G-2. "Look at this," he exclaimed.

It was a strange letter which a bewildered young ensign in the United States Navy had just turned over to our Military Intelligence. I will not use his real name, for he had no idea what it was all about. The letter was addressed to:

Ensign W. W. Blank, U.S.N.,
U.S.S. *Saratoga*,
San Pedro, California.

Please Forward.
    You need money. You can get it easily from us. Put an ad. in the Public Notices column of the *New York Times*, as follows:
    "BROWNIE—OK for contact. W.B."
    Do not inform Intelligence Service, at your peril. We are powerful and strike hard. Act quickly—we do not like delays. We must see you before you transfer to the *Enterprise*.
                                                                BROWNIE

A few days earlier we might have dismissed it as the work of a crank. It sounded so silly. But now, in view of the fantastic plots we were certain were afoot, this was worth scrutiny—particularly since we remembered that Nazi spy headquarters was desperately anxious, as witness the fake stationery plot, to get the plans and secrets of the *Enterprise* and the *Yorktown*.

We went over the letter laboriously. It was ordinary paper and envelope, purchasable at hundreds of stores, impossible to trace. We magnified the typing a hundred times to bring out every peculiarity—but that was no help until we could find the typewriter. Examination for finger-prints speedily proved worthless. The young ensign had evidently handed it round in amazement to his comrades, and it had passed through several hands before reaching us.

But one point caught our eye.

The letter—like those by "Crown"—had been mailed from Bronx Central Annex, N.Y.

A slim enough clue, but it was not much more that had led us finally to Bruno Richard Hauptmann, kidnapper and slayer of the Lindbergh baby. I had worked on that case for the F.B.I. and been in at the kill. I remembered how we had patiently narrowed the net round him by tracing the ransom bills to the section of New York in which we later found Hauptmann's home and ransom-money cache.

But whereas in the Lindbergh case there was always another ransom bill turning up, strengthening our leads, narrowing our area of search, here we so far had only these postmarks.

We turned to the G-2 files. Perhaps there, under a heading of 'Spies,' or something similar, we might find an item which seemed without importance at the time, but now, coupled with what we had, might add up to some sort of clue.

And there we did find something! Our hopes rose as we read the following entry:

"William Lonkowski. Suspected spy. Reported 9/25/35 by U.S. Customs and United States Military Intelligence."

Our hopes were almost immediately dashed, however.

Perusal of the meagre file brought us no clue—only a sinking feeling. There was only a bare outline. A William Lonkowski had been nabbed, quite by accident, trying to pass a package to a steward on the s.s. *Europa*, at New York. But the authorities, after some questioning, permitted him to go, pending further examination of the contents of the package. Not until afterwards was it realized that the package contained valuable military secrets—and by then Lonkowski had disappeared!

The full story, amazing in its implications, and revealing that Lonkowski was one of the most able and dangerous spies in the world, developed later as we progressed with our investigation, and I will set it down in its proper order. But right now the main thing that struck us hard was the realization that this was no tentative, newly born conspiracy we were up against, but that this was probably part of a Nazi spy plot which had been in operation in America for at least nearly three years. Later we were to find that Nazi spy activity in the United States dated back to 1933, the year Hitler rose to power in Germany—but that is getting ahead of the story of the investigation.

Baffled, we settled back to wait for a break. There was nothing else to do. By February 14, 1938, we had done a terrific amount of investigation but had absolutely no new clues to show for our efforts. We did not know of it until five more days had gone by, but on that date the case began to break for us.

CHAPTER III

WHILE the F.B.I. hunted the elusive "Crown," vital defence secrets were being smuggled out on virtually every Nazi ship which left our ports. Sly, clever Theodor Schütz was arranging an even deeper infestation of Nazi spies. Grim, dour Otto Hermann Voss was stealing the blueprints of our new bombing 'planes from the Seversky Aircraft Corporation, on Long Island. Honest-faced Werner George Gudenberg was taking blueprints from a 'plane factory at Bristol, Pa., as he had previously from a plant in Buffalo. In New York, at Bath, Me., in Philadelphia, and at Newport News, Va., the key designs of our fighting-ships, revealing potential weaknesses, were being stolen.

Karl Schluter was plying backward and forward, making contacts, with red-headed Jenni Hofmann as a foil. The surly, hard-drinking Schmidt, whose first name no one knew, appeared mysteriously with pockets filled with one-hundred-dollar bills, paid off spies, and just as mysteriously disappeared. Furtive groups met in Dr Griebl's office in New York.

Out at Mitchel Field a spy was copying the codes of our Air Force. The spy base in Seattle was relaying more secrets to the Japanese. Leaders of the German-American Bund in the U.S. were trying to secure for Nazi spy headquarters the confidential maps of Canal Zone fortifications. So was the spy Günther Gustav Rumrich. So were Nazi spies posing as tourists in the Zone. Pretty Eleanor Böhme opened a book of matches pressed into her hand by seductive Kate Moog and found queer symbols inside. They were the Nazi spy code. Karl Friedrich Wilhelm Herrmann, chief of the brutal Nazi

Gestapo in the U.S.A., was swaggering along the streets of New York, checking up menacingly on German-Americans who refused to sell America, their land of opportunity.

At a corner table in the Café Fatherland, East 86th Street and Second Avenue, New York, sat a tall man with a long pompadour combed back from an almost freakishly high forehead. He was making love to a blonde German girl, and confiding to her that he was a German secret agent. That was "Crown."

From Germany secret orders were coming: "We need blank American passports." Nazi spies in France and Russia had been using forged American seamen's certificates. They had been exposed. Now spy headquarters wanted to try forged American passports. The assignment went through Schluter to Rumrich, in New York.

Rumrich was afraid.

"It is impossible," he protested.

"We must have them," snapped Schluter.

"I shall be caught. . . ."

"We must have them!" repeated Schluter grimly. "If you fail. . . ."

Rumrich remembered the *Gestapo*. He paled.

"*Ja wohl,*" he said. "I will do it."

Günther Gustav Rumrich was born on December 8, 1911, in Chicago, Ill., where his father, Alphonse Rumrich, a graduate of the *Kadetten Schule* in Vienna, was secretary of the Austria-Hungarian Consulate General. That made him an American citizen, but when he was two years old, his father was transferred to Bremen, Germany, and young Rumrich grew up in war-torn Europe.

He was brought up at the home of his paternal grandfather near the spa Teplitz-Schönau, in Bohemia, then part of Austria-Hungary. That grandfather was Mayor of his native town. The other grandfather was a professor in the Royal Hungarian University at Budapest.

Young Rumrich was educated at the *Reichsdeutsche Schule* in Budapest and at the *Gymnasium* in Teplitz-Schönau. He was only a small boy during the World War, and by the time he was eighteen, in 1929, things were pretty bleak for young men starting life. But tales of the wealth in America were dazzling and exciting, and that was where Rumrich decided to seek his fortune. When he went to the American consul at Prague, Czechoslovakia, for information, he discovered that because of his birth in Chicago, he could claim American citizenship. This he promptly did, and on September 28, 1929, he landed in New York, with $100 in his pocket and only a few words of English at his command.

But he was a daring liar and a braggart even then, this youngster of not quite eighteen. He found the German colony in New York, and for one glorious week he posed as the son of a rich man in Germany. Then he was penniless in the land of his birth, in which he was a stranger.

He found a job as office-boy at George Borgfeld, Importers, East 18th Street, New York, at $15 a week. It did not take that firm long to find out he was not cut out for routine. He was fired. He roamed the Bowery, and then, desperate, he tried to join the U.S. Army. He was accepted on January 25, 1930.

In six months he was tired of Army life. He was too arrogant and conceited to take orders. He wanted to pose as a big shot, and spend freely. Soon he was in debt, hounded by creditors. On June 2, 1930, he deserted, with $30 in his pocket, took a train to Philadelphia, and then hitch-hiked west.

August found him in Pittsburgh, broke. He surrendered, was court-martialled and sentenced to six months, and two-thirds pay. In four months and five days he was out. (Imagine what they would have done to him in the Nazi Army!)

In the midst of all this restlessness and getting into trouble,

GÜNTHER GUSTAV RUMRICH TESTIFYING AT THE TRIAL

Rumrich, a queer mixture, studied hard. Scarcely out of the guard-house, he was promoted to surgical technician at Station Hospital, Fort Hamilton, N.Y. And a year later— November, 1932—he took the examination for sergeant, passed first on the list, and got his warrant as a sergeant in the United States Army—three years after he landed!

Pride in his rank and the increased pay kept him fairly straight for three years. His record was pretty clean while he served in the swashbuckling Canal Zone, where a dollar went far, from May, 1933, until he reached Fort Missoula, Mont., in July, 1935.

But in Montana he became restless again. Life was not gay enough. Romance kept him busy for a while, as he made love to pretty little Guri Blomquist, a sixteen-year-old farm-girl who lived near the Fort. He married her; she adored him; but it didn't cure the twist in his mind. He had to keep playing the big shot, spending more money than he had, throwing parties, drinking in swank places while on leave. He began to embezzle from the Fort Hospital fund. Discovery crept close —and so he lit out again.

He hopped a bus to Minneapolis on January 3, 1936, switched to Chicago to throw possible pursuers off the trail, took another bus to Pittsburgh, and then to New York. He arrived broke, a deserter, a fugitive.

He got a job as a dish-washer at Meyer's Restaurant, on Fulton Street, at $10 a week. But that didn't suit him. He quit and went to work for a former Army buddy at the Spic and Span Restaurant, 42nd Street and Eighth Avenue.

Meanwhile, in less than seven years, while drinking and gambling in and around Army posts, while fleeing as a deserter and living in the Bowery and working as a dish-washer, he had studied so hard and learned so well that he was able to get a job as a teacher of German to Americans at a language school in New York.

The idea of supplementing his income by serving as a spy for Nazi Germany came to him during this period, in 1936. He made cautious inquiries in the cafés on East 86th Street, in the Yorkville section of New York, where Nazi sympathizers and men from the German ships in New York made their headquarters. And he got the idea that Colonel Walthar Nicolai, who was head of the German Secret Service during the World War, still had that post. Actually Colonel Nicolai was a member of the Reich Institute for History of the New Germany, created by Hitler to rewrite Germany history according to Hitler.

Rumrich sat down and wrote a letter to the *Völkischer Beobachter* (the Public Observer), which is the official newspaper of the National Socialist (Nazi) Party in Germany, and Hitler's personal organ. In this letter he enclosed another, to Colonel Nicolai, offering his services as a spy in the United States.

If the Nazi spy chiefs could use him, he wrote, they could get in touch with him by inserting an advertisement in the Public Notices columns of the New York *Times*, addressed to Theodor Koerner. That was the name of a noted German poet whom Rumrich had been reading—a poet who wrote stirring battle pæans for Germany 125 years ago.

Months passed. Rumrich read the Public Notices daily, but there was nothing that meant anything to him. He decided perhaps he had misread Nazi psychology. Perhaps the newspaper had failed to forward the letter. Perhaps Colonel Nicolai had thrown it away. Perhaps they were afraid it was a trap.

He had about given up hope of a job as a Nazi spy when, on April 6, 1936, the name "THEODOR KOERNER" leaped out of the Public Notices columns to meet his eye and set his pulses racing. He read on, thrilling:

"Letter received, please send reply and address to Sanders, Hamburg 1, Postbox 629, Germany."

morrow.

NOTICE IS HEREBY GIVEN THAT SER-
vel, Inc., 51 East 42d St., New York City,
has filed its trade mark "Servel" with
the Secretary of State of New York and
recorded with the Clerk of New York
County, to be used on labels and containers, &c.

JERRY O'LEARY SOLD, FREE OF DEBTS
and bills, grocery store at 334 Lenox Av.,
New York City. Nicholas Athans, attorney of purchaser, 67 West 44th St.,
New York City.

HYMAN ROSEN, 97 EAST HOUSTON ST.,
has retired from business. Samuel Rosen
will continue under name Hyman Rosen's
Son. and assume all bills after March
31. 1936.

MY WIFE, CAROLINE SIEGMAN, HAV-
ing left my bed and board this day, I
will not be responsible for any debts incurred by her after date, April 8, 1936.
Sol Siegman, 230 Riverside Drive, N. Y. C.

THEODOR KOERNER — LETTER RE-
ceived, please send reply and address to
Sanders, Hamburg 1, Postbox 629, Germany.

MICHAEL SOTTOSANTI HAS RETIRED
from partnership of M. & S. Sportwear,
335 West 38th St., April 8, 1936.

RELATIVES OF JAMES KELLY AD-
dress to Sadie Kelly, Easley, S. C., R-5.

NOT RESPONSIBLE FOR WIFE, ALICE,
debts H. A. Francis, 1,230 Boston Road.

CONGRESSIONAL LOBBY COMMITTEE:
Please investigate proposed lawyers fees.
Senate resolution 196. Mann.

11-DAY CRUISE, $105 FLAT; 8 OR MORE
West Indian outports; outside cabins;

'Tom
mar

A
thing
was
was
tory
after
noun
fenda
Gera
hold-
"Cl
his c
had
char
rest
Jud
for
noun
ing
"L
fenda
tence
adde
the
there
you
Th
othe

ADVERTISEMENT IN THE "NEW YORK TIMES"
The fifth notice down, beginning "Theodor Koerner."

It had worked! He was as good as hired as a Nazi spy. Now he would make a lot of money—now he would be a real big shot! He sat down at once and composed a long letter, in his best style.

He boasted, he exaggerated, he lied. He said he was in contact with men in key-positions. He said he had held an important post in the Army. He said he was anxious to serve Germany in any way possible, and that money was no object—though, of course, he would need money for expenses, and to pay bribes and to buy information.

It was three weeks before he got a reply to that letter, and he spent them in both suspense and high expectation. Then the reply gave him no definite assignment, nor did it mention anything about pay. It merely asked him for more details about himself. It was a registered letter, postmarked Hamburg, Germany.

On the strength of it, however, he quit his job. It was a good move for him, as it turned out, for he found a better job as a translator for the Denver Chemical Manufacturing Company, 163 Varick Street. He got it in May, 1936.

He waited anxiously for each mail—and finally came his first assignment. It came, he noticed in wonderment, in an envelope postmarked New York. He did not yet know of the elaborate spy messenger and transport system the Nazi spy chiefs maintained on German passenger vessels plying between Germany and the United States.

But the letter looked all right. It was, like the first, on flimsy paper, such as is used in offices for carbon copies, typewritten in German, with a typewritten signature. The signature was:

"Sanders."

The letter gave Rumrich a childishly easy assignment. It apparently, even he saw, was to test him. It asked for the names of the United States Army regiments stationed in the

Panama Canal Zone, their strength and types, and the names of their commanding officers. Part of this Rumrich knew from memory, having served there. The rest he filled in by checking with the *Army and Navy Register*, a service publication.

For this information he got a letter of thanks, with two twenty-dollar bills enclosed. One bill was the kind in current use ; the other was one of the old-fashioned, large-sized bills, long since retired.

Rumrich was jubilant. This was easy. It was like found money. They must be ready to pay plenty for real information!

Three days later he got a telephone call at the chemical company's office.

"Hallo," said a guttural, unmistakably German voice. "Is this Mr Günther Gustav Rumrich?"

"Yes," he responded, wondering who this could be.

"I have just come from Germany. From Hamburg," continued the voice, stressing the word "Hamburg."

Rumrich tensed. Was this a trap—or was it full recognition? A man sent all the way from Germany to contact him!

"I have a message," the voice went on. "From Sanders—Postbox 629."

"Oh, yes," said Rumrich eagerly. "Yes?"

"Where can we meet?"

Rumrich thought quickly. He was living in a small room, with a German family, his wife being still in Missoula, Mont., where he left her when he deserted.

"The Café Hindenburg," he said. "It is on East 86th Street. . . ."

"I know," interrupted the voice. "At eight o'clock to-night, *ja*?"

He seemed about to ring off.

"But wait!" cried Rumrich. "How shall we know each other?"

The voice chuckled. "I shall know you," it said. "I have

39

seen you there, on previous visits. We know much about you."

The receiver clicked, leaving Rumrich gasping.

But at eight o'clock that evening he was at the Café Hindenburg. It is like a bit of Germany transplanted to the Yorkville section of New York. The talk is German, the food is German, the drinks are German, the music is German, the dances are German, the advertisements and signs are in German. It is in the same block where Bruno Richard Hauptmann lived, spending the ransom-money he got for the kidnapped Lindbergh baby, already murdered. It is a rendezvous for the crews of German ships when they are in port. It is where Rumrich later met several important Nazi spies, and where they gave him instructions direct from Nazi spy headquarters.

As Rumrich walked in, not knowing which way to look first, a man half rose from a table in a corner. He made a slight motion, and Rumrich walked towards him, sizing him up.

He saw a man of about forty-two, of medium height, stocky, with blue eyes and blond hair cropped in true Teutonic fashion. The eyes were bitter and glaring, and the man looked as if he had a violent temper.

This was the dangerous Karl Schluter, chief contact man in New York for that master spy organizer, Kapitan-Leutnant Pfeiffer. Some Americans who have travelled on the s.s. *Europa* might have recognized him as the steward who seemed to have surprisingly little to do, and who was treated with a strange deference by the rest of the ship's crew. They could not suspect this was only a disguise for one of the most desperate spies and important contact men in the Nazi secret service. And they could not guess he was leader of the Storm Troopers aboard the *Europa*—for no American would even dream there were such things as Nazi Storm Troopers aboard.

They might have smiled less and enjoyed the trip less had they realized that this seeming steward was a dangerous enemy of the United States—the man who smuggled back to Germany some of America's most vital defence secrets.

This was the man who motioned to Rumrich that night in the Café Hindenburg in New York and said:

"Sit down, Rumrich. I want to talk to you."

For ten minutes Schluter talked of the weather, and what a *gemütlich* place this was—'like Germany'—and Rumrich followed his lead, waiting for him to make the first real gambit.

Then Schluter motioned for more beer. He raised his glass, and a fanatical gleam came into his eyes. "*Heil, Hitler!*" he huffed, rigid.

"*Heil, Hitler!*" chimed Rumrich.

Schluter wiped his mouth.

"It is good," he said, "that young men like you, who have been in the United States Army, as a sub-officer, should volunteer to help us."

Rumrich, that glib talker and liar, promptly launched into a long speech of admiration for *Der Führer*, for Nazi Germany, and all that Hitler and the Nazi Government stood for.

Schluter listened with a pleased look for a while, but towards the end his eyes grew sardonic.

"*Ja, ja,*" he broke in abruptly. "And for money! I know."

Rumrich reddened slightly, but started to explain. "Expenses ... poor pay. ..."

Schluter cut him short.

"It will be taken care of," he snapped curtly. "You will hear from a man named Schmidt. He will pay you a regular sum each month. For real information we will pay—we will pay goot money."

He motioned for more beer.

"Listen here, Rumrich," he said. "The United States has two new ships—aircraft carriers—which carry aeroplanes. For the plans of these ships—the real plans, which will show their weaknesses as well as their strength—we will pay $1000."

Rumrich was listening, his mind already whirling. One thousand dollars! But—how could he get those plans?

It was as if Schluter read his mind.

"There are ways," he barked. "Meet young Navy officers. Get girls for them. Offer them money. We will pay. There are other ways. I don't mind telling you—we have checked up very carefully on you—that we plan to get copies of White House stationery. A letter from the President! What that could not bring!"

He drank his beer.

"Or you might make friends with a German who is also a Nazi, who is employed in the designing-offices. We get much information that way."

Rumrich was fascinated.

"Young officers. . . ." he repeated. "White House stationery. . . ." His excitement was obvious. "But how. . .?"

Schluter looked at him with cold disgust.

"That is what we would pay you for!"

But two beers later he grew a little more expansive. He even condescended to boast a little, to give Rumrich a glimpse of the fact that he was only a minute cog in a vast spy machine.

"Those plans," said Schluter, "we can get without you. We do not leave such things to one man. We have many others working on those problems, men more experienced, with better chances of success than you.

"On March 1 we are making a contact with a high naval official. We may get them from him. I have a man at Newport News, Va., in the shipyard there, a most important man, whom no one in your stupid country suspects. Somehow we will get them. We do not fail! I assign you, I assign another man, I assign a dozen. One must succeed!

"Only the money goes to whoever succeeds. As you progress in importance, the price rises. This is your opportunity to show us whether you are just a clod, or

KARL SCHLUTER

an agent of daring and skill, to be trusted with important assignments."

Rumrich's small jaw tightened. "I will do my best," he swore. "I will get them for you!"

"That is goot," said Schluter. "*Heil!* Meanwhile, tell me this.

"Do you, through your Army connexions, know of plans for a device of greater efficiency in detecting the approach of enemy aircraft? There are two such your Army is experimenting with that interest us. Do not ask me how we know; we know, that is enough. One is a method of mounting anti-aircraft guns on or directly behind the carriage of searchlight devices and synchronizing them. The other is a heat device, for detecting approaching aircraft at a greater distance than possible hitherto. We want to know about them in more detail."

Rumrich didn't know, but promised to find out.

(Schluter was right on one device, anyway. At the time he was talking to Rumrich, experimental tests were being made at the Army Signal Corps Reservation at Fort Monmouth, N.J., to establish the efficiency of just such a heat device. That was a real military secret, closely guarded. There is no harm in my revealing it now, since the Nazis have known it for two years. How did Schluter, the supposed steward on the s.s. *Europa*, know it? I don't know. I don't know if he was right about the combination searchlight and anti-aircraft gun device, but from what I discovered about the way this vast Nazi spy ring got our defence secrets, he probably was.)

Rumrich left Schluter that night with his head spinning with daring, fantastic spy plots, and a grim final warning in his ears. "If you betray us," Schluter had threatened, "you will die like a dog! And don't forget you have relatives abroad. Our vengeance will be upon them, too!"

He saw Schluter many times in the twenty months that followed. Sometimes red-headed Jenni Hofmann was with him. And, as promised by Schluter, the mysterious Schmidt came to see Rumrich at intervals and paid him off. Schmidt would telephone him at his office to make an appointment, then meet him outside, or at his home at night, or at the Café Hindenburg. A hard drinker, Schmidt sometimes became garrulous—but always managed to remain a mystery.

He would boast to Rumrich of the big things the spy ring was doing and talk familiarly of high figures in the Nazi Government and display huge rolls of hundred-dollar bills, which made Rumrich's eyes glitter. But he never explained exactly who he was, or where his headquarters were, or on what ship or ships he travelled, or how he got his orders and knew how much to pay.

Nevertheless, on the strength of this fantastic arrangement, Rumrich decided to settle down and build his future. In February, 1937, he got together $300. With it he made a down payment on furniture at the Ludwig-Baumann Furniture Store in the Bronx, and sent for his girl-wife and their baby. The child, named Günther Gerald, was born on June 22, 1936, at Missoula, Mont., while Rumrich was fleeing desertion and embezzlement charges.

He set them up in a three-room flat at 951 Jennings Street, in the Bronx, a busy, noisy neighbourhood, filled with $25- to $40-a-month flats, two and a half blocks from the Freeman Street station of the West Side I.R.T. subway, which becomes an elevated line by the time it reaches there.

By June, when the child was a year old, he decided that the spy business was good enough to warrant a larger flat. He moved to a four-room place at 1261 Merriam Avenue, in the Bronx, on the ground floor of a four-storey brick building containing about sixteen flats. It was, ironically, in a predominantly Jewish neighbourhood, and cost $48 a month.

This was some $15 a month more than the Jennings Street flat, and much more than a $22.50-a-week translator could afford.

He schemed and connived for more money. He pestered Schmidt for prompt payments. When not enough was forthcoming, he turned to love-making. In the *bierstube* on East 86th Street he posed as a single man. He borrowed $200 from Miss Emily Renn—and she never saw him again.

He started to take desperate chances in his spy activity. He even suggested daring plans to Schluter. He even got himself an assistant, a stooge, to help him. He wrote to a former Army buddy, Corporal Erich Glaser, stationed in the Philippine Islands, promising him a fine job if he came to New York when his enlistment ran out.

Glaser came. For a while he lived with Rumrich; then, lacking a job, re-enlisted, this time in the Air Corps. He got for Rumrich, among other things, some confidential code material from Mitchel Field, N.Y.

Rumrich planned to use Glaser on other, more important, more dangerous, assignments. He planned to use Glaser in the scheme to get the blank American passports which Schluter demanded. He was afraid of this scheme, but more afraid of Schluter and the *Gestapo*. He decided to have Glaser help him, and to let him take the bigger risk.

But an almost ludicrous quirk of fate intervened. Rumrich, with a feeling of peril from all sides gnawing him, was forced to attempt it alone.

CHAPTER IV

ON Monday, February 14, 1938, a man telephoned the Denver Chemical Manufacturing Company and reported that one of their translators, Günther Gustav Rumrich, was too sick to come to work that day.

The call came from a booth in a candy store on Merriam Avenue, in the Bronx. Rumrich left the booth and rode the subway to the Sub-Treasury Building, Wall and Pine Streets, Lower Manhattan. He walked past the building several times, noting the exits. There were two, and one man, no matter where he stationed himself, could not watch both. Rumrich went into a booth and called the barracks at Mitchel Field and asked for Private Erich Glaser. The odds were against it, but he got him.

"How does it go, Erich?" he asked. "Any last-minute change? Can you get away? I need you badly."

There was respectful pleading in Glaser's reply. "I'm sorry, Günther," he said. "I feel like it's my fault. I must remain here to-day, for such a crazy thing—inoculations! They won't let me off. Please forgive me, Günther."

"It makes it more risky for me without you," said Rumrich coldly. "I need you to watch one exit, while I watch the other, to see if some one leaves in response to my call. I need you to pick up the package. But you are not dependable. Never mind, I have another plan."

He hung up abruptly and left the booth. He took the subway to Grand Central Station, and there entered another booth. He telephoned the United States State Department in

46

the Sub-Treasury Building, and asked to be connected with Ira F. Hoyt, chief of the Passport Division.

"Hallo? Mr Hoyt?"

"Yes."

"This is Edward Weston speaking."

"Who?" queried a startled voice.

"Mr Edward Weston, Under-Secretary of State."

"Oh . . . ! Yes, Mr Weston. I'm sorry. I didn't expect. . . ."

"Quite natural," drawled Rumrich. "No one is aware I am in New York."

"I see," said Hoyt. "What can I do for you, Mr Weston?"

"I require thirty-five passport blanks," said Rumrich. "Please have them delivered as soon as possible to the Taft Hotel here. Address the package to Mr Edward Weston. Is that clear? Please repeat those instructions to me."

Hoyt politely explained that in view of the importance of the papers, he would have to check back. He wanted to know where "Mr Weston" was staying in New York. Rumrich made his voice imperious. He repeated the order commandingly. Hoyt seemed impressed, and promised to deliver the blanks.

But as he left the booth Rumrich felt uneasy. It seemed to his worried mind that Hoyt had sounded suspicious. He decided to take no chances, and so, instead of going directly to the Taft Hotel to claim the package as Mr Edward Weston, he waited half an hour, then telephoned the hotel from another booth.

There was no package for Mr Edward Weston.

Rumrich pondered the possible implications. Perhaps he had not allowed enough time for the wrapping and delivery of the passport blanks. Perhaps Hoyt thought it was a hoax and was ignoring the order. And perhaps the delay was because a trap was being set.

He started for the Western Union office in the Grand Central Station, but decided it was better if no one got a description of him. He stepped into a booth and telephoned the Western Union. He ordered a boy to be sent to the Taft Hotel to ask for a package for Mr Edward Weston.

Then he took the subway to 167th Street, in the Bronx, close to his home. At the corner he stepped into a pay station and called Western Union. Was there a package from the Taft Hotel for Mr Weston?

The answer was no.

He decided it was hopeless. He walked into his flat, looking so worried that his wife readily accepted his explanation that he had left his work because he was ill. He didn't even play with the baby. He sat, chin in hand, trying to figure out his next move. It looked, he decided, like a trap.

But that night Rumrich had a visitor, the mysterious Schmidt. His wife heard angry voices in the sitting room. They spoke in German, which she did not understand. Rumrich was pale when Schmidt left. He slept restlessly that night.

The next day—Tuesday, February 15—he went into a telephone-booth near his office during his lunch-hour and telephoned the Grand Central Station Western Union office again. The girl who answered shook with excitement and signalled a fellow-clerk as Rumrich asked her:

"Is there a package there from the Taft Hotel for Mr Edward Weston?"

The girl managed, with a heroic effort, to make her voice matter-of-fact.

"Yes, Mr Weston. We are holding it for you."

Rumrich thought quickly. It might be a trap, but. . . .

"Send it to your Varick Street office," he said. "I will call for it within half an hour."

He quickly ran off and went to a corner from which he

could watch the Varick Street office, to see if a boy arrived with a package. He waited until 12.55, but no boy appeared. Rumrich gave up his vigil and went back to his work as translator for the chemical company.

Hoyt had been very suspicious. He had checked up after Rumrich called him, and found Weston was in Washington. He notified the police and T. C. Fitch, special agent of the State Department. The trap had been set, first with the parcel clerk at the Taft Hotel, then with Western Union. Signals became mixed when Rumrich called Western Union during his lunch-hour on the Tuesday, however, and by the time things were straightened out, Rumrich had gone back to work. The trap seemed a flop.

But Rumrich, remembering Schluter's tone and Schmidt's words, nibbled again.

He thought it over during the afternoon and decided it might have been a case of a messenger-boy loitering on the way. At 3.30 P.M. he telephoned the King's Castle Tavern, Hudson and King Streets, where he sometimes had lunch. He asked the woman there to accept a package for Edward Weston, promising to reimburse her for the charges when he called for the package. She agreed.

At 4 P.M. Rumrich left his work and entered a cigar store and soda fountain on Varick Street, and from there he again telephoned the Western Union office, almost directly across the street. The package, they told him, had arrived from the Grand Central office.

"Send it to King's Castle Tavern," he ordered.

He sat at the soda fountain, sipping a cold drink, while he watched the front door of the Western Union office. Within fifteen minutes he saw a uniformed messenger-boy, with a package under his arm, leave and head for King Street. Rumrich paid for his drink and set out. He chose a parallel street—Houston Street—and walked down it. He arrived at

D   49

Hudson Street the same time the messenger did, and saw him enter the tavern. He waited two minutes—five minutes—ten minutes. But the boy didn't come out.

That puzzled him. He waited a little longer, then strolled in and ordered a beer. He looked at the interior carefully while drinking it. The back part was too dim for him to see clearly, and he couldn't tell whether the boy was sitting there. He finished his beer and walked out without asking for the package.

He headed towards the Ninth Avenue Elevated. At the corner of Houston Street he saw a young boy who looked as if he belonged to the neighbourhood. Rumrich approached him. "Look," he said. "There's a package for me there, but I owe the bar-tender money. Here's two dollars. Get it for me and keep the change."

As the boy entered the tavern, Rumrich walked away from the corner and watched from the opposite side of the street. He saw the boy come out with the package and walk to the corner he had just left. No one followed him; there seemed to be nothing suspicious. He whistled to the boy and motioned him over.

"Thanks," he said, taking the package and starting to walk away. But the boy blocked his way.

"Hey," he complained. "There was only twenty cents change."

"That's O.K.," said Rumrich. "Keep it."

"Whaddya mean?" argued the boy. "Only twenty cents. Is that all I get?"

"That's plenty!" snapped Rumrich—and at that moment two Alien Squad detectives closed in on him.

They took him, protesting vociferously, to headquarters. They had, in him, the thread with which the Nazi spy plot could be unravelled, but of course they did not realize it. They did not know what G-2 and the F.B.I. knew. They

THE NAZI SPY CONSPIRACY IN AMERICA

questioned Rumrich as they would any other prisoner, and Rumrich, quick-witted, lied and lied and lied to them.

At first he told them a man had stopped him in the street and told him he would pay him to get the package for him. When they scoffed at that story, he made a great show of embarrassment, and 'confessed.' The truth was, he said, that he had taken the day off from his work to do some drinking. In the Steuben Bar at Times Square, he said, he met a man who said he was Edward Weston, and they drank together. Then that man asked him to do him a favour and pick up the package for him. He huffed out his breath so that the detectives would smell the glass of beer he had drunk.

He stuck to that story so convincingly that the next day two detectives went to his office with him and sat there all day, waiting, because Rumrich told them Weston was to telephone him that day. When no call came, they were positive he was lying, and called in Special Agents Fitch and L. Clifford Tubbs, of the State Department. They questioned him at the offices of the State Department, February 16, 17, and 18, and kept him at the Hotel New Yorker the nights of February 16 and 17. Friday evening, February 18, the police took him home to see his wife and baby. They didn't know exactly how they should treat him. They really had nothing important on him so far— yet they suspected there might be more to this man than met the eye.

While at his flat they noticed a letter postmarked the s.s. *Europa*, of the North German Lloyd Line. Rumrich agreed to open it and translate it for them. He told his wife he was arrested on a minor charge and would be home soon, and went with the detectives to a restaurant, where he read the letter to them.

All this while neither I nor any other member of the F.B.I. knew of this freak arrest. I learned of it when the rest of the world did—in the morning newspaper of Thursday, February 17.

It was a badly garbled account, reading as if the man who tried to get the passport blanks was a nut. But in view of what we already knew—this man might be the break in the spy case that was baffling us!

We wanted to talk to him, and, as it happened, we did not have to ask for him. Saturday morning the Alien Squad and State Department men telephoned us and said they were bringing their prisoner to us. They had decided that the case was in our jurisdiction and that we were better equipped to handle it. They were frankly baffled, and considered the case almost hopelessly ruined because the arrest had leaked to the newspapers. The men who arrested and worked on Rumrich did their best to keep it a secret, but some fool cop who had nothing to do with the case, but wanted to appear as a big shot to the reporters, got wind of it and blabbed. It was a great break for the Nazis.

While waiting for the police and State Department men to bring Rumrich in, I got copies of the intercepted spy letters from "Crown" to "N. Spielman" and studied them again. I was deep in them when the door opened and in they walked with their prisoner.

"Here he is, Mr Turrou," they said. "We're washing our hands. Here's the statement he made to us. And here is a letter we found in his flat. It's in German. Want us to tell you what he says is in it?"

The officers were my friends, but I was anxious for them to leave. I wanted to get down to questioning this man Rumrich myself. "Never mind," I said, a little curtly, I'm afraid. "I can read it." I dropped the letter on my desk, on top of the others. They left.

I sat behind a flat-topped desk in a room on the sixth floor of the United States Court House. It was a cold morning, but clear, and the light came in from the windows behind the desk and fell squarely on Rumrich, standing there before me.

I studied him a minute, curbing my impatience. I saw a well-set-up young man of about twenty-seven, just under six feet, with black hair combed back in a long pompadour from an oddly high forehead. He had piercing, intelligent black eyes and a small, pointed chin, small, self-indulgent mouth. I'd call it a good-looking face, proud—but weak.

He stood there, erect, like a soldier, but surly.

"Why am I here?" he demanded. "What has the F.B.I. to do with it?"

That was a tip-off immediately. If he was afraid of the F.B.I., it meant he had lied to the others, that he was hiding something important. I didn't let him see I guessed that, for it was a ticklish moment. I had to find the key to his nature, the exact note, almost right away. So I watched him guardedly as he kept defiantly demanding to know why he was being held.

"Why am I being dragged from one place to another?" he complained. "First the police and then the State Department, police stations, hotel rooms, State Department office, stupid policemen questioning me, one after another—and now here! I've told all I know. What do you want of me?"

And suddenly I saw it.

It was in his eyes, in the way he carried himself. I sensed he was a braggart, that he wanted to be considered important, and that if he was pushed around he would turn sullen and defiant. I noticed he was tense with nervousness and resentment, yet I could also see that he was soldier and adventurer enough to have composed himself during the days since his capture, and to have resigned himself. That nervous, angry resentment was from something else—and now I realized what it was.

Pride! That was the keynote to this man's nature. He was one of that odd criminal type—more distressed by the minor

53

indignities of being a prisoner, the questioning and requestioning, the sneers, the blatant disbelief of his story, the being hustled from place to place—than the fate which faced him for his crime.

"Sit down," I said.

He sat down in the chair I indicated, facing me, but to my left. It was a big chair, comfortable, in which a man could relax without feeling silly. I rang for a messenger and ordered sandwiches, cigarettes, and coffee. I talked idly, stalling, while we waited, and his eyes roved over the room.

He saw a room twenty feet square, with yellow-painted walls and a grey rug, with a border of red linoleum. The desk at which we sat faced half a dozen chairs on the other side of the room. The only door was in the centre of the wall, to my left. There's something about that room. There is no hint of prison or police-station in it, yet it commands respect. It is not a soft room, yet it inspires confidence.

As we started on the sandwiches, I said:

"Well, Rumrich, I suppose you realize you're in a serious jam?"

"Yes, sir," he said, "I do."

"The other officers told me on the 'phone you've confessed to desertion from the United States Army, and to embezzlement."

"That's right, sir."

"You realize we've also got you for impersonation of Under-Secretary Weston?"

"Yes, sir."

"H'm," I said. "Quite a list." And then I added, as if half to myself, "And yet you look like a smart man."

He said nothing, but my estimate obviously pleased him.

"Now look here, Rumrich," I said suddenly. "Why did you fool those officers?"

He stiffened, but immediately relaxed further than at any

moment since he had entered the room. Of course he hadn't fooled them at all, but he liked the idea.

"Fool them, sir?" he repeated. "What do you mean?"

"This statement here," I said, picking it up. "Listen to it." I read snatches. "You're not the childish dupe this makes you out to be. This makes you out a nitwit. The dumbest jury would laugh in your face!"

It almost worked.

My statement that he was no childish dupe drew a faint smile, and the picture I drew of a jury laughing at him obviously found a hole in his armour of conceit.

"Well, sir," he said, and I held my breath, "I admit I didn't tell the police everything. It wasn't exactly like that, Mr Turrou. I didn't want to talk to those stupid policemen. Here's how it really was."

But in two minutes I knew I hadn't succeeded yet. I had heard too many tales from lying witnesses not to recognize that what he was telling me had a little more fact in it than what he told the police—but only a little more. It was still a long, long way from the truth.

I dropped my eyes from his and began to look through the papers on my desk. I was honestly disappointed, and I also wanted him to see he was not holding my interest. Sometimes a vain prisoner, his pride stung, will blurt out something he had not intended to admit, to shock back your interest.

I picked up the German letter the officers had brought along and began reading it as he droned on with his fanciful tale. It was, on the surface, merely a business letter, but my interest quickened as I recognized ambiguous words and phrases often used in spy communications. It warned Rumrich not to deal with any but accredited representatives of the writer, and referred to 'furs,' a word spies all over the world frequently use to denote secret plans. I read on, while Rumrich kept spinning his false yarn, and turned to the second page of the letter. My eye dropped to the signature—and suddenly my heart leaped and I almost jumped out of the chair. For the signature, typed, was:

"N. Spielman."

I was sure Rumrich had seen me start, but as I shot a glance at him he was still intent on putting over his story. My mind spun dizzily. Who was this man before me? It was obvious now that here was one of the Nazi spy chief's operatives. Was this not only an angle to the spy case, but the break of breaks? Was this—could this be "Crown"?

I waited a minute to marshal my thoughts. Rumrich was still going on. "And so I said to this man, 'Yes, all right, I will do it for you.' And then he told me that he wanted me to go to——"

I broke in, gambling.

"That's very interesting," I remarked. "But I know, and you know that I know, there never was any such man. Stop trying to paint a picture of yourself as a fool. I'll tell you what you are: you're a damned important spy—'Crown!'"

He jumped, eyes widening with shock. The shot had struck home! My pulse raced, for here, sitting before me in F.B.I. headquarters, picked up virtually by accident, was the mysterious "Crown" we had sought so desperately.

The game was up, and he knew it. By three o'clock the same afternoon he was ready to confess.

"All right, Mr Turrou," he said suddenly. "Let me see my wife so that I can arrange for her to go home to her folks, and I'll talk."

I picked up the 'phone and got him an outside wire. He called a store near his home and asked them to summon his wife. He stared out the window, unseeing, while he waited. When her voice came, he spoke gently, as if to a child. He told her he was all right, and that a man was coming to bring her to see him. This Rumrich was a thoroughly bad egg, an embezzler, a deserter, a liar, a spy, and a traitor to his country, but his concern for his wife seemed real.

She was weeping when she appeared; a buxom, pretty, blonde girl, not over-bright. Though only nineteen, she held a two-and-a-half-year-old son by the hand, and plainly was soon to bear another child.

"Don't cry, Guri," Rumrich said. "It's about the money I took in Montana. You go home to your mother and father in Montana. I'll come there when they let me go." He dried her tears and sent her away.

Then he began to talk. It was two o'clock on the morning of Sunday, February 20, with both of us exhausted, before I called a halt. To me he was a contradictory, fascinating character. Already it was obvious that he was merely a minor figure in this vast spy plot, yet——

He was the man who was to lure Colonel Eglin to the McAlpin Hotel. It was he who wrote the fake military orders, and was to telephone them. He was to meet the Colonel in the lobby and escort him to the trap. He was to help overpower the Colonel and steal the coast-defence plans.

He was the man who wrote those highly technical and exact instructions to "N. Spielman" for faking White House stationery.

He was the man, signing himself "Brownie," who wrote the young Navy ensign and offered him money and threats to turn traitor on the aircraft carrier *Enterprise*.

He was the spy who posed as Major Milton and thus so easily got the data spy headquarters wanted on the Second Corps Area. He did scores of other jobs for the Nazi spy ring, some dangerous, some preposterous, some silly. But all spying seems silly to our logical, orderly minds, lulled by living in a country at peace, a country secure.

Rumrich was dangerous in his way. Some of his preposterous schemes might have worked. But despite all his dangerous assignments, despite the amazing, sensational coups he was to pull off, despite his versatility and the cleverness of some of the things he did, Günther Gustav Rumrich was a sap.

He did all this for $50 a month—and the promise of bonuses. The Nazi spy leaders used him as a tool; they gave him the most foolhardy and dangerous jobs to do, and they never lifted a hand to help him since his arrest, though they aided other spies we caught.

He was even under instructions that, if ever he was caught, he was to say he was working under "Major Christopher Draper, c/o Plane Advertising Ltd., Brettenham House, Strand—Kat, London, W.C.2." That is the name and address of a British Reserve officer, who had, of course, nothing whatsoever to do with it.

But waste no sympathy on Rumrich. He was clever—almost brilliant in a way—but he had a criminal mind. I told him as much, bluntly, one day—and he admitted it. He was smart enough to read himself.

"You're right, Mr Turrou," he said. "I know it. I've got a criminal twist."

He never knew exactly for whom he was working. They kept him confused. At first he had only the name "Sanders," which he guessed was an alias, and the post-office box number in Hamburg. Some of the first few letters he got were signed "Sanders," but he was mystified by the fact that they were postmarked New York.

Then, in September or October, 1936, the letters from "Sanders" began arriving by messenger instead of by mail. Contact men like Schluter and Schmidt and Karl Weigand brought them. They explained they had mailed the previous letters to him in New York, after bringing them from Hamburg, because they had not yet completed their investigation of him and therefore would not risk approaching him.

A month later he got instructions to write to a new address. This was: "Fräulein Gisela Scheel, Gneisenaustrasse 26, Hamburg, Germany." But the letters he got back still had the same typed signature: "Sanders."

It was in November, 1937, that he got orders to use still another address—that of the Scots hairdresser in Kinloch Street, Dundee. Now he was ordered to sign himself "Crown," and that was how he got that alias.

With the change of address came a change in leadership. The name "Sanders" no longer appeared on the letters he received. The new signature was "N. Spielman," and Rumrich was never permitted to learn the true identity behind that alias. He did not know until I told him, long after, that "N. Spielman" was none other than Kapitan-Leutnant Dr Erich Pfeiffer, directing head of the *Marine Nachrichten Stelle* at Bremen. That is the Nazi Naval Intelligence, and Pfeiffer directed Nazi spies in all North and South America.

Rumrich never knew who "Sanders" was, either, or how the Theodor Koerner advertisement through which he was hired got into the *New York Times*.

"Sanders" was the alias for a Kapitan Muller, in charge of the Hamburg office of the *Marine Nachrichten Stelle*. Rumrich's first letter of application for a job was turned over to von Bonin and Menzel by Colonel Nicolai, and they in turn sent it down the line to Muller, with instructions to investigate Rumrich and hire him if he looked safe.

Muller's preliminary check through his spies and through *Gestapo* men in the United States satisfied him that it was all right to make a blind mail contact with Rumrich. So he prepared the advertisement and took it to First Officer Franz Friske of the s.s. *Hamburg*. He knew Friske, because they had served together when Muller was a captain in the Hamburg-American Line New York-Germany passenger service.

Muller gave Friske $10 and a slip of paper containing the

advertisement to be inserted. What is highly significant is that he also gave Friske a special permit, from the official Nazi Currency Exchange Division, permitting him to take the $10 out of the country. Germany is so desperate for cash that such a permit is extremely difficult to obtain, and very important reasons must be shown before one is issued. The permit places the stamp of approval of the German civil Government on the spy plot and implicates it in the conspiracy.

When the s.s. *Hamburg* docked in New York on April 3, 1936, Friske took the money and the slip of paper to Captain William Drechsel, superintendent of the Hapag-Lloyd Port in New York. (Hapag-Lloyd is the operating merger of the North German Lloyd and Hamburg-American Lines.) Captain Drechsel was too busy to examine the advertisement. If he had, I feel certain he would have torn it up. My investigation of Captain Drechsel for in the beginning I suspected him as well—convinced me he is a gentleman, a scholar, an able man of the sea, and that he had absolutely nothing to do with the Nazi spy conspiracy. He is of the highest type of the old German decent tradition, a naturalized American citizen, and would not, I feel sure, dirty his hands with anything like this.

Captain Drechsel turned the matter over to his assistant, Captain Emil Maurer, and dismissed it from his mind. Captain Maurer sent the advertisement, the $10, and a letter ordering insertions on April 6 and April 10 to the *Times* by messenger.

At the *Times* the advertisement caught the eye of Charles W. Hoyt, manager of the classified advertising department. It aroused his suspicion, for it read to him like a code, and as if it might have political meaning. Such advertisements the *Times* refuses.

So Hoyt telephoned Captain Maurer and demanded to

know if there were a hidden meaning in the advertisement. Captain Maurer assured him that it was merely a personal matter between the First Officer of the s.s. *Hamburg* and a friend named Theodor Koerner. The *Times* accepted the advertisement at a charge of $6. Later, Captain Drechsel gave Friske $4 change. Upon his return to Hamburg, Friske mailed the $4 and copies of the issues containing the advertisement to Kapitan Muller.

The history of that advertisement was important to our case in a legal sense, because it helped to establish a conspiracy. It was valuable to us in another way, too. It gave us an insight into the psychology and methods of the men we were working against, and enabled us to credit clues we might otherwise have put aside as too preposterous. After we had put together the foregoing picture of the hiring of a spy in America, nothing about this case seemed too fantastic to investigate fully, and for the first time we credited what other evidence implied— that Nazi spy headquarters was out to build the biggest peace-time spy ring here in history.

But I have, in a sense, got ahead of my story. The true identity of "Sanders" and "N. Spielman" remained a mystery until near the end of the investigation, and the Odyssey of that advertisement was the result of days of questioning, checking, and dove-tailing bits of scattered information.

The preliminary questioning of Rumrich took three long days. For two days—and far into the nights—we just talked. On the morning of the third day I called in a stenographer, and we went to work on a formal statement. It ran to 10,000 words, and took until the small hours of the fourth day.

At night Rumrich was kept in the guard-house at Governors Island, as a secret military prisoner. Even his guards knew him only as "Prisoner No. 13." Only another agent and I were allowed to see him. Each morning we got him out of the guard-house and took him to F.B.I. headquarters, and each night we saw him locked under guard again.

I wanted no further leak; I wanted no risk of losing the only prisoner-witness we had. Later events were to prove that caution even wiser than I realized at the time.

CHAPTER V

RUMRICH, of course, did some lying about his own complicity in the Nazi spy ring to the bitter end, but in the midst of his statement he suddenly blurted out a remark which blazed a trail for us and galvanized us into action.

For days he had been denying that he knew any of the other spies here. That seemed quite possible, even probable. But he also insisted that he did not know where any of the Nazi contact men could be found, how they travelled, or when one of them was next due to get in touch with him. The last part seemed preposterous, but he stuck to it steadily through the days of questioning.

And so, although we had his confession, we were really not much further advanced in smashing the Nazi spy ring. We hid an agent in his flat, and one in the office where he was employed, but we realized it was useless, in view of the fact that the arrest of Rumrich had got into the newspapers. We knew what that meant. We knew that already Nazi spies— Lord knew how many!—must have crept out of their holes and scurried in panicky flight. We knew it meant burned papers, destroyed evidence, obscured clues, covered tracks. And later I found out that was correct. The spies saw the story of Rumrich's arrest as soon as we did. It was flashed by radio, in code, to Nazi headquarters in Berlin, Bremen, and Hamburg. Nazi ships bound for this country got frantic orders on the high seas to fake their ship's manifests, change their courses, and drop off spies and contact men and *Gestapo* thugs at ports where we could not get them.

One afternoon I decided to try Rumrich once more. He

had seemed to expect that a lawyer would show up for him, or somebody arrive with bail, or with money for his wife and child.

"Well, Rumrich," I taunted, "it looks as if your fine-feathered Nazi pals have deserted you."

His eyes were bitter as he replied, "Yes, it does, Mr Turrou." He swore quietly for a moment. "That's why I want to help you smash them."

"You're not helping us very much," I said. "How about your friend Schluter?"

I really didn't dare hope it would work—but it did. Rumrich continued swearing to himself for almost a full minute; then suddenly he halted, set his small jaw, and declared:

"All right, I'll tell you. Schluter and his assistant—the red-headed Jenni Hofmann—are due in New York on the next trip of the s.s. *Europa*."

We were off!

But not at once. It was on Tuesday, February 22—Washington's birthday—that Rumrich revealed that news. But the s.s. *Europa* was not due in until Thursday, February 24. The two days that followed were the longest I ever knew. As the ship neared our shores, I began calling for frequent reports on her position. And when the huge, palatial German liner reached Quarantine, two other F.B.I. agents and I were on the Coast Guard cutter that met her. I could not wait for her to dock.

I immediately called for the passenger list and swiftly ran over it, looking for the name of "Karl Schluter." It was not there. I tried a different spelling—without the 'c.' No Shluter. I tried Sluter and Shuter and Slewter and every possible variation. I checked all the "Karls" and "Carls." But there wasn't any trace on the passenger list of Karl Schluter in any form.

Nor was the red-headed Jenni Hofmann, flirtatious *aide* to

the wily Schluter, on that passenger list. There was no trace of her there under that name, nor as Ruth Hofmann, or Johanna Hofmann, as she also was known.

We were disappointed. At first it flashed into my mind that Rumrich had tricked me, but somehow I felt that he had been telling the truth. Then it struck me that perhaps he was honestly mistaken. He had told me they travelled here as passengers, and perhaps they had told him that lie deliberately, to confuse him. Perhaps they actually lived in this country, and relayed the spy information they got from him through others.

And then another obvious answer hit me. Perhaps Schluter and Hofmann travelled disguised as members of the crew !

I called for the ship's manifest, and, scarcely concealing my impatience, ran swiftly down the list. And out of it leaped the words: "Karl Schluter . . . steward."

There it was—but it carried only disappointment. A line was drawn through it, and alongside was scrawled: "Did not sail."

Schluter had evaded us; he had escaped. Sick as I was over it then, it was nothing to what I felt later, months later in the investigation, when I realized fully how important he was, and what he would have meant to us. For Schluter was no stooge, like Rumrich, blindly following orders and knowing almost nothing about the rest of the ring. If we had Schluter and could make him talk we could learn the names of scores and hundreds of other Nazi spies here and ferret them out of their holes. Schluter knew almost all of them along the Eastern seaboard. For he and Theodor Schütz, whose trail we were to cross later, brought orders for these spies directly from Germany.

It was Schluter who got and carried back to Nazi spy headquarters the details of a secret discussion in Washington on proposed drastic changes in the design of our battleships.

It was Schluter who reported back to the Nazi high command that the armour-plates in some sections of some of our war vessels were easily damaged.

It was Schluter—with the aid of Dr Ignatz T. Griebl—who planted a contact in the offices of one of the most important firms of naval architects in the country. Through this contact he was able to give details of important American naval plans to the *Marine Nachrichten Stelle*.

Schluter had a spy posted at the Army air station at Mitchel Field; one in an aeroplane factory at Bristol, Pa.; another at Seversky Aircraft Corporation, Farmingdale, L.I.; another in an armaments plant not far from Ossining, N.Y.; another at New Haven, Conn.

But Schluter was lost to us. He was taken off the *Europa* at Bremen and transferred to a place of safety. He was assigned to a Nazi battleship, from which it would take the United States Navy to get him.

It was with scant hope, when I saw the notation beside his name on the ship's manifest of the *Europa*, that I continued and checked the manifest for the name of Jenni Hofmann. And I could hardly believe my eyes when I saw it there, with no line through it, and no notation:

"Johanna Hofmann . . . hairdresser."

My first instinct was to try to arrest her at once, but good sense reasserted itself in time. She was, so far, our lone thread reaching right into spy headquarters in Germany, and we had to be careful not to snap it. Besides, there might be other spies aboard. It would be no use to scare them off.

The problem was to get a good look at her, without her knowledge, so we could, perhaps, follow her. I didn't dare ask any of the ship's officers for aid, for I might be confiding in a Nazi spy accomplice. Just then one of the immigration inspectors, who had boarded the ship with us, went by, and I thought of the answer. I knew Chief Inspector John Mont-

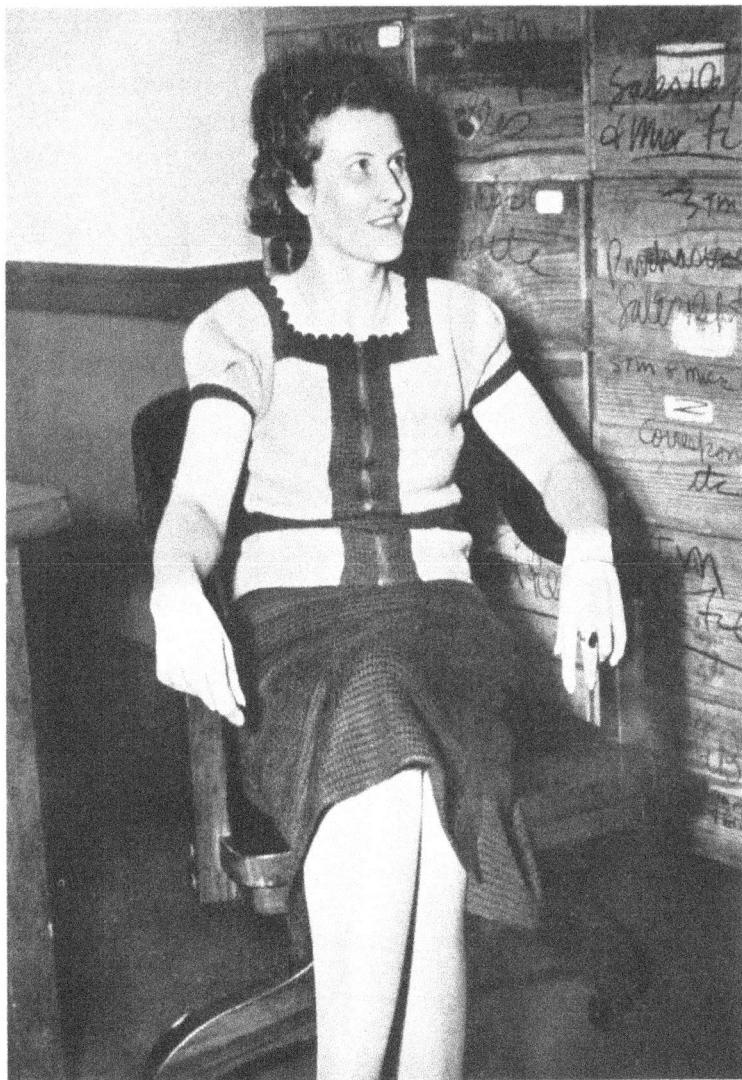

JOHANNA (JENNI) HOFMANN

gomery well enough to enlist his aid without the necessity of going into lengthy explanation.

He agreed immediately, and promptly issued a call to all members of the crew to appear in the third-class dining-room, for verification of landing-passes. That was a bit unusual, but not unique, so that no suspicion was likely to be aroused.

I sat at a table with the chief inspector, as if I were his assistant, and the two other F.B.I. agents sat at the next table, drinking beer to create the impression that the whole thing was a routine matter of absolutely no importance. Not even the two assistant pursers who called the names of the crew knew the true identity of myself and the two beer-drinkers.

"Johanna Hofmann!" called an assistant purser, and a trim young woman in a crisp white uniform, with beautiful reddish hair, came up to the table. She stood there, calmly, while the inspector asked her unimportant, routine questions so that we would have time to get a good look at her.

We saw an attractive girl, poised and sure of herself, but with a carriage and glance which revealed, even in these impersonal circumstances, that she was quite sensitive to, and aware of, men.

The photographs in the newspapers during her trial later do not do her justice. Her wealth of wavy, auburn hair framed a delicate, fair skin and set off handsomely her clear, deep-blue eyes. Her figure is quite good. When we examined her belongings later, we noted her dresses were sizes 14 and 16.

The inspector kept her standing there only about a minute, but that was enough to photograph her indelibly in our minds. We continued playing our *rôles* as assistant immigration officials as the great liner came up the harbour and was eased into her dock, coming to rest at Pier 86, North River.

Even then we made no overt move. Another agent was waiting at the pier, according to instructions, and at a signal he joined us as we went off the boat. I stationed one man where he could observe every one leaving the first-class gangway, one at the tourist and third-class gangway, and another at the crew gangway in the rear. For an hour we waited in vain. I was about to go back on board ship to investigate when I caught a signal from the agent watching the crew gangway.

And there she came, tripping lightly across the boards, apparently unaware she was being watched. There was no mistaking her; the mass of auburn hair, unconfined by a hat, the trim figure, the crisp yet exceedingly feminine walk. She still wore her white uniform, with no other protection against the February cold than a very light topcoat. Quite obviously she had come off the boat for only a few moments, and soon it was apparent that she had come to look for some one. She walked up and down, looking towards the pier-steps to the street, and when she passed us we could see a slight frown of anxiety on her forehead.

Whom was she seeking so eagerly? A lover? A spy? Or a combination of both? We lit cigarettes, and seemed engrossed in other things, so she would not suspect we were watching her. And then, suddenly, with a gesture—a little shrug which said as eloquently as words, "To hell with it—I'm not going to wait in the cold any longer," she started back for the crew gangway.

It was time to act. In a few swift strides I was by her side. I tipped my hat.

"Johanna Hofmann?"

Her eyes widened slightly, but without fright. Her looks, her visits to foreign lands apparently had accustomed her to being accosted, and in the safety of the pier, a few steps from the ship, she was unafraid.

"Yes," she acknowledged questioningly.

"Will you come with us?" I said quietly in German. "We want to talk to you."

Still she was unafraid.

"*Wer sind sie?* (Who are you?)" she demanded.

"We are Government officers," I replied, and showed her my F.B.I. badge.

For a moment I thought she was about to faint, she turned so pale.

"Where—where are you taking me?" she managed.

I suggested the pier waiting-room, because I wanted to frighten her as little as possible. A frightened man may talk more readily, but a hysterical woman is hopeless.

"*Was ist das alles?* (What is this all about?)" she asked, as we walked towards the waiting-room. But there were hundreds of people in it, and there was no chance to talk quietly there. I suggested F.B.I. headquarters would be a better place. She hesitated, then nodded agreement.

She was trembling and still pale, but said nothing more until we were in a taxi. There she began again, demanding to know what this was all about.

"Haven't you any idea, Fräulein, why the United States Government would want to question you?"

"No," she said.

"None at all?"

"None at all."

She was recovering fast and becoming bold again. "I will call to the driver," she threatened, "if you do not tell me at once what you want of me. I will scream for help."

I shrugged.

"Where is Schluter—Karl Schluter?" I demanded.

Her eyes widened with sudden realization.

"I—I don't know him!" she declared.

"Do you know Rumrich?"

She hesitated. "No," she said. "I never heard of him in all my life."

But as we passed a street light I saw that her eyes had

shadowed and now looked hunted, and her face had sagged. In the dining-room she had looked twenty-two—actually she was twenty-seven—right now she looked thirty-eight. I almost felt sorry for her, but it was no time for sentiment or chivalry. I had to look upon her in her *rôle* as my most important potential clue to the higher-ups in this Nazi conspiracy against the United States.

"It will do you no good to lie, Fräulein," I said. "Again I ask you, 'Where is Karl Schluter?'"

She did not answer.

"Do you know Günther Gustav Rumrich?"

"No," she snapped.

"Ever see him?"

"No."

"Ever hear of him?"

"No."

But, just before we reached the United States Court House, twenty minutes later, she touched my arm and said:

"Yes, I do know Karl Schluter. He is a steward on the *Europa*. That is how I know him. I didn't remember him when you first asked me."

"Where is he?" I demanded.

"He was not on board this trip."

"Why not?"

It seemed to me she paused slightly. "Because," she said, "he is on vacation."

We were entering the lift for the F.B.I. headquarters. I did not bother to point out to her that it was strange she should know the vacation schedule of a steward whom she could not at first remember knowing.

"What about Rumrich?" I asked in the lift. "Remember him now?"

She shook her head. "No, him I do not remember at all. I do not know him. I have never heard of him. Who is this Rumrich you ask me so much about? How should I know him, and why?"

In my office she sank dejectedly into a chair. I told her to make herself comfortable, and that there was a matron on duty to take care of her if she needed anything. I went slowly with her, for it was obvious she was going to prove a difficult subject, at least at first. Women almost always are. A man will avoid obvious lies if he can, and, paradoxically, tries harder to be devious and subtle under questioning. That is how he trips himself up. But women often will lie point-blank when they know full well that their answers are most obvious lies, and there is no point in lying on those lines any longer. You can confront them with plain, irrefutable evidence, and still they will deny. That very lack of subtlety can be very baffling to the questioner; for how can you get very far with anyone who lies blandly in your face and is not ashamed that you know she is lying?

I told her I knew Schluter was a Nazi spy contact man, plying between this country and spy headquarters in Germany, and that I knew she was his assistant. She denied it.

I told her she had been to Rumrich's flat, and gave the address, and described Rumrich and his wife. Still she denied that she ever saw or heard of him. I named the dates she saw him. I told her things Rumrich had said to her, and what she had said to him. She said I was making it all up. It wasn't true, she said. She didn't know Rumrich, had never been to his house, and had never even heard of him.

I told her how Rumrich had given Schluter an envelope containing U.S. Army secrets, and how Schluter had handed it to her, and how she had put it into her handbag to carry back to the *Europa.*

She said it was all a terrible mistake; that I must have her confused with somebody else.

"I am innocent," she cried. "Take me back to the ship at

once. I will have you arrested if you don't. I will complain to the German Consul. You have no right to keep me here!"

"Why don't you decide to tell the truth?" I asked.

"I have decided that if you do not release me immediately I will see that you are severely punished," she retorted.

I shook my head. "You are making a mistake, Fräulein," I said. "I advise you to tell me the truth. Again I ask you, what were your dealings with Rumrich, and for whom were you acting?"

"I told you I don't know Rumrich!" she snapped.

"For whom were you working?"

"For the North German Lloyd Line, as a hairdresser," she declared.

"But in addition to that. In your other capacity. . . ."

"I don't know what you are talking about. I tell you all I know about Karl Schluter is that he was a steward on the same boat. I know nothing about this Rumrich you talk about. I don't believe such a man exists."

I did not answer. She was facing me across my desk, but she did not see the slight signal I gave the agent in the back of the room. She read my silence as weakness, for she raised her voice and went on:

"You are just inventing a man named Rumrich. There is no Rumrich. It is a lie, a fake. I don't believe there ever was such a man Rumrich. . . ."

And then she heard the door open and saw my eyes go to it. She gave a little shriek and went absolutely white as Rumrich's voice said:

"Hello, Jenni."

Rumrich came forward, so that he stood almost alongside her. But she did not raise her eyes.

"Do you know this woman, Rumrich?" I asked.

"Yes," he said. "That is Jenni—Johanna Hofmann."

He spoke in German, as did I, for she understood almost no English.

"Is this the girl who came to your house with Karl Schluter on several occasions?"

"Yes, that's she."

"And did you give military papers to her and Schluter to take back to Germany?"

"Yes, Mr Turrou."

"And did she put those papers in her handbag?"

"Yes, sir."

"And was she present when Schluter gave you instructions and discussed spying you were to do and plans you were to steal for the Nazi Government?"

"That's right, Mr Turrou."

I motioned to the agent. "All right," I said, "take him away."

Jenni remained seated, her eyes cast down, her face pale, long minutes after the door closed behind him. I said nothing, waiting.

Then suddenly colour started coming back into her face. She raised her eyes and in a strong voice said:

"The game is over. You win. What do you want to know?"

CHAPTER VI

IT was not easy to break Jenni, however. She admitted that she had $70 for Rumrich in her bag, but insisted she did not know why Schluter sent it to Rumrich. I questioned her a little longer, then saw it was nearly eleven o'clock. Regretfully I turned her over to a matron. I did not want the argument in court later that she had been tortured by not being permitted to sleep. She was put in an F.B.I. detention-room overnight.

The next morning she was brought into my office at nine o'clock. Her lovely red hair was perfectly combed and arranged, and she again looked fresh, youthful, and sure of her attractiveness and power over men. And there was a look in her eye which told me I would probably have to start all over again.

"Whom," I asked, "besides Günther Gustav Rumrich, were you and Karl Schluter contacting in New York?"

She blinked, hesitated, then shook her head.

"I don't remember," she said.

"Now, Fräulein," I pointed out, "you yourself have just agreed that the game is over. You can see we know much already, and that you are in serious trouble. Do not act like a child. Now answer me. There were others whom you were contacting, yes?"

"Yes," she admitted.

"You must remember at least some of the names. Certainly one name. Who was it?"

Again she hesitated. Again she insisted, "I don't remember."

It was obvious that there was no use trying to drive her. A

change of tactics was indicated. Every woman likes to talk about herself, and an opportunity to tell the story of her life is a rare treat. I gave Jenni that opportunity.

"Tell me something about yourself, Fräulein," I urged.

"What is your real name?"

"Johanna Hofmann," she replied.

"And where were you born?"

"In Dresden, Germany."

"When?"

"May 19, 1911."

"Are you married?"

"No."

"Your parents' names?"

"Max and Emma."

"And where do they live?"

"No. 5 Wertherstrasse, Dresden, Germany."

Those were facts I could readily have ascertained from her passport. But already it was working. She was relaxing under questions to which the answers were familiar and easy, and about which she did not have to think or be on her guard or try to conceal anything. Soon she was talking steadily, and I was doing all the listening.

She told me how she grew up in Dresden and how she went to school there, and then to high school and, finally, to the Dresden Trade School, for three years, to learn to be a hairdresser. She told me about her two brothers, one three years older than she and one eleven years older; and about her two younger sisters, Elise and Elsie, and how Elise committed suicide on board a German steamer because a German naval officer jilted her.

She told me of her own unfortunate love-story, when she was very young, which I do not think fair to mention. And as I sat there listening to this girl's story, I had to keep reminding myself that she was not just a simple, pretty, red-headed

75

hairdresser, but the most important link I had so far to the most dangerous spy ring in the peace-time history of the United States. She looked so innocent, with the pale February sun lighting her wealth of hair. . . .

She told me how, in 1931, when she was twenty, she got a job with the North German Lloyd as a hairdresser, and was assigned to the s.s. *Bremen*, plying between Bremerhaven and New York. It was adventure to her, and she gloried in it, until that unfortunate love affair sent her home to her parents, weeping, within two years.

She remained with her parents until 1936, then went back to work for the steamship line. She made two voyages to the Far East on the s.s. *Gneisenau*, and saw Cairo and Port Said, Damascus and Java, and all the far places of which she had dreamed. She rode a camel in the desert, and went through the Suez Canal, and brought strange souvenirs from across the world to her parents.

It was on the s.s. *Gneisenau* that she first met the wily, dangerous Karl Schluter. He was nice to her. He paid her marked attention. When he was transferred to the s.s. *Europa* so that he could be of greater service to the spy ring, she went with him.

So, gradually, the story of her life drifted into the story of her part in the Nazi spy plot, and though I think she became aware where her talk was leading her, she was too fascinated by the sound of her own voice, telling all this to an interested listener, to stop.

"And one day in port at Bremerhaven," she said almost dreamily, "Karl told me he was an agent of the German Secret Service, and offered to have me made one, too."

I could see, as she told it, how the prospect had thrilled her. Schluter talked to her of patriotism and the glory of Hitler and of Nazi Germany's destiny to conquer the world.

"*Morgen die ganze Welt!*" he had cried. ("To-morrow the whole world!"—from a Nazi song.)

"He told me," she said, "that no harm would come to me. He said I need fear no consequences: He told me, 'The German Government—Hitler, *der Führer* himself!—is behind this.'"

And so she agreed. She was to be his assistant in bringing messages and instructions from Nazi spy headquarters to the Nazi spies in the United States, and to carry back the naval and military, air and coast-defence, secrets they stole here.

"When the *Europa* docked in New York the next trip," she continued, "Karl gave me a package of letters and told me to put them in my handbag. . . ." She paused, and it was apparent that the end of her spontaneous recital was drawing to a close. "That was in January of this year," she said, "and that was the first I had to do with this matter." I felt sure that was false—that she was becoming alert and careful again, and covering up activities prior to the point she suspected I knew about. But still I did not argue or interrupt.

"Karl said I was to go along with him," she went on, "to see the various agents in New York, and hand the letters over to them. He said the letters were from the German Military Intelligence Headquarters. He said that as soon as we got back to Germany I would be officially enrolled as a secret operative."

She halted, and there was silence in the room for a few moments.

"I see," I said. "And now, Fräulein, do you remember the names of the people you visited here?"

She looked steadily at me, and in her eyes grew reluctantly full recognition of what she had admitted. She even smiled a grudging admission of defeat.

"Under the bunk in my cabin," she said slowly, "you will find a brown leather bag. In it is a small packet of letters. Those are letters of instructions I was bringing here."

77

Without a word I reached into my desk and passed pen and paper to her. "Will you write a note," I asked, "to some one in authority on the *Europa*, so we can obtain that bag without difficulty?"

She shrugged her shoulders, took the pen, and wrote to Chief Officer Heinrich Lorenz, of the *Europa*, in German, the following:

> DEAR SIR: Please give to these gentlemen the brown bag under my bunk. The key is in the left-hand drawer of the bureau. I am under arrest.

I went quickly with another agent, anxious to see those letters. Chief Officer Lorenz seemed astonished. He was extremely suspicious and full of questions. He demanded our credentials. He wanted to know why she was under arrest. I told him, briefly, a half-truth. I said it was for smuggling. He asked for details, but I refused and commanded him to take us to her cabin.

It was a typical inside cabin on D deck, with panelled walls, two bunks, ventilator, washstand, and desk. It was nice enough, if small, and feminine hands had, with pictures here and there, made it quite attractive. Jenni shared it with another hairdresser, who was visiting friends in Hoboken while the ship was in port.

Lorenz entered the cabin with us and found the brown leather bag at once. He turned it and the key over to us, still shaking his head as if in bewilderment, and we sped back to F.B.I. headquarters. I was anxious to open the bag at once, but decided that in view of likely future court proceedings it would be better if it were opened in her presence.

Jenni was sitting in the same chair in my office when we returned, as if she had not moved at all while we were gone. I thought it was my imagination which told me there was a faint ghost of a smile hovering on her face. I had her formally identify the bag as hers, then fit the key into the lock and open it.

Inside was a small packet of letters, as she had said. Clipped to one of them was $70 in American money. But as I eagerly opened the packet, I realized why Jenni Hofmann had that Mona Lisa look round the lips. Most of the letters were covered with strange symbols, resembling none of the characters of any of the seven languages I knew. A glance sufficed to tell me they were not in any language. They were written in a secret code.

I looked at her, and she stared right back.

"Where is the key to this code?" I demanded.

She shook her head. "I don't have any."

"But you can decode these letters for us?"

She shook her head again, vehemently. "No," she said, "I don't know how."

And there we were, virtually back where we started from. I think every investigator must have a private prayer, "Lord, spare me from women witnesses!"

I pleaded and argued and cajoled. I got her to admit it was preposterous that she should not have the key to the code. I got her to agree that if she were in my place and I in hers she would be sure I was lying. She agreed that it was impossible that Schluter would not have revealed the code to her. But, she insisted, she had not got the key and did not know how to read the code.

I gave up questioning her temporarily, and I sat at the desk opposite her, puzzling over the coded letters and reading the two which were not in code. Even they did not make much sense. One was to a Martin Schade, 587 Riverside Drive, New York City. There were phrases in it which might or might not refer to spy activities. The other was to a Dr Ignatz T. Griebl, 56 East 87th Street, New York City. But it was just a note regretting inability to see him, and wishing him well. I set them aside for exhaustive investigation, but right now the ones that interested me imperatively were those in code.

Another agent, meanwhile, had been going through the rest of the contents of her bag, under Jenni's watchful eyes. Suddenly he held up a piece of paper.

"Does this mean anything to you, Leon?" he asked.

Even at ten feet I saw enough to bring me out of my chair. The paper was covered with symbols similar to those on the coded letters—but under each symbol was a letter of the German alphabet. It was the key to the secret code.

Jenni's voice, cool and resigned, broke in before I fairly got my hands on it.

"Well," she said, "I'll decode the letters for you now."

And, without as much as glancing at the key, she quickly and smoothly translated the letters into German. Later, when I went over them carefully with the key, I found she had not missed a symbol. She knew the code as well as she knew the letters of her alphabet, and could read the coded letters almost as easily as she could straight German. Why did she lie until the last split second? And, having lied, why didn't she keep up the pretence, so that we would not know just how much she lied? I don't know.

All the letters were from Schluter. One was to Jenni herself, apparently a note he sent her a day or two before the *Europa* left Germany. Decoded and translated it read:

Dear Jenni:

As to Miss Moog, please go on the day of departure, between 3 and 5 o'clock. Then the doctor is not there. He should not know anything about the matter.

KARL

A second page was attached. It read:

Pack your trunks. To-day we will probably go to Bremen.

YOUR KARL

NOTE IN CODE FROM SCHLUTER TO JENNI HOFMANN
"Pack your trunks. To-day we will probably go to Bremen. Your Karl."

The next letter was to Miss Kate Moog, 276 Riverside Drive, New York City. It was the first time we had run across her name in the investigation. It meant nothing to us as we read the decoded letter, which did not sound at all dangerous. It gave us no inkling that Nazi spy headquarters sought to make her the Mata Hari of this ring.

Dear Miss Moog:
  This trip I am on vacation, and Jenni is acting as my representative, who will bring you this letter.
  It was too bad that we were unable to talk to each other the last time. How are you? I hope everything is all right.
  How does the matter stand with the divorce? I have regulated the matter here to such an extent that you need only give the signal and we will then start the attack in Germany. One way or the other, the matter will turn out all right.
  You can tell all to Jenni and give her everything, since she is a good little skate. Many friendly greetings from Karl Schluter. How does the matter stand with Böhm?

There did not seem to be many startling clues in that.

The letter with the $70 in American money attached was addressed to Rumrich. It read:

Dear Friend:

1. I am sending you through Jenni $70 for the code. Kindly give $40 to the one who has got the code, and $30 for you.

2. How is it with the plans of the aircraft carriers *Yorktown* and *Enterprise*? We pay for all the plans $1000. If you can get them for $300, then the $700 is for you. So talk about the whole matter with Jenni, and tell her how the matter of the plans will be handled. You need not be afraid. As far as the money is concerned, you will see that I take care of everything promptly.

3. What about the pistol matter which we discussed?

4. How is it about the American passports? Please give them to Jenni. Please inform Jenni of the price.

5. Can you get me various Army and Navy photographs? You must state the price to me.

6. How about the anti-aircraft gun. Can you get me something along that line?

7. Addresses of American engineers who worked abroad and did not return.

8. Key procedure.

9. Everything that is known at the consulate regarding Russian orders from American industry regarding naval matters.

I sent out agents to check up quietly on this Martin Schade, this Dr Ignatz T. Griebl, this Miss Kate Moog. Then I sent for Rumrich, and had him stand by while Jenni dictated a formal confession in German.

When she was finished, and had signed the confession, I had Rumrich sit down and translate it into English. I had him read that to her in German, following which she signed the English translation he made. Then I took the German version away and had Rumrich sit down and translate the English version he just made back into German and read it to

LETTER TO RUMRICH IN CODE

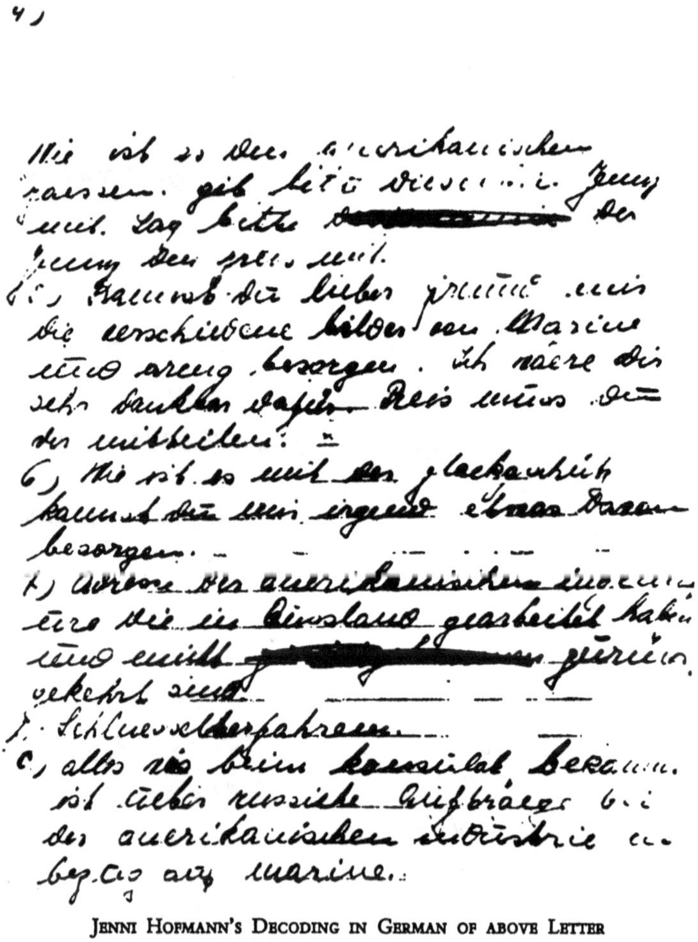

4)

Wie ist es den amerikanischen [illegible]. gib bitte diesen [illegible] Jenny mit. Sag bitte [illegible] der Jenny den Gruss mit.

5.) Kannst du lieber Freund mir die verschiedene Bilder von Marine und Armee besorgen. Ich wäre dir sehr dankbar dafür. Preis unter dir mitteilen.

6.) Wie ist es mit der Gelegenheit kannst du mir irgend etwas davon besorgen.

7) Adresse der amerikanischen [illegible] die in Deutschland gearbeitet haben und nicht [illegible] zurück gekehrt sind.

8. Schlüssel Überfahren.

9.) alles wie beim Konsulat bekannt ist über russische Aufträge bei der amerikanischen Industrie u. bez. auf Marine.

JENNI HOFMANN'S DECODING IN GERMAN OF ABOVE LETTER

her in German. That left no possibility for any lawyer to contend successfully in court that she signed a confession she did not understand.

"All right," I said. "The *Europa* is sailing this evening—but you are staying here. Do you want anything from the ship?"

"Yes," she said. She wanted her clothing and some other things from her cabin.

"We are willing to do anything in reason," I told her, "but I can't spare men to wait on the boat until the items you want are picked out. You'd better write another note to Lorenz to turn over all your belongings to us. You are going to stay here a long time, Fräulein."

She sighed, but took the pen and wrote another note. Two men went to the *Europa* and got three bags, an arm-load of dresses and coats, a camera, a typewriter, and miscellaneous articles. I cast a speculative eye at the typewriter. A hairdresser with a typewriter in her cabin. . . .

I had her taken to a detention-room, and went to work on Rumrich on the basis of the letter to him from Schluter. I demanded to know what each of Schluter's points meant, and who was the person who got the code referred to in the first paragraph of Schluter's letter. It was then that, for the first time, I found out about Rumrich's stooge, Erich Glaser.

"I tried to protect him," admitted Rumrich, "because it was my fault he got into this mess."

I sent a man to Mitchel Field to get Glaser, and went on to the other points.

The second point was just a follow-up on something Rumrich already had confessed—how he had been ordered by Schluter to try to get the blueprints of the new aircraft carriers.

The third point referred, Rumrich admitted, to a new type of pistol perfected for the U.S. Army. Rumrich had been trying to get at it for quite some time. His correspondence, as "Crown," with Kapitan-Leutnant Pfeiffer showed that, unable to get the design, he had invented an elaborate tale about a beautiful woman whom he had enlisted to aid him, and who was trying to get the design of the pistol from a drunken officer at Governors Island.

The fourth paragraph refers to the passport attempt which led to Rumrich's arrest. The one about "various Army and Navy photographs" was not as vague as it sounded. It referred to varied but specific photographs Schluter had requested. The sixth question harked back to the talk in the Café Hindenburg, when Schluter asked him, among other things, to find out about a synchronized searchlight and anti-aircraft gun.

Why Schluter wanted to know the address of American engineers who worked abroad "and never returned," Rumrich swore he did not know, and I never found out. The eighth question, about "key procedure," referred to a very secret Army code, which Schluter had mentioned to him once, Rumrich said, but never elaborated upon.

And Rumrich swore the last paragraph, "Everything that is known at the consulate regarding Russian orders from American industry regarding naval matters," was Greek to him. He said he did not even know which consulate Schluter meant. Whether Rumrich lied to protect the Nazi consulate in New York, or whether Schluter, who had to contact scores of spies, got slightly mixed in his instructions, I do not know.

For that matter, it is still a mystery why Schluter wrote that letter to Rumrich at all, since he left the ship because Nazi spy headquarters heard of Rumrich's arrest in America. The answer probably is that he took a chance on sacrificing Jenni on the slim hope that we might not have realized what Rumrich's attempt to get the passport blanks meant, and let him go. Or perhaps the person Jenni was looking for that night on the pier, while we watched her, was a contact man in New York who was to tell her if it was safe to deliver those letters. She insisted that she was not looking for anyone, and we could not budge her on that point. I am sure she, like the others, did not tell all.

At her trial Jenni and her lawyer tried to picture her completely as the naïve dupe, who knew nothing of Schluter's spy activities, and accompanied him on his rounds in New York only because he promised to take her to a real New York night-club. The story she told me, contained substantially in her signed confession, was, as I have related to you, much different, but even that was not the full account of her complicity. Two points show her to have been much more deeply involved than she directly admitted.

One is the letter found in Rumrich's flat soon after he was arrested. In it the mysterious spy chief at Bremen, who signed himself "N. Spielman," referred several times to Miss Hofmann as "Jennie, my agent," and in terms which indicated he trusted her implicitly. That letter was produced at the trial, and the references to her were read to the jury by Government counsel.

The second point did not come out at the trial because it did not directly apply to the charges on which she was being tried. But it shows even more convincingly than the first that red-headed Jenni was far from a blind dupe. The second point is that Jenni was entrusted with the task of looking over and signing up a Nazi spy in Czechoslovakia while Hitler was 'softening up' that country for conquest.

That spy recruit was Gustav Rumrich—younger brother of Günther Gustav Rumrich.

Gustav, a Sudeten German, was a student at Prague, the capital of Czechoslovakia. He was, like his brother in America, restless for adventure. He wrote Rumrich in New York that he was fed up with student life and craved excitement; that he was planning to enlist with German mercenaries in Spain.

Rumrich wrote back advising against that and promising instead, in glowing terms, to have him made a Nazi spy at home. In January, 1938, Rumrich spoke to Karl Schluter and Jenni about it when they visited his flat, and they were enthusiastic. Rumrich gave Jenni two photographs of his brother so that she could identify him. That night he wrote

Gustav again, directing him to write to "N. Spielman" through the Dundee spy relay. He told Gustav that he would get instructions from "Spielman" by special messenger —a red-headed girl named Jenni Hofmann.

That much Rumrich told me when he confessed. But there is more definite corroboration. The letter young Gustav wrote to spy chief "Spielman" offering his services was intercepted by M.I.5, which sent a copy to G-2, which in turn handed it over to us. Gustav's bid for a spy job was snapped up quickly. Jenni was sent to close the deal with him, and on February 15 she met young Gustav in Teplitz-Schönau, in the seething Sudeten area, and hired him as a Nazi spy. She admitted to me that she saw Gustav there on that date, after I showed her the copy of Gustav's letter, and references in letters from "N. Spielman" to Günther Rumrich which made it clear that she acted as the agent.

Ironically, the day she saw Gustav in Czechoslovakia was the day Rumrich was arrested by detectives of the Alien Squad here. I don't know what happened to Gustav.

However, again I have got far ahead of the story of the investigation, and where it led us, and what we discovered of the extent and intent of the Nazi spy ring in the United States.

CHAPTER VII

THE agents who went back to pick up Erich Glaser at Mitchel Field came back soon, bringing a strapping six-footer of about twenty-nine, rather handsome, with dark brown hair and dark, stupid eyes. He made no protest, they said, but came along like a soldier under orders.

He was easy to break. For half an hour he haltingly and amateurishly denied everything; but when we brought Rumrich in to confront him, his jaw dropped and his eyes looked like those of a dog whipped for something he does not understand.

"I'm sorry I got you into this, Erich," said Rumrich. "The game is up now. You might as well tell these gentlemen what they want to know, and sign a statement. I have told them it wasn't your fault."

His story was that of a typical stooge. Glaser was born in Leipzig, and, like so many other young men who grew up after the War, had trouble finding a job in post-War Germany. When he was twenty-one he decided to try America, and in March, 1930, he arrived in New York on the s.s. *Dresden*.

He had friends there, and they shipped him to other friends in Atwater, Mich., where he got a job in an upholstery factory. But the work wasn't steady, and he didn't like it anyway. So when he heard men were wanted for the United States Army, he tried to enlist. To his surprise, they took him promptly, though he could hardly speak English and was not a citizen. He became a private in the Second Field Artillery in July, 1931, and was shipped via New York to the Panama Canal Zone. There he served for three years at Fort

Clayton, and there he met Sergeant Günther Gustav Rumrich. Memories of Germany and bonds of language drew them together. Rumrich was the leader. Glaser did what he said.

When his term of service ended in 1934 he decided to try his luck in the civilian world again. But the depression was still on. The few dollars he had went swiftly, and within a month—August, 1934—he was glad to re-enlist and let Uncle Sam feed, clothe, and pay him.

This time he was sent to Fort Mills, thirty miles out of Manila, in the Philippine Islands. He became a corporal, and was resigned to Army life. But towards the end of that enlistment he began getting glowing letters from Rumrich in New York. Glaser thought it over slowly and decided that a smart fellow like Rumrich must have worked everything out and knew best. So when his time was up in August, 1937, he headed for New York and the job his pal had waiting for him.

But there was no job. Rumrich invited him to live with him as long as he wanted, but was of no help in job-hunting. He and Rumrich started to get on each other's nerves somewhat.

But the friendship between Rumrich and Glaser survived suspicions and accusations. One day Rumrich drew him aside. He swore him to secrecy. Glaser listened with open mouth as Rumrich confided that he was a spy in the employ of the Nazi Government, and that the real reason he had sent for him was to train him, too, to be a spy.

Glaser protested unhappily. He didn't want to be a spy. He didn't want to get into trouble. Rumrich handled him gently. He promised him money. He got him to do small things for him, like sending to the Canal Zone for photographs of fortifications in his name, and subscribing to the *Army and Navy Register*. That was valuable to Rumrich. He was able to sell bits of information culled from that magazine to the spy ring for a few dollars now and then, and it

F.B.I. 'ROGUES GALLERY' PHOTO OF ERICH GLASER

F.B.I. 'ROGUES GALLERY' PHOTO OF
OTTO HERRMANN VOSS

enabled him to talk to Schluter and the others as if he were in close touch with Army and Navy matters.

In January, 1938, Glaser re-enlisted. Though a trained artilleryman, able to assume the rank of corporal and perhaps, very soon, that of sergeant in that branch of the service, he requested assignment to the Air Corps, and particularly to Mitchel Field. That was Rumrich's hand. Since it was Glaser's third enlistment, he got what he wanted.

He took Rumrich on to the field and into the hangars and shops. More important, he copied for Rumrich two pages from the restricted code-book at the air-field. It was a code and a procedure for simplifying the transmission of code-messages. Both were prepared by the Signal Corps of the U.S. Army, for the sole, restricted use of the United States Army, Navy, and Air Corps.

Rumrich turned them over to Schluter, to be taken to Nazi spy headquarters in Germany. There it was decided that the material was worth $70. At least, that is what Schluter sent Rumrich through Jenni. There is more than a little reason to suspect Schluter of having cheated Rumrich, just as Rumrich intended to cheat Glaser of his share. The Nazi Government poured a great deal of its desperately scant supply of currency into spy activities in America, but only a fraction of it dribbled down to the spies themselves. The *provocateurs* and messengers and contact men, like Schluter and Weigand and Eitel and Schütz and Schmidt, got most of it, pocketing some and spending much more on hard drinking and high living.

While we were taking Glaser's statement, there came a telephone call from the German Consulate General Office in New York. A man speaking with a very marked accent introduced himself as Dr Richard Bottler, newly sent from Berlin to be counsellor at the consulate here.

He demanded to be permitted to see Jenni at once, and alone. Scribbling a note to an agent to check back at once to verify that Bottler was counsellor of the Nazi consulate, I told the telephone caller that of course he could see Jenni as her lawyer, but that an observer for the F.B.I. would have to be present. I told him to come in an hour.

Then I went to the detention-room in which Jenni was kept. I explained to her who was coming to see her, and told her that I would remain in the room during the interview. But I warned her in no circumstances to indicate, by word or sign, that I understood German.

The check verified everything, and, on the hour, Dr Bottler marched in, a pompous, officious man with red cheeks. He was typically Nazi, and as I looked at him I began for the first time to have some hope that my little act with Jenni for his benefit might work. I had arranged it only because there was no use missing any possible opportunities, no matter how slight, but with no illusions that it was clever or had a chance of success.

But with Bottler it worked. It apparently did not even occur to him that anyone but a Nazi might have intelligence, or be able to understand German. He ignored me entirely during the interview, and addressed himself to Jenni in rapid German.

His eyes began to glare as she told him the whole story— that is, as she had told it to me—beginning with her agreement to aid Karl Schluter in his spy contact work, and following through her arrest.

Bottler grew purple.

"And how much did you tell the American Government agents?" he demanded.

"I confessed to Mr Turrou," she replied. I winced inwardly, because, since she spoke so little English, that remark was as broad a hint as possible that I must understand German. "I had no alternative," she continued. "They had the code, the letters, and everything. There was no use for me to lie any more."

I breathed again when I saw Bottler had not caught on. He was too busy fighting apoplexy.

"*Haben sie alles erzählt?*" ("Did you tell everything?") he demanded.

"Yes," she nodded. "Everything."

His rage was a sight to behold.

"You didn't have to tell everything!" he muttered through clenched teeth.

It was minutes before he cooled down sufficiently to instruct her vehemently to tell no more to anyone. After a while he even reluctantly consented to see that the consulate supplied her with money each week for incidentals and food better than the regular prison fare. He told her, too, that the consulate would assign lawyers admitted to practise in New York to defend her. Then he marched out, curtly bidding me good day in English, still officious and still pompously unaware that I had understood every word.

Two New York lawyers—William J. Topken and Reimer Koch-Weser, 17 Battery Place—who handle much of the legal business of the Nazi Consulate General, arrived the next day. They, too, instructed her to talk no more, but soon they disappeared from the case. In their place appeared a man named George C. Dix. I do not know who hired him. He created a scene one day, and I had to throw him out of the grand jury room.

He made it a personal issue thereafter, and during the trial in United States Federal Court at New York in October and November, 1938, he kept making charges about me so wild and totally unsubstantiated by evidence that Federal Judge John C. Knox was forced to castigate him severely several times, and he felt it politic to apologize to me and the jury. I therefore think it fair to repeat here what I testified on the stand concerning him—that early in the case, when I asked him by what authority he sought to talk to Miss Hofmann, he told me:

93

"I'm her counsel now. Topken gave me the case. Topken's connexion with the German Government as counsel for the German Consulate here makes it awkward for him to appear in the case. It would be too obvious."

Dix took a trip to Germany to get testimony on behalf of Miss Hofmann, and spent months investigating my history and actions in America and in Europe and digging up witnesses. He told Assistant United States Attorney John W. Burke that he was spending his own money on the case.

But that does not concern this account.

Soon after Dr Bottler left, F.B.I. agents brought in Mr Martin Schade, one of the persons to whom Jenni had letters from Karl Schluter. The letter to Schade was so ambiguous in tone, and obviously so susceptible to misinterpretation, that we withheld all judgment and treated him as a witness and not at all as a suspect. And he promptly and flatly denied any knowledge of any spy matters.

Schade turned out to be a heavy man of fifty-seven, with grey pompadour, blue eyes, and a stolid, ruddy face, phlegmatic and unemotional. He is managing superintendent of a number of blocks of flats on Riverside Drive, owned by the Citizens Savings Bank of New York. The job is a good one and carries a good salary.

He was born in Hamburg, Germany, and after finishing school he went to sea. From 1908 to 1911 he was in the Imperial German Navy, but then he returned to the merchant marine and rose to be a chief engineer in the Hamburg-American Line. At the beginning of the War he was captured and remained a prisoner in England until after the Armistice.

He went back to Germany, but Germany's merchant marine was almost non-existent, and he was glad to take a job as a fireman on an American ship. Before long he was up as an engineer again, but he was beginning to get fed up with the sea, and in 1928 he came to New York to live. The next year, when he got the job of flat superintendent, he sent for his wife and family. The same year he applied for first citizenship papers, and in 1932 he became a citizen of the United States.

We confronted him with the letter from Schluter. It was not in the Nazi spy code, but it was somewhere similar in tone to the one Schluter wrote Rumrich. It requested Schade to give Jenni whatever information he had. It referred to radios and contacts with the Russian consulate.

Schade read it stolidly, and denied that it meant anything to him. It must have been meant for some one else, he said, despite the fact that it was addressed to him.

We showed him that his name was in Jenni's notebook, together with that of Rumrich and several other Nazi spies here. We read him sections of Jenni's confession. In those sections she told of visiting Schade at his home while making the rounds of Nazi spies in New York. She said Schluter had a long talk with Schade about plans of American aircraft carriers. She said Schade gave her an envelope which, she understood, contained reports to "N. Spielman," at Bremen.

Schade listened without a trace of emotion.

"She is wrong," he declared. "All that is true is that she and this man Schluter did visit me."

It was some time in December, 1937, or January, 1938, that he saw Jenni and Schluter for the first time, he said. They came to his flat and told him they were trying to get to see some friend in Brooklyn, but did not know the way, and so had dropped in for directions.

"They told me they heard of me from friends on the s.s. *Europa*," Schade explained, "and just happened to have my address. When they got lost looking for the place in Brooklyn, they noticed they were in my neighbourhood, and so dropped in."

They chatted for about half an hour, Schade said, and

Schluter talked about short-wave radio, and asked if a certain type was an Army radio. Schluter also talked about Army aeroplanes and Navy aeroplane carriers, Schade admitted, but insisted he thought Schluter was interested "merely in a commercial way."

Schade said he "happened to remark" to Schluter that he had visited one of the United States Navy's new aircraft carriers when it docked at New York a year or so earlier—just out of curiosity—but had seen only those parts of the ship usually shown to visitors.

He admitted that Schluter had told him he was interested in getting a contact at the Russian Consulate in New York. He admitted he told Schluter there were a number of Russian families in his block of flats, and that possibly he could arrange to have Schluter meet them and see if a contact of that sort could be established. But all this time, Schade explained, he had the idea that Schluter just wanted to make some kind of commercial arrangements. He was not curious enough, he said, to wonder why Schluter was interested in things like Army radios, Army aeroplanes, Navy aircraft carriers, and contacts at the Russian Consulate.

Jenni and Schluter visited him again, Schade admitted. The next time was when the s.s. *Europa* came to New York again. This time, Schade told us, Schluter offered to pay him for any information he got; but still, Schade declared, he thought Schluter merely the representative of some commercial firm.

As to the letter Jenni said Schade gave her for transmission to Kapitan-Leutnant Pfeiffer, Schade said it was merely a letter to his brother in Hamburg, concerning strictly family matters. The idea was to save postage from New York. He admitted he told Jenni and Schluter to look him up, when they got to New York again, but that was merely out of politeness, he said. And that, substantially, was his testimony when he appeared as a Government witness at the trial later.

Our investigation showed that Schade often visited German ships in port here. His explanation was that he got into the habit of dropping in for a glass of beer on the boats or a talk with any old friend from his sea-going days he might meet there. The visits were neither regular nor planned, he declared, and their purpose was partly social and partly to save postage on letters to friends and relatives in Germany. Many Germans in New York did that, he explained.

"But never did anyone ask me for any information which might be of value to the German Army or Navy," he swore. "How could I ever get any such information? I knew nothing of any spies, and I never did any spying for Germany or any other country."

We asked Schade if he had any objection to being tested under the lie-detector machine. A witness has a right to refuse such a test.

"No," said Schade. "I have no objection."

He was strapped to the machine. An expert started the test —but halted after half a dozen questions.

"Take him away," said the expert. "He is one of those rare individuals who are totally unresponsive. This machine can give no clue in such a case whether the subject is telling the truth or not."

No charge was placed against Mr Schade. He was not made a defendant at any stage of the investigation. We had no case against him, and the above is not intended as any accusation, in any degree, that he was a Nazi spy. His story is related only because it entered into the investigation at this point, and partly to show to what queer angles and what odd quarters it sometimes led. And his story is quite an apt illustration of the Nazi spy psychology running through the entire affair. Not only Schluter, but the other spies and contact men seemed to be imbued with the idea that every resident of this country who was of German origin, whether still a German citizen or not, should stand ready to betray the United States. They went after not only Schade, but scores and hundreds of others. One of the first requests Rumrich got from one of the Nazi spy contact men, for instance, was to supply him with the names of men in the United States Army whom he knew to be of German origin. Rumrich named Sergeant Arenson, of the 66th Coast Artillery, Battery "A," and Corporal Schmidt, Coast Artillery, Fort Scott, California. Nothing came of it, because—probably to their surprise—the Nazi spies found out in checking up on Sergeant Arenson and Corporal Schmidt that they were loyal American citizens.

By the time we had finished with Schade, reports began pouring in from the agents assigned to check the known activities and background of the Dr Griebl to whom one of Schluter's letters was addressed. And he turned out to be an intriguing character.

His full name was Dr Ignatz Theodor Griebl, and he had been an artillery officer in the World War with the German Imperial Army. A brother, who recently died, had been a close friend of the fanatical Paul Joseph Goebbels, head of the Ministry of Propaganda in Hitler's Cabinet, and had been considered very influential in Nazi Party circles.

Griebl studied medicine in the University of Munich before he came to the United States in 1925. Here, at Long Island University, he completed his medical course and won a degree and a licence to practise. He also spent a year at Fordham University, polishing up his English. It was gossiped in Yorkville, the agents reported, that his wife supported him during his studies. During the first stages of our investigation, his wife was in Europe on a lengthy visit.

In the thirteen years since his arrival in America he had become an influential figure in New York's German colony.

He was a widely known surgeon and obstetrician, and on the staff of several hospitals. He was also a leader in the Nazi movement in America. That began to sound interesting.

He was the friend and public-speaking companion of Dr Hans Borchers, the Nazi Consul in New York. He was the friend of the notorious Fritz Kuhn, militant head of the German-American Bund and *Führer* of the Nazi movement in the United States.

Griebl had become an open, ardent Nazi even before Hitler formally became dictator. By 1933, Griebl was so prominent in Nazi affairs that he and his wife were questioned by a Federal Grand Jury and by a Congressional Committee investigating subversive Nazi activities. In November, 1933, protests of patients and anti-Nazi groups forced him to resign as assistant clinical surgeon at the Harlem Hospital in New York.

He was vice-president of the United German Societies, and when that organization began to split over the Nazi question he organized the Friends of New Germany and appointed himself vice-president of that out-and-out Nazi propaganda outfit. Out of the Friends of New Germany, which was forced to disband when it became too notorious, grew the German-American Bund movement. Griebl avoided official titles in that, but remained friend and background adviser to the nominal leaders such as Kuhn.

An interesting sidelight to which we did not pay very much attention at the time, but which proved to be of some importance as the investigation progressed, was that he was always getting into scrapes with women. In 1935, for instance, we found, a Miss Antoinette Heim, fortyish, a free-lance real-estate and stock broker, sued Dr Griebl in Commercial Frauds Court for $3,500. She said he got the money from her by making love to her and promising to marry her as soon as he could get a divorce from his wife. Mrs Griebl took the stand

99

and testified that Miss Heim offered her $25,000 to divorce her husband. Miss Heim said Mrs Griebl demanded the $25,000, and that she offered her $300 a month for a certain period to get the divorce. Miss Heim won the suit.

Griebl, we found, was in the picture whenever Nazi affairs flared in the public eye. In 1934, he started a fight with a newspaper photographer. Griebl and Fritz Gissibl, another Nazi leader, were waiting to testify before a Congressional Committee in the Bar Association Building, 42 West 44th Street, New York City. The photographer snapped a picture of Gissibl, who was being accused by Representative Samuel Dickstein of being a Nazi spy.

Instantly Griebl was on his feet, blocking the photographer's exit. "Smash the camera," he yelled, making a move to do so himself, but desisting when the photographer cocked his fist. "Start a fight! Start a fight, and smash the camera!" he yelled instead.

He was the host to that notorious Nazi propagandist, Heinz Spanknöbel, while Federal officers were searching for him to question him concerning Nazi activities in America, we found.

His words as a speaker at Nazi rallies were fiery. We found a transcript of a speech he made before 18,000 wildly cheering Nazis in Madison Square Garden, while uniformed Nazi storm troopers patrolled the aisles and led the cries of "*Heil Hitler!*"

Germans in the United States would soon "demand adequate representation in city, county, State, and Federal Governments!" Griebl had thundered bitterly in German. "Those who fight us must perish, socially as well as economically, because of our determination to destroy our enemies completely and without any consideration whatsoever!"

Now those words are startlingly reminiscent of those of the Nazi leaders in Austria before the forced *Anschluss*, and to the speeches of Conrad Henlein, Hitler's mouthpiece in the Nazi drive to swallow free Czechoslovakia. But at the time Hitler's *"Morgen die ganze Welt"* obsession was not yet clear. Dr Griebl's words sounded merely like the rabble-rousing of a man with a money axe to grind. For we found that his income depended largely on how many Nazi organizations he could excite into making him official doctor for their members.

On the other side of the ledger, we found he was an officer in the United States Army Reserve.

He boasted often of that. He flaunted himself as a patriot. He always made sure that an American flag was displayed equally as prominently as the swastika banner of Hitler. When former Mayor O'Brien of New York withheld a permit for a Nazi mass meeting because the featured speaker was to be the notorious Heinz Spanknöbel, Dr Griebl came forward.

"I am to be the featured speaker," he announced. "I demand the permit—as a citizen of the United States and an officer of the United States Army."

The permit was granted the patriotic Dr Griebl.

I weighed the reports carefully, trying to decide whether to go after him next, or some other angle of the case. The reports were interesting, but not necessarily indicative of anything that would further our Nazi spy investigation. Dr Griebl's Nazi sentiments were none of our business. It is not a crime in the United States to be a Nazi. We noted that even Morris Ernst, though a liberal and a Jew, once went vigorously to the aid of Dr Griebl and his Nazi organizations when they were refused the inalienable right of American citizens to hold public meetings and engage in free speech.

Yet there was that letter from Karl Schluter, addressed to Griebl. Was it another Schade affair? Or was it something more concrete? I had Jenni brought from the detention-room.

"What about this Dr Griebl?" I asked her. "What did he have to do with this spy ring?"

"Oh," she breathed, "he is a very big man, an important man. Even Schluter was respectful to him. Schluter visited him every time he came here, and exchanged instructions with him. Three or four times Dr Griebl gave me big envelopes to carry back to Germany. Dr Griebl was—well, once I heard Schluter say that Dr Griebl was the most important Nazi secret-service agent in all America!"

CHAPTER VIII

THE February dusk had deepened almost into the darkness of night as the car containing two other G-men and myself drew up in front of the old-fashioned but still elaborate block of flats at 56 East 87th Street, in the heart of the German colony in the Yorkville section of New York.

A sign outside advertised: "Dr Ignatz T. Griebl, M.D."

The uniformed doorman saluted, then paid no further attention to us. I pushed the button for his office on the flat-register. The lock clicked in response, and I entered a reception room. A door opened, and out came a comely nurse, her manner as crisp as her white uniform. I was alone, having left the other agents outside to watch the exits. Agent Cotter was to follow me inside in three minutes.

The nurse regarded me coolly. "It is after office hours," she said disapprovingly. "You cannot see the doctor this evening."

"I think Dr Griebl will see me," I said quietly.

She looked doubtful. "What is your name?" she demanded.

"Agent Turrou—of the Department of Justice," I said.

Her eyebrows went up. "What do you wish to see the doctor about?"

"Go and tell the doctor I am here. He will know!" I gambled.

She turned and disappeared. I took my bearings. I was still in the reception room, beyond which I could see a fairly large waiting-room. Other doors led, I guessed, to the doctor's private office, an operating-room, and perhaps a laboratory. There were old copies of French etchings on the walls, and, prominently displayed and elaborately framed, Griebl's commission in the United States Army Reserve.

In a moment the door from the private office opened—and I had my first glimpse of Dr Griebl.

He was scared. There was no mistaking it. He was pale, and his jowls quivered. He had evidently been taking off his white physician's coat preparatory to leaving for the day when the nurse brought my name and the fateful words—"Department of Justice"—to him. Now he was trying, with fumbling fingers, to refasten it.

"Dr Griebl?" I said.

"Yes, sir," he replied, and no more.

The buzzer rang. From somewhere the nurse answered it. Agent Cotter came in quietly. Dr Griebl said nothing.

"We are of the Federal Bureau of Investigation, of the United States Department of Justice, Doctor," I said. "We want you to come with us to our headquarters."

He did not ask a question. He did not demand to know why. He made no objections. He merely said:

"Yes, sir."

And such was the military tone of obedience in his voice that for a moment I thought he was going to click his heels and salute.

I studied him as he exchanged his office jacket for a double-breasted coat and an overcoat. He was a pudgy man, of medium height, about thirty-nine. His eyes wavered behind gold-rimmed glasses. Outside his office, I learned later, he usually wore the tortoise-shell or horn-rimmed type of glasses. His clothing was very tight, accentuating his pudginess. His teeth were very white, quite noticeable. He had dimples.

Still he said nothing. It was astounding that he should not even make a pretence of wondering why we wanted him. After all, he was supposed to be a respectable, fairly eminent doctor, and here suddenly were two G-men in his office,

DR IGNATZ T. GRIEBL

ordering him to come along with them. We expected him to make some show of surprise, of protest.

But no.

I pointed towards the framed commission, and remarked on it.

"Yes, sir," he said proudly. "I am a first lieutenant. Soon I hope to become a captain."

It was amazing.

"Do you know Karl Schluter?" I flung at him suddenly.

His shoulders jerked.

"No, sir," he replied—and no more.

"Do you know Johanna Hofmann?"

"No, sir. I know no one of that name, sir."

He finished his dressing. He stood at attention, to signify that he was ready. Between us he marched out, without a word, like a man going to his execution. In his beloved Nazi Germany, that's what it would have been. The nurse, wide-eyed, watched us go from behind a door.

Not a word was spoken during the drive to F.B.I. head-quarters. He marched—and marched is exactly the word—between us into the lift, and along the corridor to my office. He stood rigidly at attention until I told him to sit down, and then he obeyed rather than relaxed.

But it was soon apparent that his obedience was in no sense surrender. He was polite, he was obsequious almost, but he denied everything, absolutely and flatly.

"No, sir, I am not a spy, sir," he said.

"No, sir, I don't know anything about German spies here. I don't believe there are any.

"No, sir, I do not know any person named Johanna Hof-mann.

"No, sir, nor Jenni Hofmann. Nor Ruth Hofmann.

"Mr Turrou, if I knew of Nazi spies here I would, as an officer of the United States Army Reserve, immediately report them to the proper authorities in this country.

"No, sir, I do not know Karl Schluter.

"No, sir, I never heard of anyone named Rumrich.

"No, sir, nor Erich Glaser.

"No, sir, nor Martin Schade.

"Mr Turrou, I do not deny I have a warm feeling for my Fatherland. I would be unnatural if I did not. But I am an American citizen first, and an officer of our Army, sir!"

"Let me try to refresh your memory, Doctor," I said. "Are you sure you don't remember Jenni Hofmann?"

"Positive, Mr Turrou. I never met anyone of that name."

"An auburn-haired girl, attractive, with blue eyes?"

"No, I do not know her."

"A girl who came to your office several times with Karl Schluter?"

"I don't know Karl Schluter, and I don't remember any girl coming to my office with Karl Schluter, sir," he said firmly.

He didn't notice the slight signal I gave the agent near the door. I talked loudly to cover the sound of the door opening as the agent, catching the signal, went out on his prearranged errand.

"Now, come, Dr Griebl," I said, "surely you wouldn't forget a pretty, red-headed girl who came to your office."

He relaxed, apparently believing he had me baulked. He even permitted himself a leer.

"No, Mr Turrou," he laughed. "You are right. I wouldn't forget a pretty, red-headed girl who came to my office."

"And yet you don't remember Jenni Hofmann?"

"Mr Turrou," he said solemnly, "I swear to you that no such girl ever came into my office."

I looked over his head.

"Jenni!" I snapped. "Did you ever see this man before?"

"Yes," came Jenni's voice calmly. "That is Dr Griebl."

I almost felt sorry for the man. His head swung round

violently, and when he saw her standing there behind him, he almost fell off the chair. I never saw a man so deflated.

"Jenni," I said in German, "is this the man from whom you took packages of spy material for delivery to spy headquarters in Bremen?"

"Yes," she said. "That is the man."

Griebl's face grew livid.

"That is a lie!" he shouted. "It is not true!"

He spoke in English, but his tone was unmistakable, and Jenni caught the meaning. A girl of fire herself, she forgot her own predicament and shouted back:

"*Ich hab' die Wahrheit gesagt.*" ("I have told the truth.")

They glared at each other. I addressed Griebl again.

"Do you still insist you never saw this young lady?"

He muttered something at her I did not catch, and then he dropped his eyes.

"Well, yes, sir," he said. "I do know this woman. But I saw her only twice in my office. She came with a man, for information concerning the Jews. That was all."

Jenni apparently wasn't one to hold a grudge. Her ire cooled as quickly as it came. She looked at him almost pityingly.

"Herr Doktor Griebl," she said in German, "it is no use. They found the codes and letters and everything, and so I had to tell the truth. Mr Turrou knows all about your connexions with Schluter and myself. You might as well tell all."

Griebl shook his head. "There is nothing further to tell," he insisted.

I called for her official statement. I showed it to him, the seal and her signature. Then, with Jenni still in the room, I read it to him, verbatim: the dates she swore she had been in his office, the remarks she said he made to her and Schluter about spy activities—the whole thing.

"Is this your true statement, Fräulein Hofmann?" I asked.

"Yes, Mr Turrou," she said.

"And now, Dr Griebl, what do you have to say?" I demanded.

His tone was surly.

"I never gave her packages containing military information," he said flatly. "I never gave her any packages whatsoever. Only notes and verbal information about the Jews."

He whirled on her and, in German, demanded fiercely: "Isn't it a fact that I gave you only information about the Jews?"

Jenni stood her ground.

"No, Herr Doktor," she replied. "I heard you tell Schluter that it was military information."

He grew apoplectic with rage. His face became suffused, his eyes stood out, and he ground his teeth. For a moment I thought he was going to leap at her with clenched fists. Then he began pouring at her such a filthy stream of vituperation in German that I had to send her from the room. He shrieked after her like a madman, "I'll see that you are repaid for what you have said. I'll see that you are shot!"

Her final retort, as the door closed behind her, was: "*Ich hab' die Wahrheit gesagt.*"

He sank back in his chair, trembling with rage. I watched a long time as I let him cool off, and then, when his breathing became even again, I said to him:

"If you are innocent, Dr Griebl, you can have no objection to our searching your office?"

He hesitated fleetingly, then looked me straight in the eye. "None at all, Mr Turrou," he said. "You are not a Jew, so you will not be offended by what you find."

He didn't explain that, and I was tired of questioning him. I figured that remark would soon explain itself. We got back to his office at about 11.45 P.M.

Indeed it soon became apparent what his last cryptic remark

meant. He had a most elaborate file, almost a library, in fact, on prominent Jews in America. In it was about every attack ever printed or publicly made on any of them, in addition to their formal biographies. The files represented quite a bit of work and investigation. I could not fail to notice that as we went through them to see if there was any evidence of spy activity in them. There wasn't. The entire file had to do solely with Jews. Men in public life were traced back to their great-great-great-grandparents. The names and addresses and occupations and histories of all their children and brothers and sisters and wives and aunts and uncles and even some third and fourth cousins were listed. Their birthplaces, school-ing, and residences at all stages of their careers, their social, business, fraternal, and political connexions, their estimated wealth, their friendships with non-Jews of note, the offices they held. It made, apparently, no difference whether they were professing Jews or not, as long as they had Jewish blood. I noted names which surprised me. All notes were inter-spersed with scurrilous, often obscene, remarks.

I am sorry now I did not note all the names in those files, but had no idea of writing a book at the time, and so kept my eye only on actual clues. The entire file, since it contained no evidence of spying against the nation, was of no interest to me as a G-man. However, I do recall that Secretary of the Treasury Morgenthau was listed, and Governor Lehmann of New York, and Felix Warburg, David Sarnoff, Samuel Untermeyer, Congressman Dickstein, Rabbi Stephen Wise, and Mayor La Guardia of New York.

We searched for an hour and half without finding any-thing like spy evidence. Dr Griebl stood by, his composure largely recovered. We were about to give up for the night when, in a corner of Griebl's personal desk, I noticed a small paper book of matches.

There was nothing suspicious about that, and I do not know

what made me reach for it. But as I did, I suddenly sensed rather than saw a stiffening in Griebl.

I toyed with it a moment, to note his reaction—and I saw that the man grew rigid, and the colour, which had partly come back into his face, abruptly vanished. Still watching him, I opened the packet.

There were no matches in it. But written in red ink on the inside of the cover was a set of strange symbols—the key to the secret spy code!

Dr Griebl was aghast when he saw me open the book of matches and look at those symbols. His face grew positively ashen, and I was convinced he would stop lying. Now he would confess.

But no. The man had marvellous recuperative powers, and was a born liar. He pulled himself together in a moment, and even managed a sickly smile.

"I meant to tell you about that, Mr Turrou," he said. "It's an odd thing, isn't it?"

"Yes," I agreed drily. "Very odd."

"You see, Mr Turrou," he continued hurriedly, "I did not tell you exactly the truth when I said I did not know Karl Schluter. I was afraid that perhaps you were interested in my activities against the Jews. But you are not a Jew, and as a man of intelligence you can appreciate that I am doing a great service fighting these Jews.

"You see, there is a man named Karl Schluter, a steward on the s.s. *Europa*. He comes to see me, and I give him reports on the activities of these Jews in America. He takes them to Germany, where they are needed to combat this plot of the Jews against Germany—this boycott you may have heard about. You see how it is, don't you, Mr Turrou? That's the way it is. That's how I know Karl Schluter—only in that connexion, Mr Turrou. . . ."

His voice trailed off as he saw the disbelief in my eyes. I

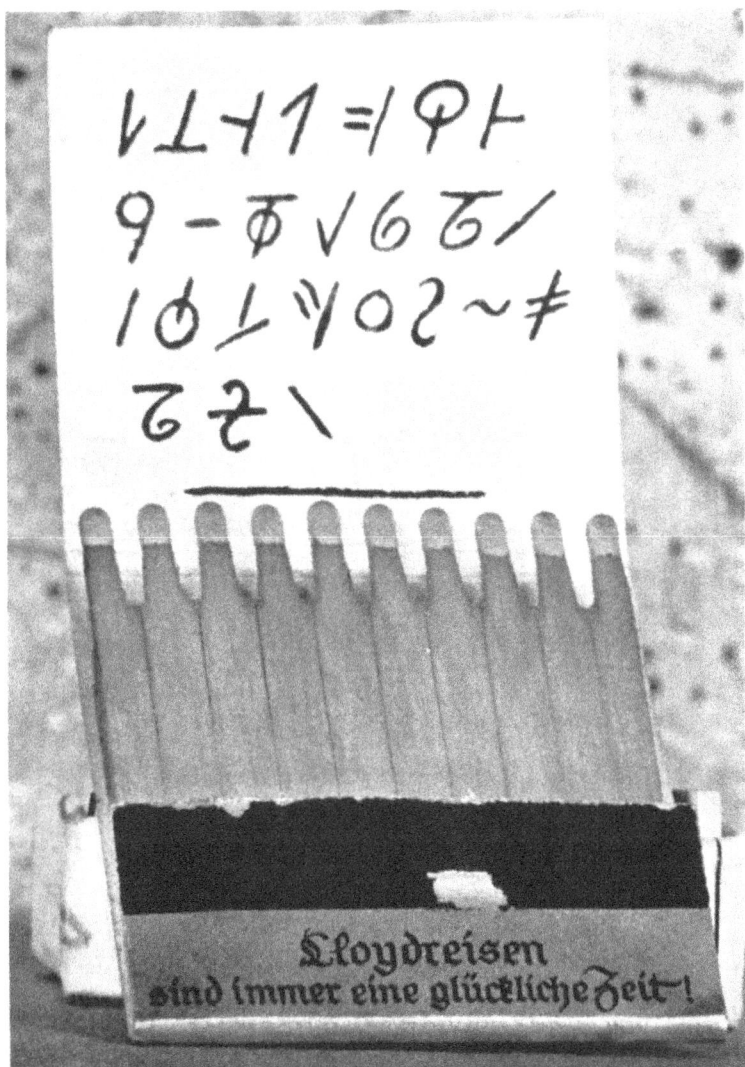

BOOK OF MATCHES WITH NAZI SPY CODE

The match-book is exactly the kind the spies used, and the code is the real spy code, but the exhibit is faked. Actually the spies wrote the code lower down, so that it was hidden by the matches. But the real exhibit did not photograph properly, so the author, for purposes of book-illustration, prepared this exhibit.

raised the match-cover, with the red symbols towards him.

"But what about this?" I persisted.

"Oh, that. . . ." he said. "Oh, yes, I was about to come to that. As a matter of fact, Mr Turrou, I don't know what that is. One day this man Schluter—about five or six weeks ago, I think it was—or maybe it was six or seven weeks ago—came to my office. He left this booklet of matches. . . . I did not even open it, Mr Turrou, I attached so little importance to it. He left it here, and asked me to give it to a Miss Eleanor Böhme, I think the name was. He said she would call for it. I placed it in my desk—and when she failed to call for it I forgot all about it, Mr Turrou, until just now when I saw you pick it up."

There was a silence in the room when he finished. He looked me straight in the eye, and I kept staring back at him, holding the paper match-cover in my hand, half raised. The muscles in his jaws contracted with the effort of keeping his eyes steady against mine, and the red crept up into his face.

Suddenly the telephone rang, clamorously in the silence.

"Answer it!" I snapped. "But say nothing. Merely tell whoever it is that you are busy."

"Yes, sir," he said, and lifted the receiver. In the silence, the diaphragm of the telephone transmitter chattered so that we could hear clearly.

"Darling!" vibrated a woman's voice, slightly accented. "Are you all right? What is the matter? What are you doing there at this hour? The nurse said two men came and took you away. . . ."

I clapped my hand over the mouthpiece. "Tell her to come down here right away," I ordered.

Twenty minutes later the door-buzzer sounded, and a beautiful young woman burst into the room and flung her arms round Dr Griebl's neck. She kissed him hungrily a dozen times, ignoring us completely, murmuring endearments mingled with frantic questions:

"Are you all right? Did they hurt you? What do they want of you? Are you all right?"

Finally he disentangled himself.

"These gentlemen are from the Department of Justice," he said. "Mr Turrou and Mr Cotter. Gentlemen, Miss Moog."

She barely acknowledged the introductions. Her eyes flashed. It was two o'clock in the morning. I stood silently holding the packet of matches.

"But what is all this nonsense?" she cried in a loud voice.

"It is nothing, my dear," he soothed her. "Some stupid girl—a hairdresser on the *Europa*—has told them I am a spy. She had a letter with her from Germany, from a man named Karl Schluter, and these gentlemen seem to think it implicates me. Everything will be all right."

He was sly, this Dr Griebl. An honestly excited man would not have bothered to explain, in his first few words to the woman who loved him and was frightened for him, that the girl who accused him was a hairdresser on the s.s. *Europa*. In a few words he had very shrewdly managed to tell Miss Moog the exact status of the case against him. I decided to look more deeply into this Miss Moog.

She whirled on us.

"He is innocent!" she cried. "You must not listen to the tales of stupid girls. Dr Griebl is a well-known man. He is innocent. You must release him at once."

We talked to Dr Griebl and Miss Moog for another half an hour that morning, though obviously it was fruitless for the time being. I decided it would not be wise to arrest them right away. If I did, I would have to arraign them shortly, and not only would I have insufficient evidence, but it would get into the newspapers and further warn the spy ring. It was better to treat them as if I was not sure of myself, and allow them to talk themselves into real trouble.

I yawned elaborately. "Well, Doctor," I said, "we'll leave you. Please be at my office at nine o'clock in the morning. Miss Moog, we will drive you home." I did not want them to compare notes.

As we went outside, unnoticed by the woman I signalled to a man who sat in a car parked near by. He was a third F.B.I. agent, and my signal meant that he was to remain on guard. Seeing us come out without Griebl, he needed no instructions to understand that it was Griebl he was to watch.

We drove her home to 276 Riverside Drive. As we bade her good-night, I instructed her to be at my office also at 9 A.M. She flounced into the house, every line eloquent of exactly what she thought of us. Cotter remained on guard outside. I went home to catch a few hours' sleep. I had no doubt that both Griebl and Miss Moog would show up in the morning. Griebl had too much at stake to flee, since so far we had only Jenni's statement and rather slight circumstantial evidence against him. He was the kind who would try to brazen it out, confident he could outwit anyone. And as for Miss Moog, one look at her face as she threw her arms round him was enough to convince anyone she would not flee anywhere without him.

At 9 A.M. they were at my office. I turned Miss Moog over to a matron and concentrated on Griebl. I went to work at once.

"Let's stop this nonsense, Griebl," I said. "You can see the game is up. What have you to say for yourself?"

"I have said it," he muttered. "It was only about the Jews—nothing more."

"Then why did you give it to Schluter and Jenni Hofmann?" I demanded. "They are spy operatives, not propagandists."

"All right," he snapped, his politeness gone. "I did under-

stand they were espionage agents as well. But I had nothing
to do with that. I used them for my purposes, because it was
convenient."

"To whom was your material addressed?" I asked.

"To Dr Paul Joseph Goebbels, head of the Ministry of
Propaganda."

"You're a fool to keep lying, Griebl," I snapped.

His head came up. "What do you mean?" he demanded
indignantly. "I am not lying!"

"The material was addressed to 'N. Spielman,' at Bremen,"
I pointed out. "He is a spy director. He is one of the heads
of the *Marine Nachrichten Stelle*, which is the Nazi Naval
Intelligence. That is entirely separate from the Ministry of
Propaganda. It is under the War Ministry at Berlin. It is
devoted entirely to spy activity. How do you explain that,
Griebl?"

It was obvious that the point struck home, but he shrugged
it off.

"I was not interested in such details," he retorted. "I
never inquired as to the mechanics of how my material
eventually got to Dr Goebbels. It could not have been of
value to the *Marine Nachrichten Stelle*. I tell you it was only
about Jews!"

It looked like a long siege ahead to break this man. I was
about to have him put in a cell to think it over while I checked
up further on his history to find another point of attack,
when the telephone on my desk rang.

"Hello," came the voice of one of the G-men assigned to
trace Griebl's activities for the past year or so. "I'm at the
Taft Hotel. Dr Griebl registered here with a woman at least
four times last year. The description doesn't fit his wife.
This was a tall, handsome woman, with flashing eyes. The
bell-boys whistled when they described her. Does that interest
you?"

I was about to say no, since I had no interest in Griebl's sex life, but suddenly a thought struck me. "Hold on," I said. "What were the dates?" The agent gave them to me. I thanked him and rang off.

Then I began chatting casually with Griebl. I asked him about his wife and his family and the associations to which he belonged, the extent of his practice, his specialities. And then I asked him, still casually, when his wife had sailed for Germany.

"In December," he replied.

I looked at the dates I had just scrawled on a piece of scratch paper.

"Then who, Griebl," I shot at him, "was the woman with whom you registered at the Taft Hotel?"

And that, somewhat to my astonishment, I must admit, worked where everything else had failed. It was apparently the element of surprise rather than the importance of the fact. It could not have been fear that we would tell his wife, for she already knew only too well that he was carrying on with other women.

"So you know that, too?" he remarked, as if to himself. He parried my further questions somewhat absent-mindedly for a few more moments, then nodded his head as if having reached a conclusion.

"All right, Mr Turrou. You win," he said. "But I must talk to you alone. . . ."

CHAPTER IX

MEANWHILE other G-men were questioning Miss Moog, trying to break her. They found themselves up against what looked like an impossible assignment. She was armoured by her love for the pudgy Dr Griebl, and nothing seemed to prevail against it.

She denied everything. She laughed in their faces when they asked her questions concerning his spy activities. He was no spy, she declared. It was ridiculous. They were a pack of fools. They would get into trouble, annoying a great man like Dr Griebl. He would show them!

They called me in from the room in which I was listening to Griebl's confession. "Maybe you can do it," they said. "You cracked Griebl." I went in full of confidence—and got exactly nowhere. She laughed at me, as she had at the others, and taunted me. "So Dr Griebl wore you out," she jeered. "I told you that you would get in trouble. I hope he gave you a piece of his mind, Mr Smart-Alec Turrou!"

But I had a trump card up my sleeve. Just as she was in the midst of giving me a piece of her own mind, I broke in quietly with: "But you are mistaken, Fräulein. Dr Griebl has confessed. He has told me everything."

She leaped to her feet, brilliant eyes flashing.

"That is a lie!" she cried. "It is not true! Dr Griebl would not. . . ."

She checked herself abruptly. Laughter came back. "You think you are smart, don't you?" she taunted. She walked up and down the office, swinging her hips, swirling her skirts.

Her laughter, high, girlish—almost like a child's—echoed through the room.

"If the doctor tells you to, Miss Moog," I said, "will you then talk?"

She halted suddenly.

"Why, certainly," she said promptly. A woman in love! It did not occur to her that her hero might have failed, might have broken down and confessed. She was so sure of his superiority to all others, so sure he never would weaken, but would triumph over these ordinary men.

"All right," I said, and raised my voice. "Bring Dr Griebl in," I called.

She swung round as the door opened. Her eyes grew startlingly wide as she saw Griebl, his head hung in shame, brought in by an agent. One look was enough to tell her the story. Her face began to twitch, and suddenly she began to weep.

He hesitated a moment, then stepped forward, put an arm round her, and began to console her. "Everything will be all right," he murmured. "It will turn out well. Compose yourself. Don't cry."

His eyes began to glitter, and he let her go. "It is not our fault!" he shouted. "It is that *dummkopf*, Schluter. Giving a girl like that—a hairdresser—the codes and the letters. They have found the letters, and we are lost!"

His fists waved in the air. "That *dummkopf*!" he shouted. "I will have him shot for this. Shot, I tell you! Shot!"

He was again the conquering male, and she looked at him timidly, and adored him.

"What shall I do, Ignatz?" she whispered, and again he put an arm around her shoulders.

"You might as well tell Mr Turrou everything," he sighed. " That is best now."

And so, obediently, she sat down and told her story. It

tallied fairly well with what Griebl told us of scenes at which she was present. At no point did it picture her taking an active part in any spy activities.

As the long hours of talking and questioning went on, through the dreary details of drawing up a statement, she recovered her spirits and became a woman once more aware of her looks. She became by turns flirtatious and coy, and turned the full power of her brilliant eyes upon me, and told me how wonderful I was, and how I was now the best friend she and the doctor had.

That was characteristic of Kate Moog. She is never the mysterious, slinky, darkly alluring woman of the spy novels. Instead she is openly coquettish and jolly. She makes her way through charm and gaiety; she has a remarkable talent for making friends. Though she is a tall woman—five feet ten inches—her childish voice and girlish ways did not seem incongruous or silly.

Her early background is shrouded somewhat in mystery. Born in Germany of well-to-do parents, she was brought to this country as a young girl. Here she completed training for the profession of nurse—but she did not remain an ordinary nurse. Her looks, her gaiety, her wit won her friends far above her station.

She travelled, on occasion, during several years of her youth, in some remarkably high circles. Von Bonin was right when he said that night in the café in Bremen that she numbered some of the most important men and outstanding officials in America among her friends. But the tense and the implications he drew were wrong. The friendships were in the past, and had been innocent. Most of the men she had not seen for years. For after several years in several cities, including Washington, she returned to New York and opened a nursing-home for convalescents and the aged. Behind her laughter and childishness lay a shrewd business brain. She did very well in the nursing-home business. At the time the spy case broke she had a fourteen-room flat, luxuriously furnished, in an upper-class block at 276 Riverside Drive, in New York City. She kept half a dozen servants, two of them fully capable of running the place during her absences. Her net income, she told me, was close to $400 a month. Ironically, many of her patients were Jewish.

Her exact *rôle* in this case is hard to determine. Her life and most of her other friends seem pretty innocent. Yet she had several strange friendships, noticeably one with Noel Scaffa, the notorious New York private detective who several times was in hot water with the police as a result of his uncanny faculty for recovering stolen goods when the rewards were quite large. But none of those friendships pointed in any way towards the Nazi spy ring, so we did not go deeply into them.

There are several other strange angles which interfere with full classification of Miss Moog. There is, for instance, that letter from Karl Schluter that Jenni had for her, saying, "How does the matter stand with the divorce?"

Just what that referred to still remains a mystery. She could not or would not explain it. Several years before she had married a man named Busch, and left him after a few days. He is another mystery. Later she got a Mexican divorce from him, claiming she could not locate him. But she was fearful of its legality.

"I have regulated the matter here to such an extent that you need only give the signal, and we will then take the attack to Germany," wrote Schluter. "One way or the other, the matter will turn out all right."

Was Schluter promising a trick divorce in Germany? And for whom—for Miss Moog from her discarded husband—or for Griebl from his wife? If the latter, why did Schluter write Jenni to go to see Miss Moog at an hour when Griebl would not be there, so that he would not know? And in either case, why should Schluter, that busy spy contact man, be taking all that trouble for Miss Moog? Had he, too, been won by her charm?

I don't know the answers. Just as she did on the witness stand in court later, Miss Moog dismissed all questions pertaining to that with the statement that she did not know anything about it. We could not press them. We had no case against her. She admitted that Pfeiffer and von Bonin and Menzel urged her to become the Mata Hari of this spy ring—to open a richly furnished flat in Washington where high Government officials and young Army and Navy officers could be lured—but denied that she agreed. We could show no overt act on her part.

The closest was the strange affair of attractive Eleanor Böhme and the paper book of matches.

"How does the matter stand with Böhme?" wrote Schluter in his letter to Miss Moog. And Dr Griebl, you will recall, told us that the paper book of matches I found in his desk, with the Nazi spy code inscribed inside the cover, had been left with him by Schluter for a girl named Eleanor Böhme.

So we hunted up Eleanor Böhme and brought her into F.B.I. headquarters. She turned out to be a strikingly pretty girl of twenty-two, a blonde, with blue eyes, fair skin, and a dimple in the centre of her chin and an oddly deep, mature voice. She was half-frightened, half-indignant.

She was born in this country, but her parents never forgot their native land, Germany. They took her on a visit there when she was fifteen and a freshman in the high school at Elmhurst, Long Island, where the family lived. Then, after a year at Hunter College, in New York, she spent two years studying in Germany, at the University of Berlin. In 1937 she returned to the United States, and was graduated from Hunter College with the degree of Bachelor of Arts in January, 1938.

Her tastes were half-American, half-German. Much of her

social life revolved round the more or less Nazi organizations in New York. And one of her ways of having an evening of fun was to visit a German ship in port at New York, to chat and dance with officers and crew members she had met through her visits to Germany.

That, she told me, was how she met Karl Schluter. She considered him merely a steward, she said, and his attentions rather annoyed her because he was so much older and apparently was of such menial rank. She denied she even suspected his spy activities, or that she ever got any hint that he was the ship's *Ortsgruppenführer* and therefore a man of power and importance.

In November, 1937, she said, he telephoned her at her home in Elmhurst, L.I., and asked her to meet him. They met at the Walgreen Drug Store, in Times Square, New York. There, she said, they had a soda and he questioned her at length as to her education, special training, background, and willingness to work. He promised, she said, to help her get a job worthy of her abilities.

A few weeks later she received a typewritten letter, on Hapag-Lloyd stationery. It was unsigned, she said, but since it referred to a job, she deduced it was from Schluter. Enclosed was Kate Moog's card. The letter instructed her to call on Miss Moog relative to a position.

"Had you ever heard of Miss Moog before?" I asked.

"No, never."

In January, 1938, she said, she telephoned Miss Moog and told her of the letter from Karl Schluter. Miss Moog showed no surprise, but cordially invited her to come up right away. It was a cold, snowy day. Miss Moog, Eleanor said, gave her coffee and questioned her for a little while about her education, special abilities, background, and willingness to work, just as Schluter had.

"Any reference to coming to live with her?" I asked.

"No."

"Did she say anything about going to Washington with her, or about a job in Washington?"

"No."

"Did she promise to introduce you to handsome young Army and Navy officers?"

"No."

"What sort of job did she say she might have for you?"

"She didn't say. As a matter of fact she said nothing about a position for me."

"A rather strange visit," I remarked.

"Very," said Eleanor Böhme.

"And then what happened?"

"Nothing."

I reached in my pocket and got the packet of matches I had taken from Griebl's desk. Eleanor's eyes widened as I opened it and displayed the Nazi spy code in red ink.

"Ever see anything like this before?" I asked.

"Yes," she admitted.

"Where?"

"Miss Moog gave me a packet like that."

"When?"

"The moment I entered her flat. As we shook hands, I felt her press something into my hand. When I looked, it was a packet of matches."

"What explanation did she make?"

"None."

"Didn't you ask her?"

"No. I didn't have an opportunity. She kept talking all through the interview."

"When did you find out about the marks inside?"

"After I left. I kept wondering why she gave it to me, and examined it carefully. Then I saw the marks."

"Did they mean anything to you?"

THE NAZI SPY CONSPIRACY IN AMERICA

"Absolutely nothing."

"Where is it now?"

"I destroyed it."

"Did you ever see or communicate with Miss Moog again?"

"No."

"How about Schluter?"

"I never heard from him again."

What Schluter's purpose in this odd incident was we can only guess. Was he following through with the Nazi spy chief's plan to set up Kate Moog in a spy nest in Washington? Was he considering Eleanor Böhme for one of the "pretty *Mädchen*" to lure Army and Navy officers into the spy ring? Were there others, already enlisted?

Miss Moog insisted she knew nothing about it. We had a hard time getting a connected story out of her on anything. Her true cleverness and intelligence are well hidden under an air of fluttering femininity and her constant coquetry. She did not openly parry questions, but talked so much round them that hardly ever could we get her down to the point. She was unpredictable. She had all the F.B.I. men working on the case, and the U.S. Attorney's staff, convinced that she was going to be a willing, helpful witness at the trial.

But when she took the stand she turned so evasive, so forgetful, that Judge Knox gave instructions to regard her as a hostile witness. With seeming stupidity and flightiness she completely baffled both prosecution and defence counsel. I admit it did me good to see that, for it made me feel less silly than I did at the conclusion of each round of verbal sparring during my questioning of her. An example of her method of answering questions, which occurred in court, is typical. Defence counsel, on cross-examination, suddenly fired at her:

"Isn't it true, Miss Moog, that you and Dr Griebl were

planning to leave the country while you were being questioned by the F.B.I.?"

Kate Moog rolled her lovely eyes and spread her hands in an eloquent, and so feminine, gesture.

"It was spwing," she lisped, "and it was so bee-yoo-tiful. . . ."

Defence counsel gave up.

At several points it got so bad that Judge Knox, one of the ablest and most even-tempered jurists in America, became so exasperated that he took over the questioning himself. He is an experienced examiner; before his years on the bench he was a United States Attorney, and he prosecuted spies during the World War.

He got particularly near in his questioning when Miss Moog told her version of the strange affair of Eleanor Böhme. She testified that she received a letter from Schluter, enclosing a packet of matches, and asking her to give it to a girl named Eleanor Böhme, who would call on her. And so, said Miss Moog with the air of one fully explaining everything, she did.

Judge Knox turned to her with his eyebrows lifted.

"Didn't it strike you as strange," he demanded, "that you should receive a packet of matches with instructions to give it to a strange woman?"

"No," replied Miss Moog, drawing out the word plaintively and casting down her eyes like a scolded child.

"You didn't think it strange," queried his Honour in incredulous tones, "even in view of what you had heard in Germany at the meeting between Dr Griebl and Pfeiffer, at which you were present?"

"No," she faltered.

"You didn't even examine the packet of matches sent you with such strange instructions and discover the markings?"

"No," she said.

Judge Knox stared at her, then shook his head.

124

KATE MOOG, ALIAS MRS KATHERINA MOOG BUSCH

Taken as she was about to enter Federal Courthouse in New York to testify.

"Well," he said, "I can hardly believe that, myself." He motioned to defence counsel to proceed.

As for the fact that Jenni Hofmann had a letter for her from Schluter in the spy code, Miss Moog declared flatly, "I don't know anything about that."

Our questioning of her at the F.B.I. during the investigation was interrupted by the fact that Griebl began to talk at great length and give us far bigger game to shoot at than a love-struck woman who might or might not know more than she was telling.

Griebl was talking partly on his own terms. After insisting that no one else should be in the room while he talked to me, he demanded that I should take no notes.

"You can't make deals with the F.B.I.," I told him.

"All right," he said. "I won't talk under any other conditions."

"We'll discuss that later," I said. "Go ahead and talk. For the time being, it will be with no one else in the room."

He remained suspicious and fidgety. He displayed surprising knowledge of secret-investigation procedure. He insisted, for instance, on remaining some distance away from the telephone on my desk. "You might have a microphone hidden in it," he said. I assured him I had not—which was true—but he carefully avoided it. He would not talk anywhere near the desk either, and watched me suspiciously every time I opened a drawer, as if he feared a microphone hidden in the desk. He kept well to the centre of the room, and spoke in a low voice, as if he knew that to-day walls literally can have ears.

For three hours that day he talked while I listened, frankly engrossed. He told me things about a vast Nazi spy conspiracy which shocked me so that I could hardly believe them. But the instant I tried to make a note, he stopped talking.

Finally I called in my superior, Reed Vetterli, and asked

Griebl to tell him the gist of what he had told me. Griebl did. For days we held such sessions, and each time Griebl told me more details and new angles of this Nazi spy plot. After Griebl left each day I made extensive verbal reports to Vetterli, and then, at his request, made an official report on the questioning and its results.

After about the sixth session, I told Griebl, "You say you are trying to help us. These notes are bound to be full of errors, particularly on names and dates. You say you despise these furtive spies, and want to help us break it up. You can prove that best by dictating a statement."

For long moments he thought it over, and from his face it was hard to tell what his decision was going to be. But at last he made a gesture of surrender with his hands, and said, "All right, I will do it. Call in your stenographer. Only—again I warn you—I will not sign it."

Vetterli stood by and listened as Griebl dictated. Griebl never did sign the statement, but that was not important. It was immensely valuable to us as it stood. For now we could swing into real action. Now began the intensive, big-scale investigation in this case. Now was no time to worry further about Miss Moog, or even Dr Griebl himself. He would keep. Now we had a hundred clues—and all of them hot.

CHAPTER X

WE could not have cracked this Nazi spy conspiracy to the extent we did, nor exposed it so completely as a deliberate plot of the Nazi Government itself, if it had not been for Dr Griebl. He gave us the clues that led us right up to the War Ministry in Berlin, right into Hitler's inner circle. For when at last he made up his mind to talk, he talked for days. I questioned him daily for more than two months. He was patently interested then only in saving his own hide. He lied about his own *rôle* in spy activities, but he betrayed the Nazi spies and higher-ups to us just as previously he had betrayed this country to the Nazis. His 'squealing' was more typical of the trade of spying than the stoicism and bravery attributed to spies in fiction. In real life there is no glamour in spies.

It was Griebl who first named the high officials in Germany, such as the august Colonel Busch, and the Kapitan-Leutnants von Bonin, Menzel, and Pfeiffer, as the master plotters in the conspiracy against the security of this country. This would have probably been merely a picayune affair, with no mention of the higher-ups and indirect indictment of the Hitler *régime*, if Griebl had not betrayed his masters in Germany. Griebl became my informer, my 'stool-pigeon.'

It was his story, I feel certain, which led the Federal Grand Jury in New York to take the drastic, unprecedented steps it did.

The Grand Jury indicted four Nazi officials who, it realized full well, were safe in Germany and could never be tried here. Griebl's story, as contained in the statement he dictated, put the Grand Jury into a frame of mind where it felt that the most vital thing was to expose this conspiracy to the American public and the entire world, and to slap Hitler in the face and make him realize that he could not get away with that in the United States. This was no ordinary Grand Jury, controlled by the District Attorney and his assistants. The members came from the so-called 'blue ribbon' panel of citizens of high intelligence, leaders in the business and professional worlds, capable of making their own judgments, and apt to take matters right out of the hands of the District Attorney if they disagreed. Included was a citizen of German birth, 100 per cent. Aryan. He was, like the others, aghast at the proofs laid before them. The jury found itself in full agreement with the way U.S. Attorney Lamar Hardy and his assistants handled the case, and the F.B.I. produced the witnesses. It said so, publicly, when it found indictments against eighteen persons, only four of whom were in custody, on June 20, 1938.

The State Department could, through pressure and the strong argument that this was a matter involving delicate international relationships, have halted such action and had the indictments confined to the comparatively unimportant persons captured. It is indicative of how flagrant and danger- ous a violation of decent international relationships this plot was considered in Washington that the State Department, though aware of what we were doing in the case, made absolutely no move to influence us against such action. It even openly showed its approval by aiding us to the best of its ability when we sought escaping prisoners abroad.

Griebl named spies in key positions in our defence industries who we never dreamed existed. He placed some of them 'on the spot' for us so that we were able to capture them, he showed us where to look for others, and he betrayed the *Gestapo* men —the brutal Nazi secret police in America—to us. He told us where the Nazi spy bases were and named the men who headed them. He betrayed Otto Hermann Voss and Werner George

Gudenberg and Karl Friedrich Wilhelm Herrmann and Fritz Ewald Rossberg and Theodor Schütz and a dozen others. He told us some things that even in this inside story of how the ring was smashed I cannot explain to you, for they touch on matters which might endanger the national defence.

Naturally we did not take his word for any of these things. We checked thoroughly. But virtually everything he told us about the Nazi spy ring turned out to be true, and I am strongly inclined to believe that some things which he told us, but which we could not corroborate and which I therefore cannot put down here, were also true. He lied a great deal, of course, but mainly about the extent of his own complicity, and by omission of full details in some matters.

Griebl revealed to us the fact that the secrets of our naval programme were known in detail to Nazi spy headquarters in Germany before some of our high-ranking Navy officers knew them.

Griebl gave us the tip that the offices of one of the foremost naval architects in this country, where many of our war vessels —the front line of our national defence—are designed, contained a Nazi spy contact.

Griebl informed us that the Nazi spy ring had a man posted in the clearing-house for the loan offices in Washington, to report which U.S. Army and Navy officers and Government sub-officials needed money, so that Nazi operatives could approach them with offers of bribes to turn traitors.

It was Griebl who revealed to me the details how a confidential discussion on naval design, held in Washington, was known in detail in Nazi spy headquarters in Germany within a comparatively few hours.

Griebl told of plans to kidnap American citizens and take them to Germany for 'punishment' because they insisted upon being more loyal to this country than to Nazi Germany.

Griebl exposed to us how Nazi agents tried to seduce

German-born engineers and designers working in key industries in America to Germany, so that they could be forced to
reveal secrets they learned in the United States.

Griebl was able to describe in detail to me the U.S. Navy's
plans for a fleet of new destroyers—their design, tonnage,
power, armament, and so forth—and when we checked up
with the Navy Department there was great consternation,
because Griebl was absolutely right! He told me Schluter
had told him those details, just as a matter of conversation,
but I believe Griebl had a big hand in securing those details,
and was only trying to save his own hide by putting all the
blame on Schluter.

Griebl tipped us off to the fact that the Nazi spy ring had
a working agreement with Japanese spy headquarters, and
sold them some of the west-coast naval secrets at 300
per cent. profit. He said that Kapitan-Leutnant Pfeiffer told
him that in Bremen, but I believe Griebl also knew of it
directly.

Griebl realized fully what he was doing in telling us all this.
He knew what to expect if the Nazis ever found out how he
had betrayed them, and then caught him in Germany. On
the afternoon of the third day of his recital, for instance, he
suddenly muttered, "*Ach, Gott!*" and buried his face in his
hands.

"What is it?" I asked.

He raised bitter eyes.

"Don't you realize, Mr Turrou," he said, "that what I
am doing is signing my death-warrant in Germany? If they
ever found out what I have told you—the secrets entrusted to
me by von Bonin, Menzel, Pfeiffer, and others. . . ."

He struck the back of his neck with the side of his hand, to
indicate beheading.

"That is what would happen to me!"

And that is what I believe will happen to him.

We handled him with gloves, for he was of more value to us as a willing witness than as an unwilling one. We did not arraign him, nor place him under bond, nor keep him under close surveillance after he began talking. In the light of subsequent events that may seem to have been a stupid way to handle the master Nazi spy in America, a dangerous menace to our country, and the most important figure captured in our spy drag-net. But it seemed sound logic and very wise at the time. All of us concerned agreed on it—the United States Attorney's office, the F.B.I. headquarters in Washington, and my immediate superior, Reed Vetterli. F.B.I. headquarters in Washington was kept informed of every development and every move, and it fully sanctioned our method of handling Griebl.

Our procedure was based on the premise that he could not flee. Mere flight from New York to another part of this country would not do him any good. We were confident of our ability to trace him anywhere he went, and, as a trained spy, he was aware that kind of flight would be useless. And, we reasoned, he could not flee to Germany, the one place where he would want to go, where he could practise medicine and obtain the kudos his ego so much needed, and where there was property for him, because all that and his life would be gone the moment the Nazis found out how much he had revealed to us.

We realized that even such careful reasoning was not air-tight, and that there still was some slight chance of a slip-up. But against it was his great value to our case as long as we could keep him talking. He was our prime witness against the higher-ups in Germany. He was our best source of information concerning other Nazi spies in the United States. He proved several times of great aid in capturing some of them. When we ran into a new name or new figure in our investigation, all we had to do was ask him, and he would identify it and help us make the capture. But we found that whenever we pressed him, whenever we treated him like a prisoner, whenever he was spoken to harshly, he shut up like a clam and lost his memory. His weakness was his ego, and as long as we treated him as a witness rather than a prisoner, as long as we let him walk out and go to his office without guard, as long as we made believe we fully believed him when he denied direct complicity in the spy plot, so long was he helpful. Therefore all concerned considered that his revelations concerning the higher-ups in Germany, and his further exposure of operatives and plots in America, more important than his immediate imprisonment. We considered the revelation of the extent and ramification of this Nazi plot more important than any one prisoner.

It was obvious, too, that wrapped in his ego, Griebl did not realize how deeply he had incriminated himself. Through all his detailed recital, he kept insisting that he had no direct part in these spy matters, but was told these things by von Bonin, Menzel, Pfeiffer, Schluter, and others merely because they wanted him to join them, and because one of his brothers had been a high official in the inner Hitler circle. Like Rumrich and Voss and some of the others, he had that queer Nazi complex of considering himself so superior to all other people that he could not see how obvious and silly and damaging his statements were. We saw he thought he was fooling us about himself, and so felt safe in letting him roam, especially in view of these two basic facts, to which we always came back in our discussions of how to handle him:

1. If he faced the music here, it meant at the most a comparatively short term in prison—and obviously Griebl thought he could talk his way out of even that.

2. If he fled to Germany, it meant death.

We overlooked one factor, as we later found out, but at the time it seemed the soundest plan. We let him roam free and concentrated on running down, verifying, and elaborating the clues he gave us.

It was in 1933—immediately after Hitler and his Brown Shirts flung the shadow of the Swastika over Germany—that the Nazi spy conspiracy began in America. That was Griebl's story to me, and that has been borne out by investigation.

There were no real German spies in the U.S. from the end of the World War until that year. The F.B.I. and G-2 have delved far back, but we can find no trace of any prior to Hitler. All we found was that Germany had the usual political and commercial informants, such as every major country has in every other country, no matter how friendly. But such men are observers and not real spies.

This is the difference between a vicious spy plot such as the Nazi conspiracy we uncovered here and the usual search for information that goes on regularly in friendly nations.

Every large country, like every business man, likes to know what its competitors are doing. A business man, unless he is out to smash a bitter, deadly enemy who threatens to wipe him out, finds out what he wants to know from the trade journals, from conversations with salesmen who sell both for him and for his competitors, from customers who deal with his rivals as well as his firm, from bankers and lawyers active in that field, and so forth. That is entirely legitimate, and a good business man must do it to keep up.

So it is with nations. One power wants to know how far another power plans to extend its foreign trade in certain quarters. It would like to know the political trends in the other nations, for their effect on trade and foreign relations. It would like to know, also, the exact status of armament programmes in other countries, even the most friendly. If Great Power A announced it was going to build a billion dollars' worth of 'planes, Great Power B, though it did not dream of war with Great Power A, would feel it must keep up. But fighting 'planes become obsolete in about three years, because of improved designs. So Great Power B would trý to find out if Great Power A was actually going to start building right away, or was going to stall for a year or so before going into construction. If the latter, Great Power B can save a third of a billion dollars by also stalling for a year.

To find out such things about foreign trade plans, political trends, and armament programmes, every large nation has in every other nation a few well-informed, shrewd observers. From them, from its diplomatic and commercial attachés, and sometimes from its newspaper correspondents, it gets all the information it needs. A careful reading of the better news-papers, a close check by an expert on import and export figures, and a couple of friendly swapping contacts with officials and informed newspaper correspondents of the other nations does the trick.

That is obviously legitimate and not at all underhanded or inimical or menacing. The men who do that are in no sense of the word spies. America does it, though not to the extent of some others. France does it, England does it, and, before Hitler, that was all Germany did in the United States.

Spies, traitors, theft of plans, bribing, and seduction of Army and Navy personnel, traps, forgeries, plots to overpower and kill men possessing military secrets, beautiful, alluring *femmes fatales*—all the melodramatic trapping of lurid spy novels and cinema thrillers—are used only by nations faced with menacing, potential enemies or nations planning aggres-sion against a friendly nation.

Yet such, in general, was the Nazi plot here. Why they should do this to America, a friendly nation, what they hoped to gain by such actions, some one better versed in the peculiar Nazi psychology will have to tell you. All the F.B.I. discovered was that such a Nazi spy conspiracy existed, that it was under the orders of, and directly supervised by, the Hitler high command, and that it began when Hitler came into power.

One day in 1933, according to Dr Griebl, there càme into his office in East 87th Street, a long-nosed man with baggy ears, who asked to be treated for ulcers of the stomach. He was a man of about forty, a little above medium height and weight, with dark brown hair, brown eyes, and a tight mouth.

That was Wilhelm Lonkowski, *alias* William Schneider, *alias* Willie Meller, *alias* William Sex, *alias* William Sexton, *alias* William Lonkis, who became one of the most dangerous and successful spies in the world.

Griebl says he didn't know Lonkowski was a spy then. He says Lonkowski thereafter organized the spy ring in America, and that he, Griebl, had nothing to do with its organization.

I doubt that. Griebl was an experienced spy. We trapped him into admitting that he was a spy for Germany as far back as 1922, while travelling in France, when still a young medical student. Whether Griebl or Lonkowski did the first spy organizing work in the United States I don't know. Lonkowski played an immensely important *rôle*, and may have been the pioneer, but Griebl could not have been far behind.

According to Griebl, Lonkowski acted merely as a patient during his first visit, and on the next couple of occasions did no more than drop hints that he was "doing something or other for the German Government." But on about the fourth visit, Dr Griebl told me, Lonkowski came out with it. It went something like this, Griebl says:

"Dr Griebl," said Lonkowski, "you are a good German, no?"

"Of course I am," replied Griebl.

"You believe in our *Führer* Hitler, and the divine principles of the National Socialist Party?"

"Yes."

"I know you do. That is why I am confiding in you. I want your help. You are prominent, respectable. No one will suspect you. I want you to help me make contacts, for I am an agent of the German Military Intelligence. I want you to help me obtain military and naval information. We must have that information—for it is the destiny of Germany, under our great leader, to rule the whole world!"

Obviously much of that scene is false. Griebl already was—and this even he admitted—a prime mover and chief clearing-house for the spread of the Nazi propaganda here. He was in constant contact with the chiefs of the Nazi party in Germany. It is quite possible that the picture is really reversed and that it was he who made a spy out of Lonkowski. My belief is that both were Nazi spies at the time of the meeting in Griebl's office, and that Lonkowski knew him or knew of him before, and that the chief reason for Lonkowski going there was to confer on plans for further infesting America with Nazi spies.

Lonkowski was a crack designer and expert mechanic, specializing in aviation work. During the World War he was a German pilot and was wounded severely when shot down in combat with a French 'plane.

When or how he came to America no one seems to know, but we traced him as far back as 1928, when he was employed as an aviation construction mechanic at the Ireland Aircraft Corporation, Long Island, N.Y. I am positive he was not acting as a spy then. I repeat: there is no doubt that there was no German spying in the United States from the close of the World War until the rise of Hitler in control of Germany.

By the time Griebl, says Lonkowski, first made contact with him, Lonkowski had given up working in aviation factories. He was too busy arranging contacts, enlisting spies, handing out instructions, and arranging for shipments of stolen secrets to Germany. He was living in Long Island, close to Roosevelt and Mitchel Fields, where he made spy contacts. He posed as a piano-tuner. That is, he carried a piano-tuner's kit, and business cards which announced he was a piano-tuner. He did not, of course, bother to tune any pianos.

For his activities Lonkowski got $500 a month salary and liberal expense allowances from Nazi spy headquarters in Germany. He also got a handsome bonus for every valuable Army, Navy, and Air Force secret he delivered.

How many Nazi spies Lonkowski introduced and planted in strategic points in America we shall probably never know. How many men he bought or cajoled or threatened or black-mailed into turning traitor and selling America to the Nazis we shall never know.

We do know, from certain damaging papers we discovered, that he was in contact with an infantry officer who was apparently supplying him with more or less secret information. We know that blueprints of many of the most vital aeroplane design secrets got into his hands. We know that almost wherever we poked into this Nazi spy mess we found traces of Lonkowski, though it had been nearly three years since he fled this country.

We know that he arranged for a spy at the Seversky Aircraft Corporation, Farmingdale, L.I., who got him valuable secrets, whom we captured, and who appears later in this account. We know he also seduced Werner George Gudenberg, an American citizen who wanted only to be left in peace with his wife and child, his job, and the home he was buying in Bristol, Pa. We know Lonkowski, with the aid and advice of Griebl, arranged for the sneaking of alien spies into America. We know that he and Griebl were local representatives of a Nazi spy plot to lure German-born engineers and designers in key positions back to Germany, with promises of huge salaries, so that they could be forced to reveal naval and military secrets learned in trusted jobs in the United States.

We know that Lonkowski, with the aid of Griebl, set up a Nazi spy base in Montreal, Canada, headed by an employee of an aircraft-designing plant. At regular intervals the spy in Canada shipped three to five rolls of film to Germany, each roll containing thirty-six negatives of confidential 'plane designs. In addition he acted as clearing agent for all Nazi spy activities in Canada. He planted a spy in an aeroplane factory near Boston, Mass., and got stolen secret designs and blue-prints from him for transmission to spy headquarters in Germany. He seems to have received confidential information from a spy at Boston Navy Yard, too.

In some manner we do not yet quite understand, the spy in Montreal got hold of secret plans for a new type of anti-aircraft gun the United States was building. The plans for this gun, which utilized an electro-magnetic device to enable it to discharge more bullets per minute, were known to Nazi spy headquarters in Germany before the gun was completed.

When we broke up the spy ring, Griebl was under orders to increase the Nazi spy staff in Canada. This was because England was planning to set up more aeroplane factories in Canada, and so that the spies could spread Nazi propaganda along the Canadian-United States border, and so that (this almost passes belief, but is fact) they could make a thorough survey of points of entry "for large groups" from Canada into mid-Western United States!

I have the name of the Nazi spy chief at Montreal, but do not feel that I should reveal it here, since that phase of the investigation belongs to the British Military Intelligence. Captain Guy Liddell, a British special agent attached to M.I.5, came to New York to get what information Major Dalton, of G-2, and I had; then he disappeared, to conduct his investigation in his own quiet way.

Dr Griebl at first denied any direct spy dealings with the Canadian base. So I confronted him with the records of his telephone calls for the past three years. They showed a number of long-distance calls to the Nazi chief at Montreal.

"Oh, that," said Griebl. "I'll tell you what that was. This man in Montreal is a stamp-collector. I am a sort of stamp-collector, too. I called him about stamps."

Then I confronted him with proof that he had at least twice sent money—$75 once and $50 another time—to the spy in Montreal.

"That," said Griebl coolly, "was for stamps I bought from him."

As anyone familiar with spy terminology knows, the word 'stamps' is frequently used in spy codes to denote plans.

We know that Lonkowski, with the aid of Griebl, set up a Nazi spy base at Newport News, Va., where many American war vessels are designed and built. We know that Lonkowski and Griebl built up the spy base in New York and had a hand in the extension of the one in Washington. Most of the Washington operations were out of their hands, however, and directed from Berlin through Nazi officials stationed at Washington. Not even Griebl, I believe, knew the identity of the Nazi spy chieftains in Washington, and it was fully to protect the identity of those men in Washington that the plans to set up the 'spy nest' with Miss Moog at Washington were presented to Griebl and Kate Moog by von Bonin, Menzel, and Pfeiffer instead of more directly.

Lonkowski and Griebl were also in touch with the Nazi spy base in Seattle, though the information secured by the Seattle base was not cleared through them, but was shipped to Germany via Japan.

Lonkowski arranged contacts and spies at Boston, at Buffalo, at Bristol, Pa., in Navy yards throughout the country. Karl Schluter took up where he left off. Both were in a sense subservient to Dr Griebl, because of his brains and position, and whenever instructions from spy headquarters in Germany did not completely cover a situation, they went to him for advice and instruction.

Lonkowski got a lot of his information from men who were not aware they were giving any. A hard-headed man, who could hold his liquor, he made it a point to make friends with men from the military air-fields. He drank with them and gave parties for them. They suspected nothing, for even the United States Army is not spy-conscious. Many an Army and Navy man, who may have been wondering whatever became of that good fellow, good drinker, and good spender William Lonkis—or William Meller—who could stand up at the bar with the best of them and almost always paid the bill, will feel sick when he reads this.

Lonkowski's spy skill ran the entire gamut. He could do the dangerous work of stealing plans himself, he could enlist other spies, and he also had the perspective necessary for a first-class spy. He saw the value of getting technicians from America over to Germany. He recognized how loosely held some of our secrets were and realized that a simple way of getting some of them was to get men who knew them over to Germany on the pretence that they were to get good jobs in the industries there.

A case in illustration of how the Nazis went about this is the story of Irwin Backhaus, 3004 47th Street, Long Island City. Backhaus was an employee of the Sperry Gyroscope Company, and an expert in the construction of the automatic pilot for aeroplanes, manufactured for the U.S. Army and Navy by Sperry Gyroscope.

In 1935 the Asconia Company, in Germany, bought the rights to manufacture the automatic pilot in Germany. It was strictly a commercial proposition, involving, naturally, no naval or military secrets.

Backhaus was well known in the field. He had worked for the German Government, and upon his arrival in America, before he got the job with Sperry Gyroscope, worked for the United States Government. So he was not very much surprised when, in April or May, 1935, he got a letter requesting him to call on an engineer from Germany, stopping at the St George Hotel, Brooklyn.

Backhaus went. Like any of us, he was not averse to listening to legitimate propositions for jobs which meant more money. And that was exactly what the engineer offered him—a big bonus and a very fine contract to go to Germany. But the size of the bonus and the liberality of the pay, considering what he knew about pay-rates in Germany, raised Backhaus' eyebrows. He kept asking exactly what he was supposed to do in Germany. If wanted as an expert on construction of the automatic pilot, he was excited at the prospect of going at such a price. But he could not see how his services in that field, able as he was, were worth that much.

Gradually light dawned. Part of the bargain, he began to see as a result of his questions, was that he should reveal in Germany everything he had learned while in the employ of the U.S. Goverment and Sperry Gyroscope. He was a most trusted employee in both places, and had access to many blueprints—and to all blueprints at Sperry. That company works closely with the Army and Navy, and some of the blueprints involved important secret devices.

When Backhaus saw the real purpose of the astounding offer, he refused to go. But how many others in somewhat similar positions were seduced we can only guess. We know of several, and they are still being watched.

An even more indicative example is the case of C. F. Danielsen, an extremely skilled naval designer, who did much of the designing on Navy destroyers built at the Bath Iron Works, at Bath, Maine.

Danielsen came to this country from Germany forty years ago, but he still had three daughters living in Bremen, Germany, and had property there. It was still, apparently, his homeland to him. That made him appear to the Nazi spy ring as an ideal subject.

Griebl says the instructions to contact Danielsen came to him from Schluter, who got them from Kapitan-Leutnant Pfeiffer, at Bremen. I suspect that Griebl first found out about Danielsen, and sent the idea of enlisting him to Pfeiffer, and that Schluter merely brought back word to go ahead. At any rate, Griebl admitted that the idea was to get Danielsen over to Germany on the pretext that a splendid job awaited him there, and then to force him to reveal everything he had learned about our naval secrets while he was engaged in designing parts of our fighting ships.

Griebl wired Danielsen at Bath, Me., and offered to pay his transportation if Danielsen would come to New York and confer with him. We subpœnaed that telegram, and the F.B.I. has a copy of it. It indicated to Danielsen that it might mean a lot of money to him to keep that appointment.

Danielsen kept it. Griebl told me that Danielsen listened to his proposition and set a price. Danielsen told me, when we brought him in for questioning, that he did not agree, but said he would think it over. Griebl is such a liar that Danielsen's version is probably the truth.

When Schluter came to New York again in his disguise as a steward on board the German liner *Europa*, Griebl told him that Danielsen had agreed in principle, but wanted his transportation to Germany paid, and had held out for a few other points. He told Schluter to tell Kapitan-Leutnant Pfeiffer that he thought Danielsen's demands should be met.

When Schluter returned, it was with word that Pfeiffer had not only agreed to everything, but had already arranged with the North German Lloyd—through Lutz Leisewitz, a director of that German steamship company—to forward immediately to New York a first-class return ticket for Danielsen.

That is not merely Griebl's story. We checked everything thoroughly and examined records. They showed that Leisewitz wrote to Johannes Schröder, general manager of the North German Lloyd in New York City, enclosing a return ticket for Danielsen. The F.B.I. subpœnaed that ticket as evidence.

Leisewitz also instructed Schröder to contact Dr Griebl to get Danielsen's exact address!

Let's add that up. We find not only that the German ships docking at our ports were used for pouring spies into the United States and shipping out our vital defence secrets, but that high officials of the German steamship lines were in direct contact with the Nazi spies in America and in Germany, and doing their bidding. We find a director of the North German Lloyd taking orders from Kapitan-Leutnant Pfeiffer, spy chief charged with supervision of the Nazi spy conspiracy in this country! Leisewitz denied, however, that he realized Pfeiffer was a spy chief.

Leisewitz was placed under bail when he visited this country in the spring of 1938, just after our case against the Nazi spy ring broke open, and was a witness at the trial the following autumn. He testified to making the arrangements I have just described.

Upon receipt of the message from Leisewitz, Schröder contacted Dr Griebl. But Griebl informed him that Danielsen had changed his mind.

Danielsen was lucky he didn't go. He was asked to sign a two-year contract, which lent weight to the story that he was being hired as an expert naval designer, and to design ships in Germany. But the ticket Kapitan-Leutnant Pfeiffer arranged for him was a return ticket, calling for a passage to Germany starting on November 27, 1937, and for return passage to the United States in December, 1937—one month later!

It becomes obvious they were going to force him to reveal

every secret he learned in America, then ship him back, regardless of contract, just as Griebl told me.

Further details of that strange deal came from Heinrich Lorenz, chief officer of the s.s. *Europa*, when we grilled him in New York. He told us that Kapitan-Leutnant Pfeiffer had personally telephoned the ship and told him that a man named Danielsen would board the liner in New York on November 27, and that Lorenz was to arrange every courtesy and privilege for him on board ship.

Pfeiffer was enraged when the *Europa* arrived at Bremen without Danielsen aboard. He grilled Lorenz and stormed at Schluter. When Schluter got back to New York, he told Griebl ruefully of the tongue-lashing he had received from the Nazi spy chief for not producing Danielsen.

For months afterwards—as a matter of fact, until we broke the ring—Griebl kept after Danielsen, trying to get him to Germany. He sent Danielsen $75 to cover expenses for trips to New York to confer with him.

Lonkowski, of course, had nothing to do with the Danielsen affair, having long since fled the country. But though he had been gone three years, he still was interested in some things in America. He was a bitter man, this master spy, who never forgot an injury, fancied or real.

He thought a girl in the United States had betrayed him, and even as we were closing in on the spy ring, was trying to get revenge on her, and had arranged for Günther Gustav Rumrich to contact her as the preliminary step to getting her to Germany for punishment.

CHAPTER XI

DARK-HAIRED Senta de Wanger might have been in a Nazi concentration camp in Germany to-day if we had not smashed the American branch of the international Nazi spy ring when we did. For the plotters were becoming bolder and bolder, and Wilhelm Lonkowski, by now safe and honoured in Germany as an official in the Nazi Air Ministry, decided the time had come to be revenged upon the woman he thought had betrayed him.

Senta is an unusual person, and her story is intriguing even before the point where it became woven in with that of Lonkowski and the spy ring. Her acquaintances refer to her— behind her back—as "*Die wilde Senta.*" That, however, does not mean what it does when translated into American idiom— a loose young woman. Actually it refers to her temper and her independence. She went her way, spoke her mind, did what she pleased, and took no nonsense from anybody.

She was born in Ulm in 1907, but as she grew up, quick-witted, eager, she found post-War Germany too dull for her. She did not like Stuttgart, where her father became a banker, and she did not like the family name of Dirlewanger. It was, she complained, too clumsy. She changed her name to Dirwa.

Before she was twenty-two, this strong-willed girl set off alone for America and adventure. She told me she was first a private secretary and then opened an interior-decorating shop at 7 Park Avenue, New York City. Where the money for the shop came from is a bit of a mystery. She may have got it from her father when she made her first visit home in 1931. I don't know.

Senta is a good-looking woman, attractive if you like them so strong-minded, and rather tall. She is five feet nine inches, weighs about 125 pounds, and has dark hair and blue eyes. Despite her dark hair, she is as 'Aryan' as Hitler. And despite her reputation for a sizzling temper, her manner is quiet and refined, and she is fairly well educated. Her voice is strong, but well modulated, and her guttural accent is rather a point of charm, as it is in many German women.

In September, 1935, she became a naturalized citizen of the United States, and took the name of de Wanger. But before that she had set herself up in another business. A smart trader, she had looked round carefully for a business which would bring in a good profit and which could be run to a fair extent by hired help. She found what she wanted, and in January, 1935, opened a good-sized liquor store at 330 Clinton Street, Hempstead, Long Island—right close to Mitchel Field.

She called it the Clinton Wine Shop—and there she met Wilhelm Lonkowski.

Actually it was his wife she met first. Lonkowski was often absent for long periods on spy business, and spent many of his other nights away from home, drinking with military airport attachés. His wife consoled herself during those absences with a bottle of her own. She preferred gin, and she came to buy her gin at Senta's liquor store. Bonds of language and fatherland drew the two women together, and they became close friends. Mrs Lonkowski confided that her husband was very ill. She told Senta he was suffering from ulcers of the stomach and had not long to live. This was quite an exaggeration, but it aroused Senta's sympathy.

The day came when Mrs Lonkowski brought Wilhelm to the store and proudly exhibited her husband. Lonkowski was in particularly good spirits that day, and bent himself towards winning Senta's friendship. He and his wife invited

146

SENTA ('DIE WILDE SENTA') DE WANGER

Senta to dinner at their flat. Then she invited them to dinner at her house. The friendship grew.

Senta had a house at 83 Lincoln Boulevard, in Hempstead, which was much too big for her. She kept it for herself because, as she put it, she didn't like "people sticking their noses into my affairs." But sometimes she grew lonely in the house with its empty rooms. The Lonkowskis appealed to her as 'regular,' as people who would not interfere with her affairs. Dr Griebl told me she was also depressed at the time because she was trying to forget an unfortunate love-affair with an Air Corps officer, but this Senta denies. At any rate, she invited the Lonkowskis to live in her house, and they accepted. She gave them two rooms for their own, and told them to consider the rest of the house as much theirs as hers, except only for her room.

Senta told me later she still thought Lonkowski was just a piano-tuner, barely making a living, and that for that reason, and because she wanted their company and not a profit, she took from them only $20 a month rent. When Lonkowski insisted on having a telephone installed in her name, though he would pay for it, she thought it quite generous of him. She says she thought he wanted it only because, as he had told her, he was a sort of free-lance correspondent for a German magazine.

They had a gay time in the house. Lonkowski often staged good parties, to which, she noticed idly, he invited lots of men from the flying-fields. But he had told her he had been an aviator in the World War, so she did not think that too odd. Other visitors, she noticed, included a grim, dour man named Otto Voss, who usually came with a small package or a large envelope, and a man of whom she had often heard as a prominent leader in German-American circles—a Dr Ignatz Griebl.

After a while she began wondering where all the money

was coming from. The Lonkowskis were spending on liquor and food for parties alone more than he could possibly be earning as a piano-tuner, even with a little free-lance correspondence thrown in. She noticed, too, that while Lonkowski set up a complete photographic dark-room in her house, and spent many hours there, he seldom displayed any of the results. And that was contrary to the conduct of any photographic fan she ever heard of.

Senta began guardedly questioning his wife. At first Mrs Lonkowski merely looked sly and parried the questions. But one day, after having applied herself with quite some diligence to the gin bottle, she blurted out:

"My husband is very smart. He gets lots of money from Germany. He is no piano-tuner. Oh, no! He is a smart man. They pay him plenty. He knows all about aeroplanes and the Army and such things. Oh, he is a big man!"

Senta could get no further details. But two days later, his face drawn in hard, suspicious lines, Lonkowski drew Senta aside and demanded harshly:

"Why have you been asking my wife questions? What did she tell you?"

Senta tried to dissemble, but he cut her short.

"You know too much already!" he snapped. "Now you must be told more, so you will know enough to keep your mouth shut. I am, what you have guessed. And you—you are going to help me!"

Senta says she drew back and refused indignantly, and ordered him out of her house.

"But he laughed at me and threatened me," Senta told me. "He reminded me that I had parents and other relatives in Germany. He told me that if I did not obey him they would be hounded, and arrested, and put in concentration camps, and perhaps killed. I knew such things did go on in Germany. I could see he was an important, powerful man."

At first she was reluctant—or afraid—to admit anything about Lonkowski and the connexion she now suspected he had with the spy ring. But when we confronted her with proof after proof, she told her story. She became a valuable witness at the trial. She asked for, and got, an armed guard. She was afraid of Nazi vengeance.

Against her will, she said, and without any clear idea of what it was all about, she became, in effect, a messenger for Lonkowski and the spy ring. She admitted that she took packages from Lonkowski to Karl Schluter, the fake steward on the s.s. *Europa*, and to Theodor Schütz, on the s.s. *New York*.

For a long time she insisted that was all. But later she confessed that she also took envelopes from Schluter to Dr Griebl, and that she received material for Lonkowski and Schluter and Griebl from a spy contact in Buffalo, though she insisted she did not know it was spy material, or the nature of its source.

Senta, like almost every other woman he met, caught Griebl's roving, amorous eye. He saw a young woman, attractive, with a good business, unmarried and living in her own house with people who would not interfere. It looked like fair game to him.

"That's a handsome woman, Wilhelm," he told Lonkowski, after he had visited Lonkowski at Senta's home and been introduced to her. "A very handsome young woman. It would be very interesting to know her better. Please tell her I would like to see more of her."

Lonkowski repeated that to Senta. She knew Griebl was married. She didn't know, she says, about Griebl's courtship of Kate Moog, but she had heard of Griebl's reputation in the German colony as one who fancied himself a 'great lover.'

"He did not appeal to me," she later told me. "What did he think I was, sending me a proposition like that! I told Lonkowski never to bring him to the house again, and to tell that dumpy fool I had no time for the likes of him!" She did, however, continue to act as messenger to and from him.

In August, 1935, Lonkowski and his wife went to Buffalo to visit George Werner Gudenberg, who had been enlisted as a Nazi spy, and who was then employed in the Curtiss Aircraft Corporation plant at Buffalo. A few days later Senta received a package from Lonkowski, postmarked at Buffalo, with instructions to take it to Pier 86, North River, New York, and hand it over to Karl Schluter the next time the s.s. *Europa* docked there.

Senta went to the pier and boarded the *Europa*, but she could not find Schluter. She said she searched and searched, and asked all the officers and employees she met, but they all eyed her suspiciously and told her they couldn't locate him for her.

Finally she handed the package to a purser, with instructions to deliver it to Schluter.

When Lonkowski came home a few days later, he asked her if she had safely delivered the package to Schluter. When she admitted she left it with the purser, he flew into a terrific rage, shouting she had betrayed him and ruined him. The package contained important plans, he cried, and would be the finish of them all if it went astray.

"I will kill you! I will kill you myself if it falls into the wrong hands!" he roared.

For days he kept close to the house, starting nervously when the door-bell or telephone rang, peering out behind the curtains to see if anyone was watching the house or coming up the steps. He kept growling and cursing and muttering threats of what he would do to Senta.

But at last a letter came, and when Lonkowski read it he was all smiles again. He apologized to Senta, explaining he had been unduly alarmed and was sorry for the way he spoke. The letter, he told her, was from Schluter, saying he had got the package all right.

Harmony reigned in this queer household until September 27 of the same year—1935.

That night Lonkowski went into New York to meet Schluter on board the *Europa*. He had a package of spy material with him. He was due back no later than midnight.

But midnight came—and no Lonkowski. At 1 A.M. his wife and Senta began to worry. By 3 A.M. the wife was screaming that her woman's intuition told her that Lonkowski was captured, and that they all would be beheaded. Senta tried to explain to her that this was the United States, and that people were not beheaded here as they were in Nazi Germany. Besides, Senta soothed her, he was probably out drinking.

But dawn came, and still no Lonkowski. His wife was in hysterics by this time. She telephoned Dr Griebl, and to relatives she had living near New York. None of them had seen Lonkowski. That convinced her he had been caught by the American authorities, and from hysterics she settled down to practical thinking. As soon as the Hempstead bank opened, she rushed to it and drew all their money and papers from a safe-deposit box. Then she prepared to go to hide at the home of relatives, cautioning Senta not to reveal where she had gone if Government authorities came to question her. As an afterthought, it struck her that maybe Lonkowski had met with an accident. Senta telephoned the local police for her, and asked guarded questions. There was no accident report on anyone answering that description. And so, after fortifying herself with a few swallows from the gin bottle, Mrs Lonkowski hurried off, and that was the last, Senta says, she ever saw of her.

Three hours later Lonkowski peered in the front window of the house, saw the coast was clear, and burst in, haggard and trembling. He refused to answer any of Senta's questions, but began packing frantically, tearing up and burning many papers.

151

He stormed so that even strong-minded Senta was afraid
of him. She left and went to her liquor store. Soon he walked
in there, furtive and wild-eyed. Breathlessly, jerking out the
words, he told her that he had been caught on the pier near
the *Europa*, had been held overnight, but had talked his way
out. Now he was fleeing the country. Would she please sell
his car and send him the money? He would write her. Then
he rushed out of the store, and that, Senta says, was the last
she saw of him too.

What had happened was a startling demonstration of how
little spy-conscious this country was. For Lonkowski had
been captured with important spy material in his possession,
including photographs of blueprints of aeroplanes and gun
sights, and letters to spy headquarters obviously containing
military information—yet he had been let go on his promise
to appear when wanted!

Here is the story·

On the night of September 27, 1935, Customs Guards at
Pier 86, from which the Nazi steamer *Europa* was about to
sail, saw Lonkowski talking to a man in a steward's uniform.
Lonkowski had a package under his arm. The Customs men
became suspicious. They thought he might be a smuggler.
They thought he had got the package from the steward, and
that it contained dutiable material.

Customs Guard Morris Josephs signalled another guard, and
they closed in on Lonkowski. They did not bother with the
steward. Not until more than three years later did they
discover who the steward was. Not until Josephs, on the
witness stand at the spy trial in New York, was shown a
photograph.

"That's the steward!" Josephs ejaculated.

It was Schluter.

The Customs men opened the package Lonkowski carried
. . . and stood puzzled. For it contained no dutiable material

THE NAZI SPY CONSPIRACY IN AMERICA

All it contained was letters, and developed films with strange designs on them.

They questioned him. He told them he was a piano-tuner on Long Island. He showed them a business card to prove it.

But what about those letters, and the films? Those, he explained readily, were reports to and material for the German aviation magazine, *Luftreisen*. He was, he said, American correspondent for the magazine.

The Customs men recognized it was too much for them. They took him and the papers and films to their headquarters and turned him over to Lieutenant Morgan, of the Customs Service. He, too, saw that this was beyond the Customs, and called in Major Stanley Grogan, at that time in charge of G-2, the U.S. Military Intelligence in the Second Corps Area.

Part of one letter read:

> Enclosed you will find an enlargement of the cover for automatic sights of machine-guns.
>
> With reference to the [next word not positively deciphered] ammunition which I am to obtain from the captain, I have as yet received no information. I understand the captain has already contacted von Papen. The captain is a Swiss, although he is in the American infantry.

Lonkowski was questioned on that by John W. Roberts, Supervising Customs Agent for this area, in the presence of Major Grogan. His answers were confusing. At one time he described "von Papen" as an infantry captain at Monticello, N.J. (There is no infantry captain by that name in the United States Army.) At another point he said "von Papen" was a person "now in Austria."

He was not asked if that was Colonel Franz von Papen, former German Chancellor, collaborator of Adolf Hitler, and a pre-War military attaché at Washington, who was cited in America prior to her entrance in the World War for flagrant and widespread espionage activities in the United States. At the time the letter referring to "von Papen" was found on Lonkowski, Colonel Franz von Papen was Hitler's Ambassador to Austria, and spreading Nazi unrest there.

There were indications in the letters found on Lonkowski that secrets of America's national defence were being stolen from Langley Field, Va., a major Army airport. There were paragraphs like these (translated from the original German):

> As regards your query reference report of July 18, 1935: reference to construction bulkheads, etc., of Seversky [aeroplane] floats. I expect sketches shortly.
>
> On Seversky aeroplanes not the running wheels but the floats are pulled in or extended. This is done by means of a small oil-pump, hydraulic. The running wheel opening in the floats has no effect whatsoever on the start. The floats are lowered so far that the wheel quickly disappears therein through the thorough-going opening in the float. The quick running off of the water is assured. I attach to this letter several enlargements of the type. At present not received.
>
> It will, of course, require some time to get the desired information about the water-tank at Langley Field. As soon as I receive same I will again refer to your query.

And paragraphs like these:

> I have just been informed that FLGZ aeroplanes, which for more than a year were used in the Army and Marine Corps, were authorized for foreign delivery. On your list also appears the NR BF2-C1, which was built by Curtiss. Please inform me at once if still interested. [This referred to an experimental Army 'plane for night-bombing flights.]

There was a photograph of the Curtiss XO3C-1, Prototype SOC-1. To that was attached a written memorandum:

> Of interest are the single strut, fully streamlined landing-gear, full enclosure for pilot and crew, short span, deep chord ailerons, slots and flaps fitted to the upper wing, trailing edge-flaps for

controlled engine cooling on the NACA cowl. 'Planes of this type are fitted with landing-gear as shown for carrier operations, but floats may be substituted for catapulting from battleships and cruisers.

Two other pictures showed the Voight SBU-1 scout bomber, for use on U.S. Navy aircraft carriers, and the U.S. Navy 'plane SOC-1. Written in German on them were:

SOC-1 ordered. Delivery here has started. Compare this with film sent in August, 1935.

There was a written memorandum in German reading:

Three new bombers being inspected by Army Air Corps. The Boeing bomber, 299, is already known. The flying fortress designed and built by Glenn-Martin Co., of Baltimore, but up to the time no photograph of this remarkable aeroplane has been available.

A new bomber has been entered by the Douglas Aircraft Co., of Santa Monica, Calif. The bombardment competition opened on August 22, and the bids cover 100 'planes. No figures concerning the various bids given out.

Another note read:

Mr —— [name suppressed by Federal Court for secret reasons] is to get in touch with Mr Eitel and report to him instead of me.

It was signed:
"Sex."
Eitel was a spy contact man on a Nazi ship. "Sex" was one of Lonkowski's aliases.

There were detailed directions of how to piece together the films found on Lonkowski, so that they would show a complete blueprint of an aeroplane, together with highly technical explanations of the blueprint. (Three years later I discovered that was the design of the Curtiss X2—the Navy's secret, experimental new light bomber.)

And yet Lonkowski was let go! The package and its contents were kept, but Lonkowski was permitted to leave under instructions to return in three days!

That is how Lonkowski, one of the world's most dangerous spies, escaped. The data found on him went into a pigeonhole in a G-2 desk. And for nearly three more years Nazi spies flourished and increased in number in America, infesting virtually all strategic points, stealing her most vital secrets wholesale!

It may help to explain why President Roosevelt, who was informed of this after the F.B.I. finally broke the case, so strongly urged increasing and strengthening of G-2, as well as O.N.I., the Naval Intelligence, which, though larger and better equipped than G-2, can still stand strengthening.

Lonkowski, of course, never showed up. But he had left his mark in America, and nearly three years later the F.B.I. found it.

Lonkowski went directly from the custody of the Customs men to Dr Griebl. He poured out the story to him. They decided immediate flight out of the country was the only answer. Griebl began the arrangements while Lonkowski sped out to Hempstead to destroy papers and gather up belongings.

From Senta's store Lonkowski went back to the office of Dr Griebl, and Griebl hid him there until late that night. Then, under cover of darkness, Griebl drove Lonkowski to the Griebl summer home in the Peekskill Mountains of Westchester County, New York. There Lonkowski remained in hiding for a couple of days, while Griebl completed the arrangements for flight. Finally Griebl supplied Lonkowski with his own car and a driver. The driver was Ulrich Haussmann, a German pilot during the World War, who was in America ostensibly as a reporter for a German aviation magazine.

Haussmann drove Lonkowski to Montreal, Canada, where they enlisted the aid of the German Consul. A German freighter was in port at Montreal, waiting for a cargo. The German Consul arranged to have Lonkowski smuggled aboard the freighter, where he was accorded the treatment of a hero and safely guarded until the ship sailed.

Haussmann is now working with Lonkowski in the Nazi Air Ministry at Berlin.

For some reason I cannot quite fathom, Lonkowski took with him to Germany a grudge against Senta. There, though all went well with him, he nursed that resentment. He sent the young woman letters threatening her and her family. Senta told me he accused her of betraying him, but that she does not know what he meant by that unless he was harping back to the time she left the package with the purser instead of handing it personally to Schluter. I know definitely that she never gave this Government any information prior to the time I arrested her as a material witness last spring and questioned her. Perhaps it was some personal matter between them . . . I don't know.

Late in January, 1938, Senta received a mysterious telephone call. A courteous male voice, speaking in German, said:

"My name is Herr Friederich von Klotz. I have just arrived from Berlin, and I have a message for you, an important message. If you will meet me on Tuesday, at noon, in the lobby of the Hotel McAlpin, in New York, I shall be happy to give you the message."

Senta wondered what it could be, but waited in the lobby of that hotel at noon of the appointed day. A bell-boy came through, calling her name. The boy told her she was wanted on the telephone. It was von Klotz, most apologetic. He was calling from Boston, he said, having suddenly been forced to go there on business. Would she forgive him? And would she meet him at the same place on the following Tuesday?

Senta agreed. But before the following Tuesday she received a letter written in German. It read:

Dear Fräulein de Wanger:

I am sorry I again have to postpone our appointment for the following Tuesday, until Tuesday, the 15th of February. Of course, I am very sorry that I have to be so ungentlemanly in this matter. However, I have to attend to my obligations here first, which I didn't know in advance, before I can tell you the announced message. I hope that you understand my point of view, and I expect you therefore without delay. This time on Tuesday the fifteenth of February, the same place and the same time.

German greetings,
FRIEDERICH VON KLOTZ

Senta kept the date. She waited for an hour and a half, but no one showed up, and so she went home, wondering what it was all about. She didn't find out until I told her.

For Friederich von Klotz was none other than Günther Gustav Rumrich. He was acting under orders from Karl Schluter, who in turn had got his orders from Lonkowski in Germany. Schluter told Rumrich to locate a Senta de Wanger because she had betrayed an important Nazi spy, and was to be forced to go back to Germany, where she could be punished.

Senta had moved twice since Lonkowski fled from America, and Schluter was not sure how to locate her. He wanted Rumrich to do it. He promised Rumrich that the actual details of getting Senta to Germany would be left to the *Gestapo* unit working in New York.

Rumrich found her easily, merely by looking in a Nassau County telephone book. He visited her store and looked her over so that he would know her. Then he telephoned her as "von Klotz" and arranged the date at the McAlpin so that Schluter could look her over.

Schluter, however, was unable to be there on the appointed

day, and that is why Rumrich put on the act of having her paged and telling her he was calling from Boston. The reason for the other delays was the same—Schluter was not available. Rumrich didn't know what to do next with Senta, without Schluter.

I got my first lead on that incident from Rumrich himself. He volunteered it towards the end of his confession. Then during the stage when Dr Griebl was confessing startling things each day and behaving in a very co-operative fashion, I laid what Rumrich told me about this odd affair before him and asked him for enlightenment. He revealed that it was Lonkowski who wanted her got to Germany for punishment— and brought Lonkowski's name into the investigation for the first time. He told me what he knew about Lonkowski— that is, he told me some things, and they were enough to enable us to fill in more through investigation. Then I had Senta brought in, and from her I drew details which further filled in the picture. She still had the letter signed "Friederich von Klotz."

From investigation of the Nazi *Gestapo* unit in New York later I became convinced that it was very lucky for Senta that we broke up the Nazi spy ring here when we did. I am convinced she was in serious danger. She was not the only woman in the United States in such danger.

The *Gestapo* was becoming very bold in America.

CHAPTER XII

A GLOWERING, hard-eyed character named Bittenberg, one of the most feared Nazi officials in Germany, came to New York in August, 1937, expressly to set up a unit of the *Geheime Staats Polizei*. From that unit the secret organization was to extend throughout the United States.

The duties of the *Geheime Staats Polizei* agents were to spy on anti-Nazis and harass them, to browbeat and threaten non-Nazi Germans in America, to trail Nazi spies suspected of selling out, to wreak vengeance on Americans who incurred the displeasure of the Hitler *régime* and deal summarily with anti-Nazis. For the *Geheime Staats Polizei* is merely the official title of the *Gestapo*, the most dreaded agency in Germany and notorious throughout the civilized world as the brutal Nazi secret police. The *Gestapo* is, in short, the Nazi strong-arm squad.

In Germany its very name strikes fear. It is headed by Heinrich Himmler, who is also chief of the Nazi "SS" (*Schutz Staffel*, the black-shirted Hitler guards), but under the control of Field-Marshal Hermann Wilhelm Göring, Hitler's right hand. Special decrees in 1936 and 1937 made it virtually omnipotent. In 1936 the *Official Gazette* revealed that the powers of the *Gestapo* had been extended to control of the offices of civil district governors. *Gestapo* men were empowered to issue commands to the governors, to assure, according to the official announcement, that "the secret police's striking power will be unhindered." It was emphasized, however, that the independence of ordinary justice would be maintained. In 1937, that, too, went. The *Deutsches Verwal-*

tungsrecht, an official Nazi publication, announced that actions of the secret police no longer could be challenged by legal process, but were subject to revision only by the *Gestapo* chiefs themselves.

"Just like the Army," said Himmler, "the secret police can accomplish its tasks only in obedience to orders from its leaders and not by living up to fixed laws."

The *Gestapo* could—and can—punish, torture, imprison, kidnap, and kill with impunity; it takes the law into its own hands, and is the law.

The *Gestapo* organization extends like a fine network from one end of the country to the other, involving porters, waiters, post-office employees, railwaymen, Custom-house officials—a mesh woven tightly about every activity, political and economic, within the Reich. The *Gestapo* moved in first into Austria, to pave the way for the *Anschluss*. It moved into Czechoslovakia to wipe out anti-Nazi agitation.

There was some *Gestapo* activity in America from 1933 on, but it was sporadic and unorganized. In 1937 the Nazi movement had become much bolder. The number of spies was quadrupled, and Bittenberg came to organize the *Geheime Staats Polizei* efficiently—as if the United States were also a Nazi province.

The first instance of *Gestapo* activity in the United States of which we have definite information was against a fellow-Nazi, the unsavoury Heinz Spanknöbel. You may recall that he was sent by the Hitler Government to spread Nazism in America in 1933. But he was a loud-mouthed man, with an offensive personality, and soon got into hot water. Leaders of the real Germans in America—the non-Nazi Germans who constitute the majority—openly denounced him. Such a storm of unfavourable publicity broke about his head that he became a hindrance rather than a help. Many of his henchmen quit under fire and disowned him.

In October, 1933, a Federal warrant was issued, charging him with violation of the United States law requiring agents of a foreign country to register with the Secretary of State. But police could not find him. He was hiding in the home of Dr Griebl.

Word came from Berlin for Spanknöbel to sneak home at once. The Nazi chiefs in Germany feared the scandal and adverse publicity of a trial. But Spanknöbel turned stubborn. He enjoyed the spotlight, even if it was unfavourable, and refused to leave.

The night of October 27, 1933, Dr Griebl, his wife, and Spanknöbel were at dinner in the Griebl flat, when there came a knock at the door and in stalked a grim-faced man. Griebl didn't know him, but Spanknöbel did, and instantly paled. It was Hellmuth von Feldman, an agent of Paul Joseph Goebbels, Nazi Minister of Propaganda, and acting *Gestapo* agent.

Von Feldman glared at Spanknöbel.

"You have your orders!" he barked. "Why haven't you started?"

Spanknöbel tried to bluster out.

"There is no hurry," he argued. "Let us talk it over."

"There is nothing to talk over," retorted von Feldman grimly. "You have received your orders."

"At least," faltered Spanknöbel, "let me finish my dinner. . . ."

"Get up!" snapped von Feldman.

"I won't," Spanknöbel whined.

"Get up!" von Feldman roared, and suddenly a heavy, ugly automatic appeared in his hand, its snout pointing at Spanknöbel's heart.

He got up, white-faced and trembling. Mrs Griebl began to weep. Dr Griebl pleaded, "No shooting here, please. You will ruin me."

Von Feldman stalked forward, jabbed the blunt nose of the gun into Spanknöbel's side.

"March!" he commanded.

Out they went. An hour later they were on board the s.s. *Europa*, docked at Pier 86, North River, New York. Spanknöbel was placed under guard by Nazi Storm Troopers aboard the ship, while von Feldman sent back to the Griebl flat for his baggage. The next night the *Europa* sailed for Germany, Spanknöbel was later forgiven, and to-day he has a good job in the Ministry of Propaganda there.

That was von Feldman's last appearance in America, too. The *Gestapo* operated only intermittently and in special instances thereafter until Bittenberg arrived late in the summer of 1937 to set up a real unit.

Bittenberg's disguise on the trip was that of an assistant purser on the s.s. *New York*. He made only that one trip—but on that trip his word was law on that German ocean liner, and his word was law in the Hapag-Lloyd piers and offices in America.

Even Commodore Fritz Kruse, commander of the s.s. *New York* and then commodore of the Hamburg-American fleet of ocean liners, had to kow-tow to Bittenberg and take his orders. For a Nazi party official is always boss. The official may be a stupid oaf, or an ignoramus or a strong-arm man, but everywhere he goes among Germans he supersedes every one except men of higher rank in the party.

Bittenberg could give orders not only because of his official rank in the party, but because for that trip he was also acting *Ortsgruppenführer*, or political leader of the ship. Every German ship has one, who usually is also leader of the Storm Troopers attached to each vessel—even the gay cruise ships. On matters of discipline and on all matters even remotely concerned with policy and party affairs, these men—usually pantrymen and stewards and dish-washers and such—can, and do, override the captains. They can order the captains to appear before them. They issue orders and mete out punishment, and there is no appeal from their orders—as in the case of the *Gestapo*—except to the leaders who put them in charge.

The jobs go only to men who served the party well in the early, brutal days of the purges. It was a sad day for the proud, able sea-captains in charge of German liners when Hitler came into power and turned much of the captain's traditional power at sea over to these men.

At the time of my investigation in the spring of 1938, the following was the set-up on the German ships touching New York:

On the s.s. *New York* a man named Richard Becker was *Ortsgruppenführer*.

On the s.s. *Bremen*, Captain Adolph Ahrens had to submit to an ex-dishwasher named Wilhelm Böhnke. This Böhnke, a burly bruiser who looks a lot like Göring and has the same passion for gaudy uniforms, plays a further *rôle* in the spy case.

Bittenberg got Commodore Kruse to introduce him to Captain Drechsel, who, as superintendent of the Hapag-Lloyd port, was ordered to give Bittenberg every courtesy and aid, and to obey every command of this supposed assistant purser. Captain Drechsel, though no Nazi, had to obey. Even the directors of steamship companies had to obey such orders, as has been indicated before and will be seen further.

Bittenberg disappeared into New York. He knew where to go, for the way had been paved for him by Dr Griebl and other Nazi propagandists and spies, and particularly by one Heinrich Bischoff, ostensibly merely a steward on the s.s. *Europa*, but actually a representative of *Gestapo* headquarters.

Bittenberg came into Captain Drechsel's office a few days later with two men.

"Captain," he ordered curtly, "give these two men passes

permitting them to enter these piers at any time, day or night, without question, and to board any German ship in port here at any hour, also without question. They are on an important assignment for the *Gestapo*, and are to be accorded every aid at your command."

Again Drechsel had no choice but to obey.

The two men were the nucleus of the *Gestapo* unit set up in New York. One was designated as chief, and that was sleek-haired, sneering Karl Friedrich Wilhelm Herrmann, who acted tough with women and peaceful non-Nazi Germans, and snivelled and squealed at once when the F.B.I. caught up with him.

I knew of him a couple of weeks before we caught him, but waited for two reasons. One was that no matter what we may think of the kind of a man who would be a *Gestapo* agent, the fact remains that being one is not *per se* an indictable offence in this country. So I hoped to get the goods on him for something definite first. The second reason was that, since I probably couldn't send him to prison, I was hoping to use him without his knowledge. I was at that time confronted with the problem of how to catch up with the mysterious Karl Weigand, a tremendously important Nazi spy contact man, ranking almost with Karl Schluter.

It was barely possible Herrmann could lead us to him. I had him trailed, and played safe by putting Senta de Wanger in protective custody, and putting a protective guard on pretty Eleanor Böhme, on Kate Moog, and on Antonie Strassman, better known as "Astra," the famous German aviatrix, for she, too, was in danger from the Nazi *Gestapo*.

But apparently Herrmann was not contacting Weigand at the time. We were exceedingly anxious to get him. We knew he was one of the men who gave orders to Günther Gustav Rumrich. We knew he was a sly, dangerous man, high in the councils of the Nazi spy chiefs. We knew that at one time he had travelled in this country as an *aide* of Fritz Wiedemann, Hitler's personal representative. We heard that Hans Dieckhoff, Nazi Ambassador to the United States, posed for pictures with him.

Yet we could find no trace of him. Rumrich knew only that he made regular trips on German vessels which docked at New York, but he didn't know which ones. We searched the passenger lists and ship's manifests of all the German ships which came here, but found no name even remotely resembling that of Karl Weigand.

Finally I asked Dr Griebl, who by this time was betraying his co-conspirators to us right and left. But Griebl was obviously puzzled by the name.

"I do not know that name—I swear—Mr Turrou," he declared.

"Would Herrmann know?" I asked.

"He might."

"Then ask him. Call him into your office on some pretext."

I realized I was taking a chance on a double-cross, but there was no choice. We were up against a blank wall.

Two days later Griebl reported back.

"That's a fake name," he said. "Karl Weigand is really Theodor Schütz. He is political leader of the s.s. *New York*. He is the most trusted operative of the Hamburg office of the *Marine Nachrichten Stelle*. He is a middle-aged man, of medium height, with strong, lined face and very clever eyes."

We checked immediately on the whereabouts of the s.s. *New York*. She was on a West Indies cruise, as was her custom during March and April each year. When she was finally due in New York, I went down to Quarantine on a Coast Guard cutter and boarded her.

There on the ship's manifest was the entry:

"Theodor Schütz, steward."

166

CAPTAIN FRITZ WIEDEMANN

Personal adjutant and confidential messenger for Hitler. Rumrich was impressed by a picture the spy contact man whom he knew as Karl Weigand displayed to him, which, Rumrich said, showed Weigand, Wiedemann, and Hans Dieckhoff, Nazi ambassador to the U.S., together.

But a line was drawn through it, and alongside was the notation:

"Signed off at Havana, Cuba."

I was blazing mad. The panicky flight of the Nazi spy ring was on. First Karl Schluter had eluded us, apparently with the connivance of the steamship officials, and certainly under orders of the Hitler Government. Then others, of whom I have not yet told you. And now this man! I headed straight for the luxurious quarters of Commodore Kruse.

"What does this mean?" I demanded.

He took a lofty tone.

"It means what it says," he declared. "The man was signed off at Havana."

I tried to control my anger, but I imagine enough showed.

"What do you mean?" I snapped. "A man signed on in Germany—signed off in Havana? That's ridiculous!"

He backed down a bit, and I noticed that underneath the bluster he was very nervous.

"It was on orders from Germany," he admitted.

"Let me see those orders," I demanded.

He put his dignity on again. "No, of course not. I can't do that!" he declared.

"All right," I said, "put on your civilian clothes and come with me before the United States Grand Jury."

That got him. He rang for the wireless operator, and finally, after long wrangling, I got a certified copy of the order. It read:

"Steward Schütz to be signed off at Havana, and to return immediately to Germany without touching any United States port. Instruct him to proceed on motor-vessel *Memel*, North German Lloyd. All expenses to be defrayed by agency connexion with stay Havana."

The cablegram was signed: "Homberg and La Salle." Homberg is a director of the Hapag-Lloyd in Germany, and

La Salle is the chief political leader assigned by the Nazi Party to keep an eye on matters at the Hapag-Lloyd main office and see that things are operated to the best advantage of the Hitler *régime*, regardless of the wishes of the company or the welfare of the passengers.

Later I discovered that the orders came directly from the Nazi Foreign Office at Berlin, and that the purpose was—as must be obvious—to keep the United States Government from catching up with and questioning Schütz. Bond was posted with the Cuban immigration authorities at Havana for Schütz by the Havana office of the Hapag-Lloyd. He was taken to one of the most expensive hotels there.

I got all set to fly there to arrest him, but was overruled by Washington. The Nazi spies must have got wind of my plan, for instead of waiting for the motor-vessel *Memel*, Schütz was put aboard the s.s. *Iberia*, bound for Vera Cruz, Mexico. There he was transferred to a ship bound direct for Germany without touching any U.S. ports.

Four weeks later, in response to my insistent demand, Captain Drechsel got a letter of explanation from the Hapag-Lloyd officials in Germany. In elaborate language it said that the reason Schütz had been taken off at Havana was that the German Government suspected him of smuggling currency out of Germany, which was against the Nazi law !

That was obviously ridiculous, because the s.s. *New York* was bound for New York at the time, where he could have been put on an express ship to Germany, without necessity of defraying his expenses at Havana. And besides, there was that damning sentence in the cablegram to Commodore Kruse: "Steward Schütz to be signed off at Havana and to return immediately to Germany *without touching any United States port.*"

What had happened was that Griebl, while aiding me, had also double-crossed me. In getting Weigand's true identity for me from Herrmann, he either intentionally or unintentionally tipped Herrmann off that I wanted Weigand— Schütz. Herrmann promptly notified *Gestapo* headquarters in Germany, and the orders sped through the ether to get Schütz off the ship and to keep him safe from us.

Now, his possible usefulness to the investigation through being at liberty gone, I closed in on the *Gestapo* chief, the feared but cowardly Karl Friedrich Wilhelm Herrmann.

CHAPTER XIII

HERRMANN was living in the flat of Miss Margaret Stevenson, a W.P.A. actress, at 75 West 89th Street, New York City. He used her telephone for his *Gestapo* affairs, and received mail in her name, but I doubt that she had a clear idea of what he was up to.

The preparatory investigation into his character and activities made me wonder, as agents started out for him, how he would react. On the one hand he was supposed to be tough, hard leader of the brutal Nazi secret police—but the investigation also disclosed that behind his back he was called "Willie." And so we were not sure whether it would be a battle with a husky bad man, or a scene with one of those sort of swishing creatures not at all uncommon in Nazi ranks.

What the agents found was a slim, dark, dapper man who dressed and combed his hair and acted as if he considered himself the answer to a maiden's prayer. He was outfitted in the Yorkville version of the height of male fashion.

"You're wanted at F.B.I. headquarters," they said, and the supposedly bad, bold *Gestapo* chief, whose name made honest non-Nazi German citizens in America quake with fear, and the hearts of Nazi maidens flutter, when he swaggered so domineeringly, turned pale and began to shake.

"Yes, sir," he said, and came meekly along.

When they brought him into F.B.I. headquarters it was just a question of getting it all down on paper. He broke more easily than any other suspect in the entire Nazi spy ring investigation. He squealed on his chief assistant before we even got down to real business.

On only one point did he remain adamant. He would not admit he was an agent of the *Geheime Staats Polizei*. He admitted acting as secret agent for undercover Nazi investigation work. He admitted reporting to contact men whom we knew to be *Gestapo* agents. He admitted doing things that come in the province of the *Gestapo*. But for some reason he would not admit the exact label of *Gestapo* man. It did not make much difference, however, for we had evidence from other sources; besides, his chief assistant later admitted it.

I was curious how such a man got to be a *Gestapo* man, and prevailed upon him to tell me his life-story. His version stood up fairly well under an investigation of the high-lights later.

Karl Friedrich Wilhelm Herrmann was born in Coblenz, in the Rhineland, Germany, in 1905, and went to the lower schools and took the courses at the commercial high school there. His ambition in life was to be a waiter, so he served an apprenticeship at the Hotel Rolandseck, and then at the Cornelius Hotel, in Düsseldorf. He served a year's military service, then got a job as a waiter in a hotel at Elberfeld, Germany.

In 1925 he thought he would like to try the sea, and got a job with the Holland-American Line as a steward. From that he went to a job on the Panama Pacific Line as a steward. By 1930 he was tired of the sea, and for four years he worked as a waiter in a dozen places in Germany, and for a short spell as a salesman for a malt company.

Hitler was making a big noise in Germany by 1932, and in that year Willie Herrmann became an ardent Nazi. He became, in fact, one of the leading Nazis of Elberfeld.

"I was of great service to the party," he remarked proudly during the questioning.

The service, it developed, consisted of spying on his fellow-workers wherever he got a job, and squealing on them. "I wrote reports," he explained, "and they were such good reports, of such value to the party, that I was considered a very reliable party member, and got much credit."

These reports, he said, went to the local unit of the *Arbeitsfront* (Labour front) of the Nazi Party.

By 1934 he was prominent enough and had proved himself so valuable a 'stool-pigeon' that he was ripe for favours and promotion. He was allowed the great honour of meeting Gustav Langhans, one of the biggest Nazis in Hamburg. Langhans got him a job as a steward aboard the s.s. *Resolute*, of the Hamburg-American Line.

Herrmann wouldn't admit it, but on that ship, too, he was supposed to keep an eye on the other members of the crew, and on German passengers who might talk indiscreetly about Hitler and his policies. I have information that Herrmann was even then a *Gestapo* man. I know that he served as a *Gestapo* agent during remarkably long shore leaves he was granted when the ship touched France and England. Then the *Resolute* went on a world cruise, and Herrmann was able to send home reports from many lands.

From the *Resolute* he was sent by Langhans to the s.s. *New York* in December, 1935, ostensibly merely as a steward. For a while—from September, 1936, to April, 1937—he served on the s.s. *Hansa* under Langhans' orders. Then he got back to the s.s. *New York*, and stayed with it until July 6, 1937. He took a vacation in Germany until August 10, 1937, and then "I decided I wanted to live in America."

That's what he says. But note this: he was given a job on the s.s. *Hamburg* as a steward for a one-way trip to the United States. It may have happened before, but neither I nor the steamship officials I questioned ever heard of a big passenger vessel taking on a steward for a one-way trip. Herrmann refused to admit that he was assigned to America by the *Gestapo*, or that the *Gestapo* arranged the one-way trip. But it was also in August, 1937, that Bittenberg came to set up a unit of the *Gestapo* in the United States.

Herrmann contends he was working under Alfred Schniewind, a high official in the *Sicherheitsdienst* at Hamburg. The *Sicherheitsdienst* is also known as the "Security Service regarding Political Activities." It is, in a sense, a sub-agency of the *Gestapo*. Its operatives are undercover men who spy on their fellow-Germans and on others who may not be wholeheartedly Nazi enough to suit the Hitler *régime*. They do not have the power to make arrests, as the *Gestapo* does, but the nature of the work is much the same.

Herrmann also admits that when he decided to come to America he first visited a "Herr Schleckenbag," at Hamburg. Schleckenbag is head of the Nazi secret police at Hamburg. Schleckenbag thanked him for his services in the past, and said he hoped Herrmann would continue in America.

"I said I would be glad to continue," Herrmann admits.

He also admitted to me that Schleckenbag told him to contact Heinrich Bischoff, a steward on the s.s. *Europa*, as soon as the *Europa* docked at New York, and to turn his reports over to Bischoff.

"But Bischoff is a *Gestapo* man," I pointed out to Herrmann. "How can you still deny you are a member of the *Gestapo*?"

"I don't know what Bischoff is," he insisted. "I only know I was told to report to Bischoff, and I did."

Herrmann got into the United States through fraud. He got a visa from the American Consul at Hamburg on the strength of an affidavit by a man in this country who was supposed to be a close relative. The man was Herman Umbreidt, then an owner of the Café Hindenburg, on East 86th Street, in the heart of the Nazi colony in the Yorkville section of New York. It was at that café that Karl Schluter first talked to Günther Gustav Rumrich, you may recall, and it was over the

173

beer-tables there that many of the Nazi spy schemes against the defence of America were hatched.

Despite the depression and widespread unemployment, Herrmann had no trouble getting along in America. He got a place to live in right away, having met and become very friendly with Miss Stevenson some ten years previous on a visit here. And he got work as a waiter readily. He worked at the Longchamps Restaurant at 59th Street and Madison Avenue, and at the Brooklyn Club, Remsen Street, near Borough Hall, Brooklyn. His earnings as waiter never exceeded $30 a week. He denied that he got any pay for his Nazi activities.

From this point on, except when he squealed on his partner and assistant, Herrmann did even more lying about his exact *Gestapo* duties. It was obvious during the questioning, and borne out later when he was submitted to the Polygraph, better known as the 'lie-detector.'

For instance, he admitted that he handed Bischoff reports "involving Communistic activities of a number of individuals in New York."

"Of course, you investigated carefully before you made these reports?" I asked him.

"Yes, sir," he said.

"Well, name some of those individuals."

"I—I don't remember," he faltered. And his memory got no better under questioning.

He admitted he knew Theodor Schütz, *alias* Karl Weigand, but denied that he knew Karl Schluter. He admitted he knew and often visited Dr Griebl—which he could hardly deny, as it had to be obvious to him that it was Griebl who betrayed him to me. But he insisted that his first visit to Dr Griebl was to sell him a form of treatment for varicose veins! The picture he tried hard to paint of himself was that of merely an investigator for the Nazi Party in this country of anything anti-Nazi, with no intention of doing anything about it further than making a report.

In the summer of 1937, he said, he investigated the murder of a butcher on the s.s. *Deutschland*, at Pier 86, New York, on the theory that the butcher might have been slain by Communist agitators because he was an ardent Nazi. Herrmann was vague on the details of what his investigation comprised, but said his report was that there was nothing political about the killing.

Next, he said, he investigated reports that employees and officials of the Hamburg-American Line were letting Communists ride free on the boats to Germany. He got nowhere with that, he said.

Following that, he said, he investigated a "Mr Nisselbeck," and his supposed relation with the *Schwarzefront*, which, Herrmann believed, was some sort of a Communistic outfit. Apparently he wasn't much of an investigator, for he seemed to have no clear idea of what he was investigating or what to do about it. Only on one point was he positive—and that was that always it was Communists at the bottom of whatever was suspected.

He said he made an investigation to find out where Communistic pamphlets, particularly the *Schiffahrt*, were coming from, because it was suspected that they were being issued by German sailors, or as a result of information from German sailors. But he got nowhere with that, either, he said.

Then he "conducted an investigation concerning a man named Kramer," supposed to be a German Communist, on board the s.s. *New York*. "I managed to secure a picture of Kramer," Herrmann said, "and turned it over. But I don't know what happened to Kramer. It was long ago."

He said he was told to investigate reports that a bar-tender on Eleventh Avenue near 23rd Street, New York, was dealing in forbidden bank-notes with German seamen, but that he never got on to investigating.

Not very exciting, his account. But there are huge gaps in it. He admitted that he told Dr Griebl of his activities.

"Wasn't that a dangerous thing to do?" I asked. "How did you know Dr Griebl was safe?"

"Well," he said, "I got to talking with him, and I knew he was an ardent Nazi."

"Did you know he was a spy?"

"No, sir!"

"Did you help him in spy work?"

"No, sir!"

"Yet you told this stranger all about your secret work? How did you come to go right to him?"

"Well, I heard about him."

The lie-detector is not accepted in most courts as yet. So this fact is not evidence—the fact that the lie-detector reacted violently whenever Herrmann insisted he had nothing to do with the Nazi spy ring here.

I cannot explain why Herrmann so readily squealed on his chief assistant, Ewald Rossberg. I don't know why, except perhaps that he had an idea he could save his own skin that way.

Rossberg's real name is Orlamunder, but for some reason he took the name of Rossberg in America. The change may have been connected with the fact that he, like Herrmann, got into this country through fraud. Though he entered this country in 1927, he never tried to become a citizen. He was married, lived with his wife at 944 Park Avenue, New York City, where she was employed as a housekeeper for a railway executive, and worked as a mechanic at the Silvertown Process Co., in New York.

Rossberg was a rabid Nazi, and I believe he did what he did without pay because of his faith in Hitler and the Nazi movement. He was of sterner stuff than the snivelling Herrmann,

though he followed the latter's leadership unquestioningly.
This was because he considered Herrmann smarter than himself
and looked up to him.

He was surly and defiant when he was brought into my
office for questioning. I looked him over; five feet ten inches
and very husky, weighing almost 200 pounds. If the Nazi
Gestapo found any rough stuff necessary here, Rossberg was
built to do it. He was strong as an ox, and almost as stupid.
His dull blue eyes, under the light brown hair, showed that
plainly. But it took more than two hours to crack him.

"What did you do for the *Gestapo*, Rossberg?" I demanded.

He shook his head. "I don't know anything about it," he
muttered.

"I know you are a member," I declared.

"No, you don't," he retorted.

I told him when he had joined up. I told him some of his
activities with Herrmann. A brighter man would have become
worried, and seen that I must know a lot, and have begun to
crack. But Rossberg had room for only one idea in his head
at a time, and at the moment it was to insist stubbornly that he
knew nothing. Besides, he had that typical Nazi scorn for anybody not a Nazi.

"How about your orders to kidnap Antonie Strassmann—
Astra?" I flung at him.

"It's a lie," he said.

"How about your reports to Bischoff, the steward on the
Europa?"

"I never made any reports."

"How about your contacts with Erich Kubatsky, the
Ortsgruppenführer on the s.s. *New York*?"

"It's a lie," he retorted.

I flung bombshell after bombshell at him, any one of which
would have blasted a man of ordinary imagination and nerves
into confession. I hurled names and dates at him. I might

just as well have been punching a concrete wall with bare hands.

"No, I didn't," he said doggedly, over and again; or, "It's a lie."

Finally I shrugged my shoulders.

"All right," I said, "if that's the way you feel about it. But your pal, Willie Herrmann, had sense enough to confess. And he told me all those things, and implicated you."

Wild anger flamed in his eyes.

"That's a dirty lie!" he roared.

I took Herrmann's confession out of a drawer and began reading parts of it. Painful puzzlement appeared in Rossberg's eyes, but still he refused to believe it. It was obvious that he adored Herrmann and couldn't get it through his head that his idol could crack and squeal.

"Don't kid me like that," he muttered. "Herrmann would never do that."

"No?" I said, and signalled an agent. The door opened, and in came Willie Herrmann.

Rossberg looked at him like a stricken ox. Herrmann had a hangdog air. His eyes avoided Rossberg.

"Herrmann," I demanded, "is this man here, Rossberg, your assistant, the man who worked with you on these Nazi investigations?"

"Yes, sir," said Herrmann in a low voice, without raising his head.

"Now, listen, Herrmann. And you, too, Rossberg."

Slowly I read, word for word, line for line, the parts of Herrmann's statement referring to Rossberg.

"Is that what you said about Rossberg?" I demanded.

"Yes, sir," mumbled Herrmann weakly.

Herrmann was led away. Then I turned to Rossberg. His head, too, had dropped. I almost felt sorry for him. His last illusion was gone.

"Now, Rossberg," I said, "how about it?"

His head came up slowly. The bewildered look in his eyes was turning to one of bitterness.

"I sure wouldn't have believed it of Herrman," he said, as if to himself. "I sure wouldn't. . . ." And then suddenly his eyes blazed, and he shouted:

"All right, now I'll tell my story!"

And he did, putting all the blame on Herrmann, and telling things about him which Herrmann had refused to admit.

The silly things these *Gestapo* men did! If the fantastic motives and the almost insane drive behind them were not so potentially dangerous, some of the ideas these dreaded *Gestapo* men get into their heads would be downright funny. There is, for instance, the time and energy and money they wasted checking up on two women here. One was the handsome Antonie Strassmann, fondly nicknamed "Astra" when she was a famous German aviatrix a few years ago. The other was the elderly, kindly Mrs Thomas Manville, mother of Tommy Manville.

Somehow the Nazi master-minds in Germany got it into their heads that Miss Strassmann and Mrs Manville were dangerous counter-espionage agents, working for some unknown power against the Nazi spy ring.

This is how they worked it out:

1. Miss Strassmann had been the toast of Germany and Germany's feminine flying star until the Hitler *régime* cracked down on her because in her family tree there was some Jewish blood. Therefore she must be an enemy of Nazi Germany.

2. She was a friend of old Mrs Manville, and Mrs Manville was always entertaining and giving presents to employees of German ships. That was very suspicious. Why should she give presents to employees of German ships if she were not a counter-espionage agent? Ho, there must be dirty work afoot there!

179

Mrs Manville is a nice old lady who lived at the Savoy-Plaza Hotel in New York and had both the inclination and the money to travel. And when she travelled she often took a German boat. And she was the kind of woman who believed in being nice to people who were nice to her. And so she remembered the maids and hairdressers and stewards and other employees who served her on those German ships. She gave them gifts at parting, and invited them to call on her whenever they were in New York. Being no fools, they made it a point to call on her, for she entertained them splendidly and gave them more gifts. But then again maybe they were fools, for they promptly became suspect in the eyes of the Nazi spy chiefs and the *Gestapo*.

The case of Miss Strassmann was slightly more complicated. She was a world figure. She travelled in high places (not only aeronautically speaking) and made friends high in the business, social, and diplomatic life of the United States and other countries. And she did have ample cause to despise the Nazis.

Astra was born in 1901 in Berlin. Her father is Professor Paul Ferdinand Strassmann, professor of obstetrics and gynaecology at the University of Berlin and head of a private hospital at Schumann Strasse, 18, Berlin—until Hitler came into power. Professor Strassmann was a Christian, his wife was a Christian, and Astra was a Christian. But there had been Jews in the family, and that meant thumbs down. Professor Strassmann lost his professorship and his hospital. He was expelled from his medical societies, sports clubs, other organizations. He was German representative of the American Interstate Post-Graduate Medical Association, but the Nazis put a stop to that. He remained, however, an honorary graduate of Birmingham University, England, and an honorary member of several American medical societies. That is about all the aged professor had left; that and his memories, which included those of a time when he was physician to the Kaiser's family.

So it went with all the family. Astra's eldest brother, Helmuth, was killed in action November 5, 1916, fighting for the Fatherland—but that did not lessen the Nazi terror against that family. Astra's second brother, Dr Erwin O. Strassmann, was a brilliant young physician, connected with the University of Berlin. But the taint of Jewish blood resulted in his being forced to leave the University. He was expelled from all clubs and medical associations of which he was a member. In 1936 he fled to America and was for a while with the Mayo Foundation.

Astra's sister married Max Gutzwiller, a Swiss who came under even the Nazi definition of 'Aryan,' then with the Swiss Embassy in Berlin. He joined the law faculty of the University of Heidelberg. But because his wife had Jewish blood, he was forced to resign.

As a child Astra went to *Luisenschule* in Berlin, then to a select *Gymnasium*, where she took a classical course until 1918. At seventeen she dreamed of a career on the stage, and began studying for it. She made her first stage appearance at Stolp, Pomerania, a ten-months' success beginning a few months after the War. Then Magdeburg and Stuttgart, and triumphantly in Berlin.

She met and became close friends with Emmy Sonnemann, the blonde actress who afterwards married Wilhelm Göring. Astra twice visited her friend Emmy in Berlin on visits to Germany following her marriage, but Göring always avoided greeting her or exchanging any words with her.

Astra came to America in 1925 for a few weeks with her husband, Dr Wilhelm Joseph, whom she divorced later. After the divorce she went back to the stage in Berlin and to radio.

Meanwhile she became interested in flying, and took her training at *Fliegerschule Bornemann*, in Staaken, near Berlin. (I know all these facts about her because we made a most

181

intensive investigation. If she were a counter-espionage agent operating in this country, as those Nazis seemed to believe, we wanted to know about it.) In 1928 she made widely publicized flights to Austria, Czechoslovakia, Jugoslavia, and Turkey. Pre-Nazi Germany took the daring young aviatrix proudly to its heart, and she was the toast of Germany, particularly after she took her stunt-pilot examinations at Würzburg in 1928 and put on a notable exhibition of stunt-flying.

In 1930 she went to the United States, under the auspices of the *Deutscher Luftsport Verband*, in conjunction with Gimbel Brothers' stores, to exhibit German aeroplane models in America. She lectured before Chambers of Commerce and boys' clubs in New York, Philadelphia, Pittsburgh, Milwaukee, Akron, and other American cities. That same year she flew American sports 'planes round the country on exhibition tours, and took part in the air-races at Chicago and in the All-Florida State Air Tour.

Her next international fame came when she flew in the giant German aeroplane, the Dornier Do-X, from North Beach, via Newfoundland, the Azores, Vigo, and Calshot, to Berlin, in a flight beginning in May, 1932.

But by this time the Nazis were in the ascendancy in Germany, and a scurrilous article appeared in the Nazi newspaper, *Der Angriff*. It denounced her as a Jewess, under the heading, "*Wer Hat Antonie Eingeladen?*" ("Who invited Antonie?")

However, the Nazi terror was not in full bloom yet, and Dr Hugo Eckener, the airship genius, invited her to go in his Zeppelin to South America. She did, and took with her a small eighty-horse-power Klemmplane, which she demonstrated and sold in South America for a German firm.

When she returned to Germany in 1933 the Hitler *régime* was going full blast. Her father and whole family were ostracized. She was expelled from the German Aero Club.

She was no longer Germany's darling; she was an enemy to be crushed, a Jewess by blood if not by faith.

Details become monotonous. For a long time she couldn't believe her Germany had gone so mad. There still were many fine people left. Important men and women sympathized with her, and secretly aided her, and some even risked Nazi vengeance by openly befriending her. The names of those who remained her friends, which I cannot give here because it would bring Nazi rage down on their heads, read like a list of all that was fine and decent and civilized in Germany.

She came to America as representative of several German firms interested in exchange of patents with American firms. I suppose that is what gave rise to ideas in Nazi minds that she was an enemy spy. Actually she was working as a legitimate business contact. She toured the country, visiting Washington, Akron, St Louis, Dayton, Kansas City, Wichita, through Oklahoma to Sante Fe, Durange, Ship Rock, Grand Canyon, Boulder Dam, Los Angeles, San Diego, Yosemite Valley, Tioga Pass, Sacramento, San Francisco, Redwood Valley, Crater Lake, National Park at Mt Ranier, Seattle, Spokane, Yellowstone, Black Mountains, Chicago, and back to New York.

She was still loyal to Germany. When representatives of German aviation firms for whom she did business wanted to come to America and visit aviation factories, she made all arrangements. She worked for the Junkers Company, and Klemm Corporation, and Siemens Corporation, and Bendix Corporation, and the Heinkel Company, and Messerschmidt, or Bayerische Flugzeugwerke. She dealt with the Goodyear Tyre Company, and Edward G. Budd Company, Philadelphia, and Fleetwing, Bristol, Pa., and General Tyre, Akron, O., and a dozen other American firms. She proved a smart business woman, and made a fine living out of arranging sales and swaps of international patents. She had charm and wit and made

happened, even abduction of Astra and Senta de Wanger. There were men on the German ships who would aid even with things like that, as certain things to which I am coming indicate strongly. There were other *Gestapo* men, their identities unknown even to Herrmann and Rossberg. We could not uncover them; we saw only traces of their work.

Herrmann's and Rossberg's confessions included another picture, too, perhaps, in its implications, one of the most important of the whole mess. They told me facts and named names which led us right into the German-American Bunds and implicated them in the spy conspiracy.

CHAPTER XIV

IN January, 1938—shortly before the tip from the M.I.5 opened our eyes to the fact that a desperate Nazi spy ring was operating in America—United States Senator Reynolds, of North Carolina, warned the U.S. Senate that there were twenty-six Nazi camps in the country, with 8000 uniformed, drilling Nazi Storm Troopers.

"I ask you," Senator Reynolds demanded rhetorically, "if any other country in the world would permit uniformed foreign soldiers to march in their land?"

Senator Reynolds was referring to the camps and the *Ordnung Dienst* of the *Amerika-Deutsche Volkesbund*. His talk was embalmed in the *Congressional Record*. Not much attention was paid to it. Congressman Samuel Dickstein had been shouting the same thing, and much more, for years without creating much of a furore. The typically American reaction (and if I may be permitted an editorialism, the healthy reaction) was: "So what?"

We in the F.B.I. knew roughly the history and status of the *Amerika-Deutsche Volkesbund*, better known as the German-American Bund. It grew out of the organization known as the Friends of New Germany, created in 1933 by Heinz Spanknöbel and Dr Griebl and a few others. The first president was Spanknöbel, self-elected. When his Nazi propaganda became too raw and he too notorious a figure, he handed the presidency over to Dr Griebl, whose American citizenship and rank as an officer in the United States Army Reserve put him above suspicion. So much so that when on July 27, 1937, Congressman Dickstein read Griebl's name into the *Congressional Record* with the charge that he was a Nazi spy, no one paid the slightest bit of attention, including, I must admit, the F.B.I.

By 1936, under repeated exposures and attacks, mainly by the respectable, non-Nazi German organizations in this country, the Friends of New Germany was so notorious that a change of name was imperative. Then was born the German-American Bund, with burly, swaggering Fritz Kuhn as the American *Führer*.

Griebl and most of the other original organizers dropped into the background. By the time we had the goods on Griebl as a dangerous Nazi spy, he had long since given up all open participation in Bund activities. He remained, however, the friend and adviser of many of the leaders.

Kuhn is a Bavarian War veteran who came to America in 1923 and got a job as a chemist at the Ford car factories in Detroit. He was active in German affairs from the beginning, but how he suddenly got to be *Führer* of the Bund is somewhat of a mystery. So are a great many things about the Bund. Last year, while claiming in various speeches that the Bund had "200,000 members," or "180,000 members" or "230,000 members," he told the F.B.I. it had exactly 8299 members. All those figures are false. The 8299 figure is made ridiculous by the fact that in the New York area alone there were sixty-five branches last spring, with the number growing daily. Hitler's annexation of Austria gave the movement in America great impetus, the number of branches in New York and its immediate vicinity jumping from fifty-eight to the sixty-five mentioned above within a week of the *Anschluss*. Membership-drive advertisements in the German-language newspapers in the United States were patterned closely on the Nazi propaganda flooded into Austria just before the seizure, and the Bunds were preparing to celebrate the capture of Austria a week before it happened. Membership took a terrific leap upward when England and France handed over Czechoslovakia to Hitler recently. I think the best guess—though only a guess—would be that in the autumn of 1938 there were 75,000 Bund members in the United States.

There are Bunds in New York, in a dozen communities surrounding it, Philadelphia, Chicago, Los Angeles, St Louis, Boston, Salt Lake City, Minneapolis, Seattle, Detroit, Portland, Ore., Kansas City, Milwaukee, Cleveland, Georgia, and Texas. In March, 1938, eighteen American newspapermen were summoned to the Austrian Embassy in Washington and offered jobs in a chain of Nazi newspapers to be started in eleven cities in the United States.

There is no intention on my part to indicate that the Bund is subversive or illegal. But since the F.B.I. has proof—including confessions—that some Bund leaders actively tried to aid the Nazi spy ring and to furnish it with military defence secrets of the United States, some background of the Bund, some picture of its methods, is entirely called for at this point.

The twenty-six camps referred to by Senator Reynolds are for the most part but summer recreation camps for Germans in America. In the main what goes on in them is perfectly harmless and innocent and proper. The majority of the people who visit them do so to get fresh air and sunshine, play games, sing songs, talk over the old country with others of German birth, drink beer, eat wieners and sauerkraut, and have a perfectly decent good time.

But included are other things. Speakers thunder hoarse visions of the morrow, dreams of German world dominance. They shout demands for German representation in America, shockingly similar to the words of Henlein in Czechoslovakia. They quote Josef Hünerfauth, a leading Nazi philosopher: "Primarily we are not citizens of states but racial comrades." They quote the slogan of the People's League for Germanism Abroad: "In admiration and deep faith, our racial comrades in foreign States look up to the Reich and its *Führer*." They

189

sing the Nazi marching-song, the Horst Wessel song, in memory of the pimp who became a Nazi hero, with its bloodthirsty lines. The speakers cite the names of anti-Nazis in America, and after them words that have become ritualistic in Nazi camps, "He will be dealt with when the day of reckoning comes." And frenzied cheers arise.

They drill and march and practise at rifle ranges. And outstanding among them are the members of the *Ordnung Dienst*—the Bund version of the Nazi Storm Troopers, in uniforms, with Nazi emblems and sheathed knives. It was a simple uniform at first, with variations according to purse and taste, but in 1937 Nazi tailors in New York were given a boost by the following style decree: greyish-blue tunic, with black cuffs and neckband, black forage-cap with silver braid, black trousers. They used to display the Nazi flag—black swastika on a white disk in a red field, but in April, 1938, *Führer Kuhn*, in view of charges that the Bund was controlled from Germany, decreed a new flag. It carries in the centre the gold emblem of the Bund (a swastika obliquely on the base of an inverted pyramid) against a background of black, white, and red rays in the pattern of a Maltese cross.

They give the Nazi salute. They make strenuous efforts to be friendly with, and enlist men and officers of, the United States Army and Navy. They have had quite a bit of success. They have penetrated fairly deeply into the National Guard in some sections of New York. In February, 1937, there was an advertisement in the New York Nazi weekly, the *Deutscher Weckruf und Beobachter,* urging Germans to enlist in Battery D of the 244th Coast Artillery. And at a Fascist ball, jammed with Nazi Storm Troopers in full regalia in New York on November 13, 1937, there appeared thirty men and officers in the uniform of the United States Army. There were also two guests of honour in the uniforms of officers of the United States Navy.

The Nazi salute is given definitely on many occasions. At the trial of six Nazi Bund leaders in an up-State New York court in the summer of 1938, on charges of failing to register properly, one defendant demonstrated the Nazi salute in the Court-room.

"Is that what you call the salute of an American citizen to his flag?" demanded the District Attorney.

"No," retorted the Nazi, "but it will be."

"I saw things in this Court-room," commented Judge L. Barron Hill later, "I never thought I'd see in this country. I am saddened."

But enough of the background and the general picture. Now down to specific facts about some Bund members and their connexions with the Nazi spy ring. It was no secret in the ranks of the Bund that such a spy ring was operating here. Instead a number of the members went out of their way to aid it.

Take, for instance, Wilhelm Böning, 315 East 95th Street, New York City.

Böning was—and probably still is—an important member of the German-American Bund. He was also a leader of the *Ordnung Dienst.* Böning, 200 pounds, five feet ten inches of Nazi *Führer*, goose-stepped pompously at the head of the 1500 Storm Troopers who paraded in a Nazi demonstration in New York's Madison Square Garden in October, 1937. They saluted the Nazi flag and huffed: "*Heil* Hitler!" with out-thrust arms while thousands cheered. They had police protection.

Yet Böning was trying his best to aid the Nazi spy ring against the United States. In December, 1937, at a Bund meeting in the Grand Central Palace, in Yorkville, he got to talking with a group of other Nazis who were boasting of their War experiences.

One of these was John Baptiste Unkel, an official of the Bund at New Rochelle, N.Y.

Unkel had been in the United States Army, and he was boasting that he had helped build the Philippine Island fortifications. At least, Böning got the impression it was the Philippine Islands. It turned out later that Unkel was talking about the Panama Canal Zone, but Böning's knowledge of geography was rather limited, and he thought the two places were the same.

In the midst of his boasting, Unkel announced that he had a complete set of plans of the fortifications. Böning pricked up his ears. "I saw," he confessed to me later, "a chance to help my Fatherland."

He immediately hunted up Fritz Ewald Rossberg, the assistant chief of the *Gestapo* in New York. He met him at the Franz Siegel Tavern, on East 84th Street, in the Yorkville section of New York.

"Those plans will be valuable to Germany, don't you think?" he demanded.

Rossberg became excited. "Arrange to see those plans," he ordered Böning. "See if they look like the real thing. If they are—we must have them!"

Rossberg thought them so important that he reported the matter to his chief, Karl Friedrich Wilhelm Herrmann, and to Dr Griebl, who later passed on the story to me and thus led me to grill Böning and Unkel. I could not find out, however, what made them think them so important. I have not been able to clarify in my mind what good plans—rather old plans, at that—of the fortifications at the Philippine Islands or the Panama Canal Zone would do Nazi Germany, unless the Nazis looked forward to war on America, which is, of course, ridiculous. Yet you will recall that Rumrich was asked by Nazi spy headquarters for information concerning Panama Canal Zone fortifications and defences, and that it came through as apparently a serious assignment. And in November, 1938, Nazi spies were caught taking photographs of the restricted sections of the Zone, containing the fortifications. The motive still eludes me, just as the psychology which made these Bund members—American citizens—think immediately of turning military information over to the Nazi Government.

Böning got in touch with Unkel, after his conversation with Rossberg, at the *Ordnung Dienst* Club, in the headquarters of the German-American Bund, at 178 East 85th Street, Yorkville, New York City.

"Those plans you spoke of the other night," Böning said. "They are of great value. You must produce them."

Unkel wanted to know who wanted them. Böning refused to tell him. Whereupon Unkel, according to the story they tell, declined to turn them over. "It is a dangerous matter," Unkel is supposed to have said, "and I must know the name of the man I am dealing with."

Böning reported back to Rossberg, explaining at the same time that it developed that the plans were of the Panama Canal Zone, not the Philippine Islands, fortifications. Rossberg showed even more interest then.

"That is highly important," Rossberg declared. "We must get those plans!"

"But Unkel refuses," Böning pointed out.

"We must get them—by force if necessary," Rossberg cried.

Böning went back to Unkel the next day. He told Unkel he would introduce him to the man who wanted the plans.

Here the story becomes rather confused. Somebody— Böning, Rossberg, or Unkel—or all three—lied here.

Böning said he was approached at a New Rochelle Bund meeting a little later by a man whose name he did not know. This man, he said, walked up to him and asked to be introduced to Unkel. So Böning introduced him to Unkel, according to the story he told me later, but didn't hear what the man said to Unkel.

Unkel's version is that Böning brought up a man and introduced him, but that he didn't catch the name.

Rossberg, Unkel, and Böning said it wasn't Rossberg. Rossberg, like the other two, said he had no idea who it was. Herrmann said he didn't know who it was. I suspected it was Rumrich, because the tie-up between the spy ring and the *Gestapo* was very close. But Rumrich denied it, while admitting more damning things. Was this still another spy, of such importance that all feared to name him? It might have been. I already have confessed that it is highly possible we only scratched the surface of this spy ring in our investigation. There were probably other spy cells so far untouched by the investigation.

Unkel's story is that the mysterious man immediately demanded of him:

"Are you a loyal German?"

"I was surprised," said Unkel, "and asked him what he meant. I told him I was an American citizen. He kept asking me was I a loyal German, and finally came out with it and asked me if I had the plans of the Panama Canal fortifications."

Unkel's story is that he was shocked—oh, so very shocked! So shocked, he says, that he asked the mysterious man:

"Are you a German secret agent?"

And the man, according to Unkel, said, "No."

The upshot of the conversation, Unkel claimed to me, was that he told the stranger that he hadn't got the plans any longer, and didn't want to get mixed up in anything like that, anyway. And that, Unkel claimed, is what he told Böning later, too.

"It was all just a lot of beer-drinking talk in the first place, anyway, Mr Turrou," he told me. "I'm a loyal American citizen. I was in the United States Army. I'm an American, not a German. I don't like Germany and these Germans, anyway."

THE NAZI SPY CONSPIRACY IN AMERICA

"That's an odd way for you to talk," I remarked. "And you an official of the Bund."

He shrugged that off.

Unkel was born in 1886 at Linz, on the Rhine. He came to this country in 1910, and in 1913, after three years as a steward, enlisted in the United States Army. He was sent to Fort Slocum, then to Fort Washington, Md., to the 44th Coast Artillery, and thence to the Panama Canal Zone. He deserted while there, was caught, and served eighteen months in prison at Fort Jay.

Later things were arranged so that his desertion was not held against him when he wanted to become an American citizen. In 1917 he re-enlisted, and served at Fort Slocum, New York, until January, 1919, while the A.E.F. was overseas fighting German troops. Unkel is married, has a grown son, and for nine years was a chauffeur for Miss Mosby, 16 Chestnut Avenue, Larchmont, N.Y.

Böning, a thin-lipped, ruthless-looking man, was born in Delmenhurst, Germany, in 1907. He is married, has four children, and worked as a machinist at the Edward Ermold Co., 652 Hudson Street, New York City.

He told me he became an ardent Nazi early in the movement, and in April, 1934, joined the *Ordnung Dienst*.

At first he denied that he ever went beyond membership in the uniformed Storm Troopers of the Bund except the one time he tried to arrange to get plans of the United States defences to the spy ring.

"Then how did you get to be a leader of the *Ordnung Dienst*?" I challenged. "I thought you had to have done some special service for the Nazi Party to get such an honour?"

He still denied any other activities, but by confronting him with certain facts, I got from him the admission that he had known Rossberg, and that Rossberg was a *Gestapo* man, for some time.

"You were a member of the *Gestapo*?" I demanded.

"No, sir, I was not," he declared.

"But I know you helped Rossberg," I told him.

"Well, yes, I helped him."

"How?"

"I gave him information."

"What kind of information?"

"Oh, about Germans living here."

"What kind of information?" I persisted.

"Well, lots of kinds . . . things the German Government asked Rossberg to find out."

"Spy information, for instance?"

"No, sir!" he declared vehemently.

He stuck to his denials, beyond the admission that he aided Rossberg. All I could get out of him concerning the nature of his work with Rossberg was that he checked up on non-Nazi Germans, and Germans suspected of being anti Nazi and Communists. Whenever I got him into a corner, his answer was, "I investigated Communists."

Rossberg remained interested in the plans even after Unkel told the stranger he would not turn them over. He asked Böning about them again later. He got Böning to give him Unkel's full name, his exact address, and the description of his home in Larchmynt.

"We must get those plans," Rossberg declared. "I think Unkel is lying when he says he hasn't got them any longer. If we can't get them any other way, we will break into his house and get them!"

But soon afterwards Rumrich was arrested, and Böning became frightened and Dr Griebl and Herrmann ordered a halt for the time being.

What I have related of this incident so far comes from the joint version of Griebl, Herrmann, Rossberg, Böning, and Unkel. The lie-detector indicated that there was more to it than that. But the whole thing seemed so silly. It was too ridiculous to dignify with severe action and indictment, though the fact that there was a conspiracy to get such plans— even though the conspiracy failed and even if there were no such plans—is sufficient for indictment. It seemed to Mr Hardy and the Grand Jury and myself, however, that exposure of the fact that such things were going on in this country, and revelation of the twisted Nazi psychology that led to such things, was enough.

Besides, things began happening too fast. We were more interested in getting to the bottom—or top—of this Nazi spy ring than in cluttering up the jails with small fry. We didn't consider Rossberg important enough to watch closely even, particularly when he found he had a good job, was married, that his wife had a good job, and that a Nazi lawyer in New York told him that if he kept his mouth shut, our legal case against him was weak—which was true.

But that night—the night of March 30, 1938—Rossberg disappeared.

The first inkling of his flight came the morning of March 31, when his wife telephoned me.

"Where is my husband?" she demanded. "How long are you going to keep him?"

Twenty minutes later his employer rang up with the same question. But then I was convinced he was gone, but there was no use wasting men searching for him. The odds were he had sneaked out on the first German ship sailing away from New York.

I checked with Captain Drechsel at the Hapag-Lloyd Piers and found the German motor-vessel *St Louis* had sailed for Germany the night after we released Rossberg on his promise to appear when wanted. It seemed a good bet that Rossberg had gone on that ship, and so I ordered Captain Drechsel to radio the ship for information. Captain Drechsel did so, explaining in his cablegram that it was the United States Government demanding information. But arrogantly the Nazi captain of the *St Louis* violated all the traditions of courtesy of the sea and international procedure. He did not answer.

It took two weeks of strong protest before the Government got any official reply. That came in the form of a cablegram from the home office of the North German Lloyd Line at Bremen. It said that Rossberg had stowed away on the *St Louis* and had not been discovered until the ship was at sea. Then, according to the cablegram, he had produced money and bought a third-class ticket, and therefore had been treated as a passenger thereafter. Despite the fact that he had no passport, he was permitted to leave the ship at Bremerhaven. That is a point to remember later, when we come to the escape of another of our witnesses, and the alibis with which the Nazi officials baulked our efforts to get him. As for Rossberg, we made no further efforts to get him. Political offenders are not extraditable, and Rossberg was, furthermore, of such small value to our case that we had not planned to seek his indictment.

In April there came a letter from Rossberg. It came to Ernst Ramm, 101 West 52nd Street, New York City. Knowing that Ramm was his best friend, and suspecting Rossberg might try to get in touch with his wife through Ramm, I had warned Ramm to inform me of any mail he got from Rossberg, or be considered an accomplice.

Rossberg wrote Ramm that he was being treated splendidly in Germany, and that he now felt prouder than ever of what he had done for the Nazi Party against the United States while living here, and that he would do it again if he had the chance. The letter closed with "*Heil* Hitler!"

Enclosed was a letter to his wife. But Ramm turned that over to her before notifying me, and when we questioned her she said she had torn it up and refused to tell us what was in it. We did not press her, but let her go.

CHAPTER XV

BEFORE we examine the results of the lie-detector tests upon some of the witnesses in this Nazi spy case, it is necessary to understand exactly what the lie-detector is and how it operates. So much bunk has been written about it, and so much misinformation and so many misconceptions engendered, that some people think it a magical instrument which peers into the heart and mind of the subject, while others dismiss it as a silly, worthless gadget. Actually it is an extremely valuable, soundly scientific device—but worthless except when operated by an expert. I am referring only to the type used by the F.B.I., the Polygraph, developed by Professor Leonard Keeler in the North-Western University Scientific Crime Detection Laboratory. Of the merits or demerits of other types I know nothing, therefore can make no comparisons. I have seen the Keeler Polygraph in operation many times. I began with scepticism and wound up with enthusiasm.

The inventor calls it "a diagnostic method for detecting deceptions." It does not report whether the subject is lying. All it does is measure and record the rate of respiration and the rate of the systolic and diastolic pulsations of the heart. Sometimes it is arranged also to record the muscular reflexes of the arm or leg. From these measurements and recordings the expert deduces whether the subject is lying.

Basically the machine is a sort of twin aneroid barometer; it is in principle much like the apparatus for recording atmospheric pressure. Its active principle, like that of the twin aneroid barometer, is the effect of pressure upon a thin-walled vacuum chamber. If the pressure increases, the walls are depressed, and the change in pressure is reflected in the rise of a column of mercury. If the pressure decreases, the thin metal walls react outward and the column of mercury drops.

In the barometer the atmosphere supplies the fluctuations in pressure. In the Polygraph the fluctuations are caused by the rise and fall of the chest, due to expansion and contraction of the lungs, and by the systole and diastole of the heart-action—the contraction and expansion as the heart pulses blood through the network of arteries.

Repeated tests have proved that normal persons—that is, all except madmen, low-grade morons, and idiots, and sometimes (I am not being facetious) women in love—show definite distortions in the rate of heart-beat and breathing when lying. That has been demonstrated so often that it is accepted as scientific fact. Why that is leads to some argument, however, with the leading theory being that deliberate lying, based on fear and a desire to mislead because the truth would be dangerous, does something to secretions of the endocrine glands, which in turn affect the breathing and heart-beat.

Here is how it is applied:

The subject is ushered to a chair close to the apparatus, an innocuous-looking box about the size of, and with somewhat the appearance of, an old-fashioned table radio. Two, and sometimes three, rubber-covered tubes lead out from it. One ends in a blood-pressure cuff, such as used by your physician. It is fastened round the bared upper right arm, where it can be affected by the pulsations of the brachial artery. It is inflated to midway between the systolic and diastolic blood-pressures—to neutral, in other words. The second tube ends in a broad rubber tube, which is fixed round the chest at the point of maximum expansion during normal breathing. The third tube, not often used, is fastened round the bared leg, to check on muscular reflex. Let's drop that third tube in this picture.

Inside the machine the tubes are connected to slender steel pens, each of which touches a strip of paper about six inches wide which unwinds from one reel on to another at the rate of six inches a minute.

The preparations so far have, naturally, not aided the subject's poise if he has anything to hide, or expects to tell lies. With everything set, the tiny motor activating the machine is started. Not a word is said as the two needles write down the simple record of the subject's breathing and heart beat in order to determine 'normal.'

Let Professor Keeler take up the explanation from there, as he did in an article in *The American Journal of Police Science*:

A record is obtained for two or three minutes to ascertain the individual's normal fluctuations, heart-condition, and respiration. Following this brief period of silence a preamble is read: "This machine to which you are connected has been used for some years on criminal suspects, and so far has proved a very reliable means of detecting the innocence or guilt of a man, and I'm sure we will not fail in your case. Now sit as quietly as possible and answer my questions just 'Yes' or 'No.' If you have any explanations to make, just reserve them until the completion of the test."

A few irrelevant questions are then asked. An innocent individual will seldom react in any marked degree to these questions. He takes them at their face value. A mentally defective (border-line), whether innocent or guilty, will show but slight disturbance at these questions. However, a mentally alert, guilty individual will construe these as being camouflaged questions regarding his crime.

Following the irrelevant questions, direct questions pertaining to the supposed crime are asked in a quiet, monotonous voice. Time is allowed between questions for the bodily responses to occur and to return to equilibrium.

The guilty individual becomes more disturbed as the test progresses, the general blood-pressure curve rising and the rapid fluctuations increasing in intensity and frequency. The blood-pressure response to each lie causes an increase in both systolic and diastolic pressure.

Ordinary physical abnormalities, such as high blood-pressure and irregular pulse, or emotional instability caused by fear unrelated to the fear of detection, anger, or other disturbing factors, do not interfere with the test, because these irregularities are brought out in the control part of the record and by the questions asked.

I must stress again the point that the machine or the tests are of no value except in the hands of experts. I have watched and taken part in scores of such tests, yet I would not take it upon myself to consider my reading of the results absolute. Though I stood by and aided in the tests in the cases in which I was interested, I never allowed myself to draw conclusions until the report of the expert, based on careful study of the results, came in.

Remember, too, that in most Courts the results of lie-detector tests are not admissible as evidence. Therefore in the following examples of some of the results of the tests on some of the spy witnesses, there is no intention of pointing an accusing finger. I am citing those examples merely because I found them highly interesting and think that perhaps you will, too.

The subjects we placed under the Polygraph test in the Nazi spy investigation were:

1. Martin Schade, the New York flat-manager, who was accused by two members of the spy ring of working with them, and to whom Karl Schluter, spy contact man, addressed a letter, but who denied any complicity and was released completely.

2. Captain William Drechsel, superintendent of the Hapag-Lloyd Piers in New York, who aided our investigation, and who was placed under the test to determine if his co-operation was real.

3. Karl Friedrich Wilhelm Herrmann, *Gestapo* chief in New York.

4. Wilhelm Böning, Bund official and Storm Troop leader, who tried to aid the spy ring.

5. John Baptiste Unkel, Bund official, who boasted he had United States defence secrets.

6. Miss Kate Moog, sweetheart of Dr Griebl, whom the Nazi spy chiefs tried to get to play the *rôle* of a Mata Hari in this Nazi spy ring.

7. Dr Ignatz T. Griebl, director and clearing-house for all Nazi spy and propaganda activities in the United States.

The tests were made in my office in F.B.I. headquarters at New York, by two F.B.I. experts from Washington. The questions were carefully thought out and chosen to give the maximum and most enlightening results, and I first went over them with the experts, explaining their significance and enlightening them on the background so that they could better understand the results.

Some of the questions were without meaning, such as: "Have you had breakfast this morning?" Those questions were to 'cool off' the subject, and to be used as controls to determine whether the subject's reaction to other questions were due to lying, or to other emotional disturbances.

With Martin Schade we got nowhere. He turned out to be one of those extremely rare individuals—so stolid, phlegmatic, and controlled that the test was worthless. The experts spotted that almost immediately, and after a few questions, gave up. He was freed with a clean slate. The experts' formal comment was: "This subject was quite unresponsive in so far as any changes in blood-pressure or respiration were concerned during the test. This unresponsiveness is believed to be physiological in part and to be characteristic of the subject. For this reason no opinion whatsoever can be rendered concerning his truthfulness or sincerity, and the test was discontinued after the preliminary stages."

Captain Drechsel came through with flying colours. The experts reported, after a lengthy test, that "the attitude of this subject was that of unusual frankness and the Polygraph does not reflect any reactions which are particularly inconsistent with this attitude." At one point we got a reaction which looked bad. It came when he was asked if he had been sending any information to Germany. But further questioning developed that when he answered "No," he realized that was not the truth since he had been reporting to his superiors, the steamship officials in Germany, our activities with regard to employees of the German steamship lines, as was his duty. Unable to explain, because the experts' instructions were to answer just "yes" or "no" with no explanations, he had become upset, and his disturbance was reflected in the machine.

The results of the test on Karl Friedrich Wilhelm Herrmann were quite different. The experts reported that "pronounced reactions were obvious whenever we gave him a question which would involve him directly in the spy ring."

It is difficult to give samples of the questions and answers which led the experts to those conclusions. As you can see by the case of Captain Drechsel, an isolated example, a question and answer torn out of the context, or even a series of questions and answers, can be misleading except when studied by experts. It is particularly difficult to illustrate the test and results in writing, for what the experts study are the wavy and jagged lines made by the steel pens on the moving paper. But in writing reports on such tests, a system of asterisks has been devised to give some indication of results. Thus, one asterisk after a response indicates a mild emotional reaction, two asterisks indicate a strong emotional reaction, and three asterisks, quite an emotional reaction, such as would be found when the subject is telling a 'whopper.'

Here are the last dozen questions asked Herrmann, and his replies. I cite them only to show how the apparatus works, and not as judgment one way or another on whether Herrmann was lying:

Q.—Was it your ambition to do espionage work in this country?
A.—No. ★★★

Q.—Did you give plans to anyone on the s.s. *Europa*?
A.—No.

Q.—Did you follow anyone on the s.s. *Europa*?
A.—No.

Q.—Did you conspire with Dr Griebl?
A.—No. ★★★

Q.—Did you ever talk to Dr Griebl about (military) plans?
A.—No. ★★★

Q.—(repeated) Did you ever talk to Dr Griebl about plans?
A.—No. ★★★

Q.—Were you born in Germany?
A.—Yes.

Q.—Did you tell Griebl about the plans for the fortifications of New York?
A.—No. ★★

Q.—Have you had breakfast?
A.—Yes.

Q.—Did you ever talk to Griebl about plans Unkel had?
A.—No.

Q.—Did you discuss the price of the plans with Griebl?
A.—No.

Q.—Did you ever discuss other plans of fortifications or ships?
A.—No.★★★

The point of the questions about whether he was born in Germany, as he had been and had told us, and as to whether he had his breakfast, were to determine how much the strong emotional reactions to other questions were due to nervousness and general fear. They were control questions. If he had shown reactions when answering truthfully those inane, harmless questions, the expert would have discounted considerably the reactions to the other questions.

Wilhelm Böning was next. After studying the results of the test on him, the experts concluded that while Böning was not entirely frank, and did not reveal everything, the case in which he confessed—the effort to get fortification plans from Unkel for the Nazi spy ring—was the only spy case in which he was implicated.

Some queer reactions popped up in the questioning of John Baptiste Unkel. But the experts drew no strong conclusions from the results, except that he was not telling all he could tell.

The questioning of Miss Moog under the lie-detector, and her reactions, would have been amusing if the case were not so serious. She sat there smiling and flirting with us, and the atmosphere created by the preliminary stages had little effect on her. The results were not of much value. We have to be very careful in reading the results of a Polygraph test on most women. I am not necessarily referring to Miss Moog when I say that we have found that it is true that women can lie better than men. And as for a woman in love. . . .

For instance, we knew definitely that Miss Moog was aware that her sweetheart, Dr Griebl, was a member of the espionage ring. And when we questioned her about her own connexion with the spy ring, the Polygraph showed reactions. But when we asked her if she knew Griebl was a member of the spy ring, she blandly said "No." We expected a whopping reaction. The machine showed absolutely none!

We did not question her very long. The experts reported she was not telling the truth, but that there was no use continuing with further tests on her.

Dr Griebl proved the most interesting subject of all.

The machine works best on intelligent people. The more alert, the more aware, the more quick-witted the subject, the more marked the reactions. As a scientific man, Griebl knew what was happening. He knew that no matter how he tried, the chances were that whenever he lied his respiration and blood-pressure would betray him.

He sat there with a half-smile on his face, but the corners of his mouth were twitching.

Here is the record:

Q.—Do you live in New York City?

A.—Yes.

Q.—Do you object to this test?

A.—No. (He had already given his permission. We always obtained consent first.)

Q.—Have you ever furnished military information to Kapitan-Leutnant Dr Pfeiffer at Bremen?

A.—No.★★★

Q.—Have you had breakfast?

A.—Yes.

Q.—Did you accompany Lonkowski to Canada? (You will recall that Griebl aided Lonkowski, the Nazi aviation spy, to escape to Canada, but did not accompany him. The following answer was therefore true. Note the absence of reaction, despite the disturbing nature of the question.)

A.—No.

Q.—Are you now a practising physician?

A.—Yes.

Q.—Did you ever give Schluter military information?

A.—No.★★

Q.—Is to-day Friday?

A.—Yes.

Q.—Did Schluter ever pay you for any military information?

A.—No.★★★

Q.—Have you had breakfast this morning?

A.—Yes.

Q.—Did you take Lonkowski over the border?

A.—No.

Q.—Were you an espionage contact for Pfeiffer?

A.—No.***

Q.—Have you had breakfast?

A.—Yes.

Q.—Have you ever visited Rumrich's home?

A.—No.**

Q.—Is to-day Sunday?

A.—No.

Q.—Did Danielsen (a ship-designer they tried to get to Germany) ever give you any military information for transmission to Pfeiffer?

A.—No.*

Q.—Personally, have you obtained military information in Washington?

A.—No.

Q.—Did anybody ever give you any military information for transmission to Pfeiffer?

A.—No.*

Q.—Do you live in New York?

A.—Yes.

Q.—Have you withheld any information from the F.B.I. agents?

A.—Yes.

Q.—(repeated) Have you withheld any information from the F.B.I. agents?

A.—Yes.

(Note that while this was a very dangerous question, and Griebl must have realized that his answer was damaging to him, the Polygraph showed no reaction when he replied truthfully in the affirmative.)

Q.—Have you conspired with Miss Moog?
A.—No. *
Q.—Have you told me any lies?
A.—No. *
Q.—Is Miss Moog involved in the espionage ring?
A.—No. **
Q.—Are you double-crossing the agents?
A.—No.
Q.—Do you know the German contact with Gibbs and Cox?
A.—No. **
Q.—Have you been in Philadelphia?
A.—Yes.
Q.—Have you personally furnished espionage information to Dr Pfeiffer?
A.—No. ***
Q.—Is Miss Moog presently connected with this ring?
A.—No.
Q.—Are you presently conspiring with any of the ring?
A.—No. **
Q.—Are you sincere in present efforts to assist Federal agents?
A.—Yes.

Again let me warn against laymen trying to read those results too closely. The experts' reaction was: "This individual was unusually responsive on the Polygraph. His reactions were so pronounced that it is believed they can be definitely isolated, and for this reason it is believed that the conclusions were unusually reliable. As a result, it is believed that he was deeply involved in the espionage ring and in direct contact with Dr Pfeiffer. It is not believed from the questioning that he personally took Lonkowski over the border. It is believed that his present co-operation with the F.B.I. agents is sincere up to a certain point, but that he is still withholding much information concerning his own complicity in the espionage work."

It was on May 5 that he was questioned. He left F.B.I. headquarters with a worry he tried vainly to disguise. He knew he had given himself away. Yet there were two questions and two answers which made us relax all vigilance, all watchfulness over him.

They were, as you may have noted above:

Q.—Are you double-crossing the agents?

A.—No.

Q.—Are you sincere in present efforts to assist Federal agents?

A.—Yes.

I still believe he was telling the truth there—at that time. He was honestly working with us to expose the Nazi spy ring in order to save his own hide, and lying only about his own complicity also to save his own hide. Something happened later to make him change.

To understand that picture, and what Griebl told us, and what it led us to, and how his love-life was mixed up with his spy activities and with a house in Germany, we must go back to the time he visited Kapitan-Leutnant Pfeiffer, and Colonel Busch and Kapitan-Leutnants von Bonin and Menzel in Germany.

CHAPTER XVI

GOING back on Griebl's career, we find women playing a prominent *rôle*. Sometimes it reads like the script of a romantic film. Even on the battlefield he found romance.

He enlisted in the Army during the World War and became an officer in the Imperial German Army, assigned to fighting on the Austrian border, against the Italians. He fought in the scene where Ernest Hemingway's *Farewell to Arms* is laid.

There, wounded, he met the woman, Maria Glanz, who later became, and to-day still is, his wife. She was a nurse with the Austrian Army on the Italian front. They met at Udine, where he was wounded, and where she nursed him. She, already trying to think up an alibi for him, told me he was kicked by a horse and was unconscious from that for three weeks. That apparently was to establish an insanity defence, if needed, for my later information was that it was a bullet, not a horse's hoof, which laid him low.

Their meeting progressed like fiction. The Austrian nurse fell in love with the young German artillery officer, and after she nursed him back to health and he was invalided back home, they corresponded. Three months before the end of the War she was captured by the Italian forces and kept in a concentration camp until the end. Released at the end of the War, she joined Griebl at Munich, where he had entered the University to prepare himself for a career of medicine. She helped him, working as a nurse, and in 1922, sailed for America, because that, she heard, was the land of opportunity, and there she could earn more money to help her dear Ignatz become a doctor, and could pave the way for him to come to her.

In America she worked day and night, obtaining nursing-work in hospitals and private homes. In two years, by denying herself, she had earned enough, even over what she sent him in Germany to help him along there, to buy a steamship ticket for Ignatz. He arrived in America early in 1925, and they were married shortly afterwards. He lived on her. She paid his way by nursing through Long Island Medical University for a year, through his internship, and through a year at Fordham University to perfect his English. She supplied his tuition fees, bought his books and clothing, paid his board, and gave him pocket-money. "I slaved for him and worked my fingers to the bone for him," she wept to me later. "And then he ran after other women. That Moog woman was not the only one."

Truly he had a roving eye, this Griebl, and fancied himself God's gift to women.

Finished his studies and admitted to practice, he heard of an office in Bangor, Me. Maria put up the money, and they took over the practice there. But this young German doctor with the roving eye and hands which reached out for any woman who came near him didn't do so well among the 'down easters' up in Maine.

So they moved to New York, and he opened an office in Yorkville, right in the heart of the German colony. Immediately he prospered. He joined all the German societies in sight, patted all the men on the back, and made passes at most of the women, and became very popular and was chosen official physician for most of those organizations. In that way he got not only juicy annual retainers, but also a lot of other medical business. He decided that the most lucrative practice among Germans was in obstetrics and varicose veins, and so, at once, he became a specialist in those two fields.

MRS MARIA GLANZ GRIEBL

And so he waxed well-to-do and prominent and respected, and became the ideal clearing-house for the Nazi spy ring which developed later. He punctuated his other activities with affairs with women.

German women fought for the man. The answer, partly, lies back in the World War, when five years of slaughter left the cream of Germany's manhood on the battlefield. For years afterwards, women far outnumbered the men. A man was a prize, to be fought for by women—particularly a doctor, a prominent man ! The attitude persisted, even among Germans who emigrated to this country, where the balance was evened.

Miss Moog came later. They met at meetings of the *Deutsche Gemeinschaft für Literatur und Kunst* (the German Association for Literature and Art), actually a Nazi outfit, in New York

Deutsche Gemeinschaft für Literatur und Kunst
1353 Lexington Avenue   New York City

WINTER - HALBJAHR 1937-38

1. VORTRAGS-ABEND

Dr. I. T. GRIEBL
„Deutsche Geschichte in Amerika"
Ein Beitrag zur Richtigstellung anglo-amerikanischer
Geschichtsdarstellung.

ÜBERREICHUNG der HUGO ECKENER-EHRENMEDAILLE
an Frl. KATIE MOOG

EHRUNG VERDIENSTVOLLER MITARBEITER

FREITAG, den 8. OKTOBER 1937, abends 9 Uhr
NEW YORK TURNHALLE, 85. Str. und Lexington Ave.
25c

ADVERTISEMENT OF A NAZI MEETING WITH GRIEBL AND KATE MOOG
LISTED AS CHIEF SPEAKERS

Turnhalle, 85th Street and Lexington Avenue. Dr Griebl was a featured speaker at that Association, while Katie Moog was its belle.

Now let us go ahead to a day in May, 1937, when Dr Griebl received a letter from Germany which put him in high spirits, but which also set him acting very mysteriously, particularly with his wife. The letter was from Kapitan-Leutnant Pfeiffer, the spy chief at Bremen, and urged him to come to Germany as soon as possible. Important matters were in the wind, it indicated, and promised that he would be allowed to meet the highest chiefs of the Nazi espionage service.

Griebl began packing at once, though it meant leaving his very busy and lucrative medical practice. Several of his women patients were nearing confinement, and several operations were on his schedule. But he turned them over to another doctor, and on June 1, 1937, he sailed for Germany aboard the s.s. *Europa*.

As he was about to leave his flat for the ship, his wife put on her hat and picked up one of the bags.

"What are you doing?" he demanded.

"Why—I'm going to see you off at the ship."

"No, you're not!" he shouted. "I don't want you seeing me off at the ship. I can take care of myself. I don't like scenes and messy farewells."

His wife stared at him with startled, hurt eyes.

"But, Ignatz," she faltered. "I only wanted. . . ."

"I won't have it!" he roared. "That's final!"

And he rushed out, slamming the door.

For a while she wept. Then suspicion grew in her mind. She remembered what the maid had told her, after she had returned from two weeks in the country the summer before.

"I think you ought to know, Mrs Griebl," the maid had said. "A woman has been calling the doctor on the telephone at least fifteen times a day. It was that flirty Katie Moog."

And she remembered the times patients had called and asked for Dr Griebl, after he had told her he was going out to call on them. She remembered the nights he did not come home until very late, though there were no meetings, she knew, of the Nazi organizations to which he belonged. She remembered the nights he did not come home at all.

"My woman's intuition told me something was wrong," Mrs Griebl told me long afterwards. "I knew there must be a reason why he didn't want me to see him off at the ship."

So she dried her eyes, called a taxi, and went down to Pier 86, North River. It was little more than an hour before the ship was to sail. She stood on the pier, steeling herself to go aboard and face his wrath, when suddenly, on an upper deck, she saw her husband.

He was smiling, but not at her. He was smiling at beautiful Kate Moog, and he had his arm round her.

"I felt as if some one had stabbed me in the back with a knife," Mrs Griebl recounted later. "I nearly fainted. Everything began to swim and go black."

But in a few minutes anger gave her strength, and she boarded the ship. Dr Griebl saw her coming, and went towards her to head her off.

"Now I know why you did not want me to see you off," she cried. "Now I see it all."

The man had amazing gall. He brazened it out.

"You are a suspicious fool!" he exclaimed, his apparent anger smothering hers. "You should be grateful to Miss Moog. She put me in touch with important officials in Germany, so that I can get the property of that Jew, Berliner. Now you may have spoiled it all!"

She knew he was lying, but he was too clever for her. Before she could collect her wits, he made the most brazen stroke of all. He demanded that she should go up to Miss Moog and thank her for what she was doing for them!

She refused. He began berating her for lack of appreciation. The cry of "all visitors ashore" became more and more insistent throughout the ship. She was confused, bewildered, and before she knew it he was hustling her off the boat, as if she were the one in the wrong.

"I cried for days after that, and was miserable all the six weeks he was gone with that woman," Mrs Griebl told me later. "But I forgave him. What else could I do? It is not true, what that Kate Moog says, that I consented to divorce him, for $150 a month alimony, so he could marry her. No, I wouldn't do that."

She was, quite obviously, very much in love with her husband. "He is a born skirt-chaser," she told me sadly, "but I still loved him. I had to get used to his chasing other women long ago. He had affairs with dozens of women. He could have been one of the greatest surgeons in the world, my Ignatz, if it hadn't been for that. Women ruined him. Every time a woman looked at him, every time a woman flattered him, he fell in love with her right away. He thought he was a great lover and that no woman could resist him.

"Yet it was I who made it possible for him to come to America, to become a doctor, to be a success! I slaved and worked for him, supported him and encouraged him—and this is the thanks I got."

But she loved him so much that she would do anything for him, she said. "I would even have divorced him, if I thought it was best for him. I told him that when he came and told me he was in love with that Katie Moog, and wanted a divorce. I loved him so much I would do anything I thought would make him happy."

That is very interesting in view of what happened later, and worth remembering.

She was in many respects a pathetic creature. But she was also a strong-willed, bitter woman. I would feel more sorry for her if her history, under investigation, did not show her to be a leader in the Nazi movement among the German women in this country, and did not indicate that she knew far more about this Nazi spy ring, and the vicious Nazi propaganda here, than she lets on. She preached hate among the women of Yorkville, and shrieked vituperation upon all non-Nazis.

She was in close contact with Kapitan-Leutnant Dr Erich Pfeiffer at one time herself. She said it was only with regard to the property in Germany that she and her husband were trying to get the Nazi Government to force the Jew, Berliner, to give up to Griebl. She was called as a witness by the Federal Grand Jury in New York in 1933, which was investigating the disappearance of Spanknöbel. She refused to swear on the Holy Bible before testifying, declaring that all of it, including the New Testament, was "a pack of Jew lies." She offered to swear by the American flag instead.

Soon after Spanknöbel escaped, after hiding at her flat, she sailed for Germany, and it was suspected that she took some of the things he left behind with her. The description of a woman who conferred with Spanknöbel in Germany soon afterwards fitted her exactly:

About 40, five feet four inches; 115 pounds, bleached blonde hair; blue eyes, rather prominent nose, many jewels, particularly large diamond on the left hand; heavily rouged.

That was in 1934. Mrs Griebl went to Europe again in October, 1937, though she was by this time bitterly suspicious —and suspicious is an understatement—of Griebl and Miss Moog. She consented, however, when Griebl told her it was necessary for her to go to complete with Kapitan-Leutnant Pfeiffer the arrangements for depriving the Jew, Berliner, of his property.

It was a property at Giessen, Germany, valued roughly, according to Griebl and Mrs Griebl themselves, at $100,000.

To lend a semblance of legality to the deal, they were going to make over to Berliner their summer cottage in Westchester County, New York. Griebl himself placed the value of this property at less than $20,000—and Miss Heim, who is a broker and real-estate expert, said it was built with the $3,500 Griebl got from her on the promise of marriage.

Berliner, under heavy pressure, had already consented to the deal. But suddenly the Nazi Government put an extra squeeze on him, and wanted him to pay it a huge sum of money in addition. Berliner was protesting that he could not raise the money, and the whole situation became complicated. That is why Mrs Griebl, with the power to act for Dr Griebl, had to go to Germany.

> Please [wrote Berliner plaintively in a letter to Kurt Griebl, brother of Dr Griebl, at Würzburg] write a letter to the Foreign Currency Exchange Agency [at Berlin] to the effect that Mrs Griebl, your sister-in-law, wants to know where she stands.
>
> I believe that you should give an ultimatum of this kind to the Foreign Currency Exchange in Berlin, and not to me. [Kurt Griebl had written him curtly, demanding that he should act at once, but Berliner insisted he could not raise the money the Nazi Government now demanded from him as the price of his release.]
>
> You know [Berliner continued] that I, being a Jew, cannot ask them to answer my letter. I wish that you have more success than I. You know that Mrs Griebl would be more successful with the Government than I, because I am a Jew.
>
> I hope to hear from you at your earliest convenience. I am to-day quite exhausted.
>
> I am not the man I was in June, 1937.
>
> Very truly yours,
BERLINER

It was in June that Dr Griebl had arrived in Germany with Miss Moog to discuss spy affairs with the Nazi spy chiefs, and to see that the screws were put properly on Berliner to make him agree to the one-sided deal. Faced with the inevitable, for he was being forced to leave the country because he was a Jew, Berliner had sadly agreed—only to be confronted with additional and new demands by the Nazi Government.

I know the above letter is authentic. Mrs Griebl produced it when we wanted to know why she went to Germany in October, 1937, and remained there until April, 1938, which was after we caught her husband as a spy leader, and what she was doing there. We tested the letter, and others she gave us, in the F.B.I. laboratories. They were completely authentic.

The correspondence she showed me revealed that the Nazi Foreign Currency Exchange demanded 50,000 Reichsmarks from Berliner. It showed that finally, in desperation, Berliner offered 10,000 Reichsmarks. It showed that, in an effort to meet the demands, he tried to get his partner, an 'Aryan,' to agree to liquidate their business. The partner refused, and so Berliner was unable to raise anything like 50,000 Reichsmarks.

Berliner had, under bitter pressure, and before the Nazi Government made additional demands for itself, signed a contract to make the uneven swap with Griebl. How Mrs Griebl and her brother-in-law then squeezed him was shown by later correspondence, which also contained an almost direct admission by the Nazi Government that the deal was being forced through in return for Griebl's spy services.

Mrs Griebl, as per Berliner's plea, finally wrote to the Currency Exchange Agency. Here is the reply she got:

> Replying to your letter of recent date, we agree that *the peculiar circumstances* in your case make it justifiable to grant you the exchange with Berliner if he is willing to pay $3000 and 15,000 Marks in the German Gold Diskontbank in Berlin.

The italicizing of the words "the peculiar circumstances" is mine. Since both Dr Griebl and his wife admitted to me that the squeezing of the Jew Berliner was in payment for

Dr Griebl's Nazi activities in America, I believe I am rather justified in presuming that "the peculiar circumstances" indicates that the official Nazi Government, including the Foreign Currency Exchange, knew and approved of the Nazi spy conspiracy in the United States. The Foreign Currency Exchange heads had to know about it, for they issued the permits which allowed currency to be released from Germany for payment to spies and propagandists in America, as you may recall the investigation into the case of the spy Rumrich definitely proved.

Dr Griebl's brother, Kurt, wrote to Berliner, enclosing a copy of the letter Mrs Griebl got from the Foreign Currency Exchange. It blackjacked Berliner with the fact that he signed a contract, without mentioning the fact that he signed it before the Nazi Government made its additional demands. Kurt Griebl's letter included a sentence which stuck in my mind as indicative of the whole tone:

> It is very clear to me that you still expected that the German Reich will do favours for you which of course could not be expected.

So that is Nazi patriotism. Griebl, posing as a patriot in America, hiding behind the fact that he was a lieutenant in the U.S. Army Reserve, sold the United States to the Nazi spy ring—but at a fine price. For this deal was not the only payment. As Griebl told me himself, he was offered also the rank and pay of a German Army captain. The pay was to accumulate for him in Germany until such a time as his usefulness in the United States would be ended, and he was recalled to Germany or had to flee there. Under the cloak of patriotism Griebl drew pay for betrayal; under the cloak of despising Jews, he robbed them.

The deal finally went through, and the summer cottage was registered in Berliner's name in exchange for a $100,000 property and $3000 and 15,000 Reichsmark ransom to the Nazi Government, but it took a long time.

In the beginning of this chapter we left Griebl on the s.s. *Europa*, sailing for Germany with Miss Moog. What happened there; how he met the august Colonel Busch, supreme chief of all the far-flung Nazi spy system, in the offices of the *Nationale Geheim Abwehr*, in the German War Ministry Building, 72 Tierpitzufer Strasse, Berlin; how he discussed spy affairs with him and began the negotiations for Berliner's property; how he conferred with Kapitan-Leutnants von Bonin, Menzel, and Pfeiffer of the Nazi Naval Intelligence; how they boasted to him of the vast and devious reaches of their spy ring, and of how they asked Miss Moog to open a swanky spy nest in Washington and lure United States officials and young Army and Navy officers into the spy web—all this has already been told.

But we have not nearly covered all the things Dr Griebl confessed to me, including many of the things he said von Bonin, Menzel, and Pfeiffer told him; nor have I yet told you of all the men we captured and the plots we discovered and the spy traces we found as result of his tips.

CHAPTER XVII

SOME of the amazing things that Dr Griebl revealed to us about the Nazi spy ring still are not completely explained. Investigation of some of his disclosures carried us only so far that we were forced to consider them seriously. We would find proof of the truth of virtually all the surrounding details —and then run into a blank wall. Consider, for instance, what Kapitan-Leutnant Dr Erich Pfeiffer told Dr Griebl that night—June 23, 1937—in the Bremen Café, when they discussed the ramifications of the spy ring in America.

"The United States must be ridden with graft," said Pfeiffer sneeringly. "The way you keep changing the plans of your Navy destroyers shows that. It keeps us busy keeping up with all the changes.

"And the money you pay your workmen! We could build the same destroyers at a fraction of the cost.

"The new destroyers your Navy plans to build within the next few months are nothing but suicide squadrons," Pfeiffer scoffed. "They are suicide craft because they are of very poor quality, misconstructed, with hulls so thin and weak that they can be damaged easily."

And then Pfeiffer, according to Griebl, went on to describe the projected United States Navy destroyers in detail. At least, Griebl, whether he got it from Pfeiffer or elsewhere, was able to tell me all about them. And Griebl was right!

It is like locking the stable after the horse is stolen, but I do not feel it right to reveal all the details in public print. However, no agency can complain if I tell you that Griebl told me we were planning to build four squadrons of destroyers, with a leader for each, and a flagship for the fleet—a total of twenty-one ships. The destroyers, he said, would be of 1500 tons each, with 52,000 shaft horse-power. The squadron leaders were to be of 1800 tons each.

How did Pfeiffer—or Griebl—know all that at that time? It is hard to tell. Griebl told so many different versions. At one time he said he understood the information came from a Nazi spy station at Bath, Me. Another time he said it came from the offices of certain naval architects, into which a spy had wormed. The firm itself is above suspicion, but it has hundreds of employees. Precautions are taken against spying there. They have been increased and tightened since, though we have no indication except Griebl's that that is where the leak was. Our desire to find that leak was one of our reasons for letting Griebl wander around loose.

Griebl told us that Nazi spy headquarters got the exact design of a newly developed under-water sound-chest apparatus, with which the presence or approach of submarines could be detected far better than by means of any previously existing device.

He said that Pfeiffer got copies of the very latest U.S. Navy device—an apparatus whereby the officer on the bridge could release immediately six depth-bombs to destroy any near-by submarine, merely by pressing a button.

Previously, orders had to be relayed from the bridge, which meant that often by the time the bombs were released, the ship had sped past the spot where the submarine was detected.

"It cost a lot of money to get such information," Griebl told us. "Pfeiffer's office pays as high as $300 a blueprint, and sometimes scores of blueprints are needed to complete just one design.

"Lonkowski told me once that he paid out $30,000 in one year for spy information to one group of men."

That's all we could find out about that incident. The trail

is cold now, and the answer will probably never be fully disclosed. But with some of Dr Griebl's other tips we were much more successful.

Otto Herrmann Voss, for instance, is serving six years in a Federal prison because Dr Griebl 'put the finger' on him as a Nazi spy. We had no idea of Voss's activities or even his existence until Griebl named him and told us he was an important Nazi aviation spy. He told us of meeting with Voss and discussions of spy work.

I asked Griebl to put Voss 'on the spot' for us, so that we could trail him and check up before we closed in. Griebl agreed at once. He agreed to everything those days, trying to save his own skin. He called Voss to his office for a medical examination—and two F.B.I. agents were sitting in Dr Griebl's waiting-room when Voss entered at eight o'clock one evening in March, 1938.

Griebl came out of his inner office, greeted Voss by name, shook hands with him, then left him to wait a few minutes, so that the F.B.I. men could get a good look at him.

They saw a man of close to forty, tall and gaunt, six feet two inches, weighing about 160 pounds. He wore silver-rimmed spectacles and had sparse blond hair, infested thickly with dandruff. "Teutonic type," the agents reported back. "Shrewd blue eyes. Pock-marked face. Poor teeth, long nose, prominent ears, yellowish complexion, taut skin. Shabbily dressed. Looks like a fanatic."

For a solid week we were able to trail him, night and day, and check on his bank account and connexions, without arousing his suspicions. We found that though Voss earned only an average of $45 a week, he had between $7000 and $8000 in the bank. He had a new car, for which he had paid cash. He had taken two trips to Germany, within a short period, with his wife. On the second trip he took his car along, paying heavy freight charges. He was gone three and a half months that time—July 15 to October 29, 1937. (He conferred with Kapitan-Leutnant Pfeiffer at Bremen that trip, we found out and made him admit later.)

Where did the money come from?

He was working in the experimental section of the Seversky Aircraft plant at Farmingdale, Long Island. Seversky was building fast chaser 'planes for the United States Army, embodying important military secrets.

On March 9, 1938, we closed in on Voss. F.B.I. Agents W. Callahan, J. T. McLaughlin, and E. Davie, who worked day and night with me on the case, and did immensely valuable work, went with me out to the Seversky plant. We got the general manager to call Voss into his office. He came in, poker-faced, apparently unsuspecting the purpose of the summons.

Voss paled when I told him who we were, but showed no other sign of emotion.

"Yes, sir," he said. His voice was thickly accented. "What do you want of me? If it is about aeroplanes I must have the permission of the general manager before I can help you."

This was a shrewd remark, but the manager merely said, "Go with the Government men, Voss, and tell them anything they want to know."

Voss nodded and said no more until we were in the car and on our way.

"Where are you taking me?" he asked.

"To F.B.I. headquarters in New York," I told him.

"But—why?"

"Because, Voss," I shot at him, "you are a Nazi spy!"

His sharp blue eyes, behind the silver-rimmed spectacles, widened under the shock, then narrowed.

He shook his head.

"That is not true," he muttered. "It is a mistake."

"We will soon see," I said.

He relapsed into what seemed to be habitual silence for about ten minutes. Then he said:

"I would like to stop at my house. I want to tell my wife."

We knew from our surveillance that his wife was not at home, and that he knew she wasn't. What, then, was his motive? I guessed there were probably papers he wanted to destroy and hoped we would let him go into the house alone. I decided to appear to play his game and let him lead us to those papers. We drove to his home, 225 Jericho Turnpike, Floral Park, Long Island.

That turned out to be correct. He hesitated when he saw we were determined to enter the house with him. But I said, "While we are here, we would like to see if you have any confidential aeroplane blueprints hidden in your house."

He could not very well refuse, realizing that we could quickly get a search-warrant, and that his refusal would look suspicious. Besides, he knew he had no blueprints in the house. So he gave his permission.

He was a very methodical man, this Voss. In his desk we found every letter, every bill he had received in the last ten years, neatly filed. We also found a diary—and that was what finally broke him. We took it along with us.

At F.B.I. headquarters he stolidly maintained his innocence under hours of questioning. It began to look bad for our case against him, since we had only Dr Griebl's statement so far that Voss was a Nazi spy.

I turned the questioning over to another agent and retired to a quiet corner with the diary, and as I flipped through the pages of the diary, I saw the following names which looked interesting:

Karl Eitel.
Herbert Jänichen.
Werner Gudenberg.

I saw from the entries that Eitel was apparently a steward on the German liner s.s. *Bremen*, and that he had visited Voss often from 1935 to 1937. Then Eitel's name dropped out of the diary, and Jänichen's replaced it. Jänichen seemed to have got Eitel's job, and to have adopted his custom of getting together often with Voss. Gudenberg seemed to be an old friend of Voss, with whom he exchanged visits and discussed aviation matters.

Then, folded between two pages, I ran into something which made me sit right up. It was a note for $185, dated three years previous. And signed to it was the name of— Wilhelm Lonkowski!

Diary and note in hand, I walked in to confront Voss. I waved the note and flipped the pages of the diary before him, staring at him grimly.

"Make up your mind fast, Voss," I said. "You've got a lot of explaining to do."

His lips tightened, and his fanatical eyes glared at me. For perhaps fully two minutes we stared at each other thus. Then his eyes dropped, and he said:

"All right. I will tell you."

And here is his story of how he became a Nazi spy, and how he aided the Nazi spy conspiracy in the United States—even while he was becoming naturalized as an American citizen.

Voss was born in Hamburg on November 5, 1899. Two brothers, Friedrich, 33, and Heinrich, 35, still live there, running a meat-business. He went to school in Hamburg, and after being graduated from the *Realschule* (high school) there in 1915, he became an apprentice machinist. In August, 1917, he was drafted into the German Army. He served with the Engineers, Battalion 9, in Finland and France, rising to the rank of corporal.

After the World War, he served in the German Army Volunteer Corps, until December, 1919, when he enrolled in

Floral Park and introduced himself as Eitel's successor. He said his name was Herbert Jänichen, and that he, too, was disguised as a steward on the *Bremen*. He produced a letter from Pfeiffer identifying him as a Nazi spy operative, and a letter from Eitel, requesting him to follow through with Jänichen.

Voss says he doesn't know why Eitel dropped out of the picture, but I know that Eitel was 'knocking down.' If given $300 by Pfeiffer, for instance, to pay a Nazi spy in the United States for services rendered, Eitel would hand over only $200, or $150, and tell the spy that was all headquarters had allotted.

I don't know how he was tripped up; I presume through the *Gestapo*, the Nazi secret police operating in New York. I don't know exactly what happened to Eitel. He was not 'liquidated,' but assigned to other duties in which he would not be handling money.

It apparently was not unusual for the spies to cheat and double-cross one another. This investigation taught me that spies are rats by nature, even when they claim to be working for love of country. The double-cross seems to be just as truly a Nazi spy symbol as the Swastika. Here is the translation of a letter from "N. Spielman" (Kapitan-Leutnant Pfeiffer), to Rumrich, which pretty well illustrates their continual suspicion of one another:

Dear Friend:

I have looked once more to your business reports, and on your behalf I must call your attention to a few business mistakes. You must above all things keep strictly separate the representatives of the various firms.

Also, there exists in Europe a certain amount of business discretion, because one firm will never tell another firm what or where it has purchased its material. For this reason you must also accept this method because whatever I purchase for my firm

THEODOR SCHÜTZ, ALIAS KARL WEIGAND

[*Left to right*] GLASER, VOSS, AND RUMRICH

does not concern any other firm. Only I, or my representative, Jenni, are responsible for it.

For this reason I beg you never to communicate to any other firm anything regarding our business transactions, what I want, or what I purchase. Also never to tell what you have sold me or what I have taken with me. Also you must never state a fixed price, because this might lead to many misunderstandings.

I shall always name to you a price of whatever the merchandise is worth to me after it has been evaluated, and you can then decide whether you can deliver this merchandise at this price.

I am not interested in what you pay for the merchandise, because every man, if he wants to live and to live up to his business obligations, must naturally make a living.

I believe that in time you will become acquainted with European business procedure. Also you should never make known your correspondence with the various firms. All correspondence must be always your own affair.

If you wish to become a good merchant you must pay heed to these little things and hints. As far as the price for the lastly mentioned furs is concerned, my representative Jenni, at her next visit there, will tell you what these furs are worth to me. As previously mentioned, I have no interest in your purchase price.

Regarding the radio business, a matter is in order and my representative Jenni will regulate this matter, too—that is, if you can take care of this item for me alone. I was glad to be able to meet your brother on February 15.

N. SPIELMAN

The letter is easier to understand if you know that in spy terminology throughout the world the word 'furs' is commonly used to denote plans, and 'merchant' means spy, and 'merchandise' means stolen secrets. The friendly, chatty tone is not natural with the autocratic Pfeiffer; it was intended to throw off suspicion if the letter was intercepted.

It is easy to see from the letter how distrustful Pfeiffer was of some of his own agents. Besides, he was jealous of the agents of other spy chiefs in other branches of the Nazi spy service. The various branches regularly cut in on one another, double-crossed one another, and stole one another's agents.

With Jänichen, Voss swung into action. Three weeks after he met him, Voss gave Jänichen details of seventy-seven Army chaser 'planes, known as Model P-35, which were being built at Seversky. Nazi spy headquarters showed great interest in these. For months Jänichen pumped him each trip for more details concerning these 'planes.

In June, 1937, Voss reported that something was wrong with the model—that it failed to develop the expected speed. He drew sketches to show Jänichen and spy headquarters how the landing-gear could be folded into the wings. He showed him how each wing had five panels, instead of the usual two, making it theoretically less vulnerable to anti-aircraft fire. He showed Jänichen how the duralumin spars were set into the wings.

Jänichen showed extreme interest when Voss talked of the petrol storage in this model 'plane. Jänichen made him show exactly how this was done. In this type of 'plane the petrol was stored in compartments, rather than in a separate tank. The compartments were located in the centre of the wings, close to the fuselage.

The next time Jänichen was still hungry for details concerning this ship. Spy headquarters wanted to know exactly how the petrol compartments were constructed and how they were armoured.

Voss told him they had no armour-plates. Cotton tape, impregnated with bakelite varnish, was used to make the fuel compartments gas-tight. He drew a sketch for Jänichen to show exactly where the bomb-racks were under each wing, and drew another sketch to show the exact location of the gun-sights.

He explained to Jänichen that each 'plane was equipped

with two machine-guns—one on each side—mounted on the motor and on the hood. He told Jänichen that .30-calibre guns were standard for these 'planes, but that a few carried .50-calibre machine-guns. He showed the spy messenger how the bullets were fed into the guns, and where the cartridge ejectors and ammunition containers were set.

It took a long time to get all that from Voss. It came out piecemeal. Some of it he admitted only after we questioned his wife and obtained a statement from her in which she said, among other things, that Voss told her Pfeiffer had promised him money and a home in Bavaria in return for information.

Even when he opened up, Voss for some reason refused to admit that he had direct spy dealings with Lonkowski. It seemed obvious that he must have supplied Lonkowski with spy data.

After capturing and grilling Voss, I had talked again to Senta de Wanger. Previously she had told me about a man who very often visited Lonkowski when he lived at her home in 1935, but could not remember his name. When I asked her if it was Otto Herrmann Voss, and described him, she said that was who it was. Voss later admitted visiting Lonkowski at Senta's home frequently, but denied that the packages he bore on those occasions contained spy data.

"It was ice cream and cake," he declared on the witness stand during his trial later. When it was pointed out that it was quite a distance from the store where he said he bought the ice cream to Senta's home, and that often he had to wait for Lonkowski, he replied:

"Well, it was the home-made kind of ice cream, which you don't expect to be hard like the other kind, anyway."

The jury apparently did not think much of that explanation.

Questioning of Voss about Lonkowski reminded me of the films found in Lonkowski's possession the night in September, 1935, when he was nabbed on Pier 86, but allowed to get away. The films, I found, were at G-2 headquarters, on Governors Island, N.Y. I sent a request for them, which had to go through several agencies, taking several days.

Voss was held on $10,000 bail at first. His wife produced a cashier's cheque for $10,000. Half was his own money, Voss said, "and half I borrowed from a friend." Later, when other witnesses mysteriously disappeared, the bail was raised to $25,000. Unable to raise that, Voss went to jail pending trial.

Jänichen, I discovered, was due in New York on the *Bremen* the day after Voss signed his confession. I went down to Quarantine and boarded the ship. I checked the ship's manifest, and found his name on it all right, listed as a "*chef de range.*"

But a line was drawn through the name in red ink, and alongside was the notation: "Did not sail." I noticed that the stamp of the American Consul, to verify the notation, was missing, but I did not want to ask too many questions, hoping Jänichen might be on board the next trip.

Later I learned that Jänichen had been on board ship all the time.

Word of Voss's arrest had been flashed to the ship in code, and the ship's manifest had been deliberately faked to prevent the United States Government from seizing Jänichen.

CHAPTER XVIII

AT six o'clock on the morning of May 11, 1938, the operator at my hotel in New York called me and told me that a Miss Kate Moog was on the 'phone, insisting she had something of tremendous importance to tell me.

I was annoyed as I said: "All right. Put her on." I wondered what in blazes she could want at that hour.

"Oh, Mr Turrou," came her high, rather childish voice over the 'phone, "something terrible has happened!"

I fought a yawn, engendered of weeks of working half through the nights on the case.

"Yes?" I said.

"Ignatz—Dr Griebl—he has disappeared!"

That stopped the yawn dead and brought me up with a jerk.

"He has been kidnapped! They have taken him on a ship! They will kill him in Germany! Oh, Mr Turrou, do something!"

She was too hysterical to handle the telephone.

"Go right down to F.B.I. headquarters. I'll meet you there," I ordered. "Talk to no one—absolutely no one—understand?"

The news stunned me. As I sprang into my clothes, I tried to figure out what could have happened. Could Griebl have fled of his own free will? It was hard to believe. He had shown no signs of planning flight while pouring out all that testimony about the Nazi spy ring. He had not tried to touch his bank account. He had not tried to get rid of his new car, or any other belongings. He was obviously passionately in love with Kate Moog, and it would have been just as easy to take her along in premeditated flight. Why, then, if his disappearance was voluntary, did he leave her behind? But most important—death faced him in Germany!

Just before I started for the office I telephoned two agents for a fast check for any signs of premeditated flight. When their report came in later in the day it showed no such signs. On the contrary, it revealed that he had some fifteen appointments with patients for that day, and two operations scheduled. I leaned heavily towards the abduction theory then.

The stories of Miss Moog and of his wife seemed to bear out that theory, at least in some respects. And since Mrs Griebl, according to her account, was the last person to see Griebl in New York, let us examine her story first. I found her at her flat, after I left Miss Moog. She was red-eyed and very pale under her make-up, and her bleached blonde hair was stringy. But whether her appearance was from weeping or lack of sleep, or both, I could not tell.

Griebl had been unusually attentive to her the night before —the night of May 10—she said. He had invited her to go with him when he drove to Greenwich Village to see a patient. That was about nine o'clock, she said.

"I was so happy to go with him, Mr Turrou," she sobbed. "I thought perhaps he was changing for the better, and through with Miss Moog and those other women."

He told her to wait in the car while he attended to the patient, and when he came out, she said, he turned the car north, towards Pier 86, North River.

"I didn't ask him where he was driving. I was too happy just being with him."

It was a clear, cloudless night, with nearly a full moon. As they drew abreast of the pier, they could see two German liners docked—the s.s. *Bremen* and the s.s. *Hansa*.

"The doctor parked the automobile across Twelfth Avenue

from the pier," Mrs Griebl said, "in front of a sort of saloon. He said he was going inside the saloon for a minute—that he had to go to the men's room."

He remained inside the saloon about fifteen minutes. When he came out, he told her, according to her story, "I have an appointment on board one of those ships. I will be back soon." That, she said, was about 10.30 P.M.

She watched him cross Twelfth Avenue and go towards the *Bremen*, which was all lit up and full of bustle, for it was due to sail in two hours. Griebl left his physician's case in the car. He had no extra clothing with him. He wore just a business suit. Her eyes followed him until he was swallowed by the pier—and that, said Mrs Griebl, was the last she saw of him.

Half an hour passed, then an hour. Activity on the *Bremen* increased. Taxis came rushing up with last-minute passengers. She saw gay *bon-voyage* parties pouring into the pier.

Midnight, and no Dr Griebl. She was tired, waiting alone an hour and a half, but decided he would be along any minute. She heard the warning cries of "All visitors ashore!" Now, surely, her husband would appear any minute. Then she heard the last cries of farewell from the pier, and the thrilling clamour that signals the moment of departure of a great liner; she saw the huge ship and its lights begin drifting away from the pier. Now he must appear, she thought, but the crowds of well-wishers who had seen the ship off came out and departed—and her husband was not among them.

Panic seized her, she said, and she got out of the car and ran over to the pier.

"I looked all over the pier, but he wasn't there. I went over to the *Hansa* and asked there, but, no, he wasn't on that boat."

Back in the car, she said, she thought it over and suddenly became suspicious. She decided, she said, it was all a plot for a rendezvous with Miss Moog. Her husband could have slipped out of another exit from the pier and hastened off to keep a tryst with the beautiful Kate.

Tight-lipped, she went grimly to a telephone and called Miss Moog's flat. Bitterly she accused the younger woman of harbouring Dr Griebl. But Miss Moog denied it vehemently. So vehemently that Mrs Griebl's conviction became shaken. She began to fear that something had happened to him. But then another suspicion entered her mind: perhaps the tryst was with still another woman.

She couldn't drive the car, so she telephoned the New Niagara Garage, 1832 Second Avenue, to send a man to drive her home. That took a long time, and when she got home at nearly 3 A.M., she was again convinced, she told me, that it was Miss Moog her husband was with.

So she telephoned Miss Moog again, and again accused her. But gradually Miss Moog's protestations and great show of fear and worry over what could have happened to Griebl wiped out her belief he was with Miss Moog, and a deep fear, she said, grew in her.

"Now," she sobbed, "I was convinced he had been kidnapped by the *Gestapo*. I was sure they were taking him to Germany to kill him or do something terrible to him."

Mrs Griebl knew about the *Gestapo* from personal experience. Her remark about the *Gestapo* reminded me of that tale. It happened on April 6, 1938, as Mrs Griebl was ready to sail back to this country after her visit to Germany to make final arrangements with the Nazi Government to squeeze the property of the Jew, Berliner, out of him as a reward to Griebl for his Nazi services.

Mrs Griebl had booked a passage well in advance on the s.s. *Europa*, and was in her cabin an hour before sailing-time from Bremerhaven, when two *Gestapo* men stalked into her cabin.

"You can't sail. Come with us!" they commanded.

Her protests were in vain. She told me later they gave her no explanation. They took her passport away from her and made her leave the ship with them.

I found out about that because I went out to Quarantine to meet the *Europa* that trip, so that I could question her before she had a chance to talk to her husband. I found her name on the passenger list, but no trace of her. Investigation through Captain Drechsel revealed that she had been taken off the ship at Bremerhaven just before sailing. A few days later I learned she was to sail on the s.s. *Bremen* from Cherbourg, arriving in New York on April 21.

On that day I went down to Quarantine again and met her. She was well-nigh hysterical. She wept as she told me how roughly the *Gestapo* men had taken her off the ship. But she became very evasive and more hysterical than ever when I tried to find out from her what happened after that, and where the *Gestapo* men took her, and what went on in the next few days, and what they said when they finally permitted her to sail. I had to give up, as she seemed about to collapse.

Later I learned she had been taken off on order from Kapitan-Leutnant Pfeiffer. Nazi spy headquarters was in a panic. They knew we had got Dr Griebl and were grilling him. They knew we had Miss Moog, too, for their *Gestapo* men and undiscovered spies were keeping them closely informed. The detention of Mrs Griebl grew out of that panic. But I was unable to determine whether Pfeiffer had some wild idea of holding her as a sort of hostage to keep Griebl from squealing, or wanted merely to drill her in what to tell Dr Griebl when she arrived back in America.

Nazi spy headquarters were positively frantic. Not only Mrs Griebl was yanked off the ship that day. Three members of the ship's crew were suddenly pulled off. First was Heinrich Bischoff, the *Gestapo* man disguised as a steward on the ship, whom we wanted to question. He was called off the ship an hour before it sailed.

Then, soon after the *Europa* pulled away from Bremerhaven, Nazi spy headquarters had another brain-wave and had a cablegram shot to the captain of the ship, ordering him to drop off his chief officer, Heinrich Lorenz, at Southampton. Lorenz was instructed to hustle right back to Bremerhaven. Somehow Nazi spy headquarters, in its excitement, got Lorenz mixed up with Franz Friske, the officer who, you may remember, delivered the advertisement which was inserted in the New York *Times* and led to the hiring of Rumrich as a Nazi spy.

We did want Lorenz, too—but not very badly—in connexion with the matter of Danielsen, the ship-designer who was to have been lured to Germany. Lorenz, you may recall, got instructions to take good care of him. Lorenz was also the chief officer of the *Europa* when we took Jenni Hofmann off, and it was to him that she wrote the note permitting us to take her things. Neither matter made Lorenz an important witness. But soon after he was yanked off the *Europa*, there came a second message, announcing he was promoted to captain of the s.s. *Chemnitz*, a German freighter. Maybe that was just coincidence, but the method was certainly odd.

I eventually got to question Lorenz, anyway. I got him when the *Chemnitz* came into Boston Harbour in May. He told me that after being recalled to Bremerhaven, he was summoned before Kapitan-Leutnant Pfeiffer, and that Pfeiffer questioned him closely as to what he had heard on his trips to America about the progress of our case against the Nazi spy ring. Lorenz tried to convince me that he urged Pfeiffer to surrender Karl Schluter, and anyone else we wanted. Perhaps Lorenz did that, for while he is a Nazi, he is more intelligent than most of them, and honestly believed such frank action would be best for Germany in the long run.

The third man yanked off the *Europa* that frantic day was Second Officer Werner Jarren. We wanted to question him concerning his conversations, while First Officer of the *Bremen* in 1937, with Jacobus Mauritz, a supervisor of construction of anti-aircraft carriers at Newport, News, Va. Mauritz says Jarren tried to convert him to Nazism and to get information, but failed.

Half an hour before the *Europa* sailed that day, Jarren burst excitedly into the office of Captain Scharf and announced he could not sail. He would not explain why. Captain Scharf suspected Nazi Party reasons, and so did not dare press the point too hard. Jarren had his job as a reward for party services, particularly as an organizer of Nazi organizations in Buenos Aires, Argentina.

Nazi spy headquarters even tried to yank a fourth man off the ship that day—but he already had been yanked off. He was Karl Schluter. They forgot they ordered him off a previous trip, so as to baulk our investigation.

Recalling all those frantic orders and drastic yanking of men from ocean liners in desperate efforts to circumvent us, it seemed entirely possible, as I talked with Mrs Griebl and Miss Moog, that Griebl might have been kidnapped. He might have been lured on to the *Bremen* on a pretext, then overpowered and kept against his will. In view of other incidents in this affair, the idea did not seem too lurid. And there was, recurring again and again, the knowledge that Griebl knew that if Germany ever found out how he had squealed, death awaited him there.

Miss Moog's story verified Mrs Griebl's as far as the telephone calls at 1.15 A.M. and 3 A.M. She said Mrs Griebl had called her and accused her of having Dr Griebl in her flat. She had herself become frightened, she said, and tried to tell Mrs Griebl that Griebl must have come to harm. She said she had begged Mrs Griebl to notify me at once, but that Mrs

Griebl had refused. And so, after a sleepless night, she had started trying herself at 6 A.M. to reach me.

That's the story as told by the two main women in Griebl's life. There were holes in it, and serious flaws, which might be due to hysteria, or to something sinister. But there was no time to sit down and grill them. The job was to try to get Griebl back.

A check-up showed that the *Bremen* was almost already two hundred miles at sea. I ordered Captain Drechsel to radiophone Captain Adolph Ahrens, commander of the *Bremen*, to find out if Griebl was aboard.

The answer came back:

Yes, Griebl was aboard—as a stowaway.

Lester C. Dunigan, Assistant U.S. Attorney, got in touch with the United States Coast Guard. A seaplane was warmed up, made ready. Dunigan and I were going to fly out to sea, overhaul the *Bremen,* and take Griebl off. We sent a query to Captain Ahrens by radio as to whether he would surrender him.

We did not anticipate much difficulty. Spies operate at their own risk and are promptly disowned by their Governments when caught. We did not yet realize how brazen, how defiant the Nazi Government was going to be towards the United States authorities, how much they would smash all precedent.

Captain Ahrens did not give us a direct answer at first. He radioed instead that the weather was very bad at sea and the visibility poor, and that it would be too hazardous for us to make the flight. His solicitude was really quite touching. But we replied curtly that the Coast Guard pilot and Dunigan and I were willing to take the chance.

Then Ahrens pointed out that he would have to stop the ship and lower a boat to put Griebl off. This, he argued, would frighten the 1300 passengers aboard, and he flatly refused to take that responsibility.

When he put it on that basis, we were licked, and the flight was off. But we radioed Ahrens to be ready to surrender Griebl to the proper authorities at Cherbourg, France, first stop of the *Bremen*. Ahrens agreed by radio to hold Griebl as a stowaway, and to surrender him to the French authorities upon presentation of a warrant.

We got busy with the State Department, which promptly cabled Ambassador Bullitt at Paris to arrange with the *Sûreté Générale* to take Griebl off at Cherbourg.

That afternoon there came a new cablegram from Captain Ahrens. Griebl, he reported, had just paid for a tourist-class passage, and so had been released from the brig. It was easier now to surrender him at Cherbourg, Ahrens reported, for if he had remained in the status of a stowaway, company rules would have made it mandatory to deliver him at the home port of Bremerhaven.

That is interesting to remember, in relation to late alibis.

United States Attorney Lamar Hardy summoned Johannes Schröder, general manager of the Hapag-Lloyd in New York, his first assistant, Christian Ahrenkiel, and Captain Drechsel, in his capacity as Port Superintendent, to his office. In no uncertain terms Mr Hardy advised them to inform their home office in Germany of the seriousness of this matter, and of the fact that the United States Government was bitterly aroused. Mr Hardy made it plain that he was convinced that members of the crew of the *Bremen* aided in the escape—or kidnapping—of Griebl, and that grave repercussions would ensue if Griebl were not surrendered.

Schröder, Ahrenkiel, and Captain Drechsel so notified the German office; I know, because I saw the cablegrams. They told their home office their business would be ruined if the German Government slapped the American people in the face by refusing to surrender Griebl. They also radioed Ahrens to co-operate in every way possible with the American authorities. On the strength of that I engaged passage on the s.s. *Normandie*, to sail to Cherbourg and get Griebl when he was surrendered there.

It did no good.

On the high seas Captain Ahrens got a cablegram from his home office at Bremen, warning him that the steamship line had just received firm instructions from the Nazi Government not to surrender Griebl to either American or French authorities at Cherbourg. Captain Ahrens was commanded not to permit Griebl off the ship in any circumstances until the *Bremen* touched German soil.

And so, though we cabled a warrant to Cherbourg, with the consent and aid of the State Department, it did no good. Griebl remained safe on the ship until it reached Bremerhaven. The Nazi Government had stymied us again.

Even more direct proof of the official Nazi Government's concern and interest in the escape of the spy Griebl is available. The files of the Hapag-Lloyd agency here showed that the Bremen office wired the New York office to get in touch with Ambassador Hans Dieckhoff, at Washington, for further advice and instructions in the Griebl matter.

But suppose we now go back and see what really happened to Griebl on the night of his disappearance. How did Griebl really get on board that ship? Was he actually kidnapped— or did he sail willingly, after long planning to flee? Was his wife's story of how he disappeared true? How much did she know of his plans—and did she play an active *rôle* in the plot?

Well, part of the answer is that Mrs Griebl was lying. She knew that Dr Griebl was not coming back off that ship. The whole story about his suddenly having to go to the men's room of the saloon across the street from where the *Bremen* was docked, and suddenly remembering he had to visit some one on the *Bremen*, was obviously a lie from the beginning. But the question was—whose lie, Griebl's or his wife's?

The story of Jack Hayes, night mechanic at the New Niagara Garage, threw some light on the picture when we questioned him. It was he who came and got Mrs Griebl and the car across the street from the *Bremen*'s pier, and drove her home. He said she appeared calm and normal and did only one strange thing. That concerned the doctor's medicine and instrument bag, which was in the back of the car, where he often left it overnight.

Hayes thought it strange that Mrs Griebl insisted on taking it with her.

"The doctor won't be using it for a long time," she said. "He went on an emergency trip!"

Later she shipped a trunk to her husband, through friends. Then, in June, 1938, I caught her and friends trying to ship Griebl's new car to him. And finally I discovered her buying a passage on the s.s. *Bremen* to sail to Germany on June 14. That is why Federal Judge Leibell held her in $5000 bail as a material witness for a while—an action which Seward Collins, apologist for the Nazis here, promptly shrieked was persecution. What do you think your Nazi pals in Germany would do to her there in similar circumstances, Collins?

Incidentally, we released her later and allowed her to sail to Germany when she complained of feeling ill.

The question arises: why, then, did Mrs Griebl telephone Miss Moog and accuse her of harbouring her husband? We cannot be sure what she said to Miss Moog. Remember, she had discovered that Griebl was in love with Kate Moog and wanted a divorce so that he could marry her. Could Mrs Griebl have telephoned Miss Moog to gloat over her—to tell her that he was 'safe from your clutches' now? I wonder just what those two women did say to each other that night over the telephone.

I know that as far back as April of the same year, while coming back to this country, Mrs Griebl wept to Wilhelm

Böhnke, leader of the Storm Troopers on the *Europa*, that her husband was in love with another woman, and that she wished she could get him to Germany, away from "that woman."

And I know that Böhnke played the leading *rôle* in getting Griebl aboard the *Bremen*, to which he was transferred after the trip during which he met Mrs Griebl.

Let's go into what happened that night of Griebl's disappearance on board the ship.

Twenty minutes before the *Bremen* sailed from Pier 86 that night of May 10, Böhnke came to Captain Drechsel in his office, at the pier, acting in a peculiar manner. He was always somewhat in awe of Captain Drechsel, because Drechsel is an upright man who knows his job and brooks no nonsense.

"I thought I ought to tell you, Captain Drechsel," Böhnke said, "that two members of the crew have just informed me that two strangers appeared on board the ship this afternoon and said they were making arrangements for Dr Griebl to leave on the *Bremen* to-night as a stowaway."

Drechsel was immediately indignant.

"I will not countenance such goings on, Böhnke," he stormed. "If Griebl is on board I will hold up the ship and notify Mr Turrou of the F.B.I."

But Böhnke swore that he had searched the ship and Griebl was not aboard.

Böhnke became all tangled up in his stories when I took him off the *Bremen* the next time the ship reached New York and questioned him. That's why he was held in $15,000 bail for a long time; it was so obvious that he was lying and had a major share in the spiriting away of Griebl.

This Böhnke is of some interest. When I boarded the ship at Quarantine, he was dressed in civilian clothes, waiting. He knew he was in for it. Though listed on the ship's manifest as an ordinary pantryman, he had two big rooms, one used as an office and one for his quarters. Pantrymen get about

100 marks a month; he got 300. For this big, six-foot, fat brutal-looking bruiser, almost a ringer for Göring, was a big shot in the Nazi ranks. He was not only in command of 180 Nazi Storm Troopers on the *Bremen* (why Storm Troopers on a passenger ship?) but also *Ortsgruppenführer*. On questions of discipline, political actions on the ship, and handling of the crew, he superseded even the captain.

And what training equipped him to be such a power on a ship carrying as high as 1300 passengers a trip across the ocean? He was born in Bremerhaven, thirty-three years ago. His education ended when he grew too big for public school. He claims he was a salesman until 1922; my information is that he was a pedlar. Then he went to sea as a fireman on a freighter. After that he was a dish-washer on the *Seidlitz*, *Sierra Ventane*, *Sierra Morena*, *Sierra Cordoba*, *Sierra Nevada*, and *Columbus*. The *Sierra* ships were German ships plying between South America and Germany.

Böhnke was one of the earliest Hitlerites. He joined the *Stahlhelm*—the Steel Helmets—as far back as 1927 and remained with them until Hitler came into power. He was unemployed at the time, but under Hitler he got a job on a ship as a pantry-man—and also leader of the eighty Storm Troopers on that ship.

His limited ability and intelligence kept him a dish-washer or pantryman, but otherwise he rose rapidly. In November, 1934, he came aboard that great German liner as a dish-washer —and leader of 180 Storm Troopers.

In 1935 he had a run in with Leopold Zeigenbein, of the *Bremen*, then commodore of the North German Lloyd fleet. Böhnke left the ship and went to a party convention at Nurem-berg, for he was an important party man. Captain Zeigenbein is no longer either commodore of the fleet or captain of the *Bremen*.

After three weeks at the convention, Böhnke was enrolled

THE NAZI SPY CONSPIRACY IN AMERICA

in a Nazi political school at Hamburg for four weeks. Then he was sent to a school for party leaders at Hirschberg, in Silesia, South-eastern Germany, and spent four weeks there.

That equipped him, a dish-washer and pantryman, to be not only Storm Troop leader, but the powerful *Ortsgruppen-führer* on big ships, and that is what he became.

Böhnke's first tale to me was that at 11.30 on the night of Griebl's disappearance two strangers walked up to him in his office on the *Bremen* and asked him to help them stow away Griebl on the ship.

"Do you know Karl Friedrich Wilhelm Herrmann?" he says they asked him. "Well, we are working with him."

Böhnke claimed he refused indignantly, and that when he saw Captain Drechsel ten minutes later he told him about it.

"Now, listen, Böhnke," I snapped. "I have proof that Griebl was already on board the ship by that time. What kind of a cock-and-bull story do you call that?"

"It's the truth," he said sullenly.

But when I confronted him with the fact that he told Captain Drechsel it was two members of the crew who had been approached by the strangers, and that the approach was in the afternoon, he became nervous.

"Captain Drechsel is wrong," he muttered.

"Do you want to match your story against Captain Drechsel's before the Grand Jury?" I demanded. "Do you think they will believe you instead of a man like Captain Drechsel?"

That seemed to pull him up short. Suddenly he hit his head with his fist.

"Oh, I remember now," he exclaimed. "It was two members of the crew, and it was in the afternoon. I—I must have been thinking of something else!"

"You certainly must have," I agreed. "Who were the two?"

He thought a long time. Finally:

"Walter Otto and Johann Hart," he mumbled.

The two obviously bewildered seamen denied any knowledge of what Böhnke was talking about when I questioned them. I believe their denials.

Now let's try to piece together the picture of Griebl aboard that ship. Where he hid—or was hidden—until the ship was well at sea, we do not know. Captain Ahrens said that the first thing he knew about Griebl's presence on board the ship was 4.30 in the morning of May 11.

At that time, Captain Ahrens told us, Dr Griebl appeared on deck and surrendered himself to Fourth Officer Kruger.

"He told Kruger he was an American citizen and had gone on board ship to visit some friends and fell asleep," Captain Ahrens said. "He had no baggage and no passport. All he had was a pistol permit issued by the New York authorities, a driving-licence, a card showing membership in a medical association, and $180 in cash. Kruger locked him up under guard.

"The next day Griebl offered to pay $156 for tourist-class passage, and was released and treated as a passenger thereafter."

One of the first things Griebl did was to write a letter to his wife, and another to Miss Moog. They were virtually identical, and both, I feel sure, were intended to be turned over to me. Read the one he sent his wife and see if you don't agree with me that it is a crude, deliberate smoke screen:

Dear Mitzi:

I am undergoing very unpleasant experiences—every one wants to cover himself up and nobody knows nobody. I am in custody and locked up under guard.

I was forbidden to communicate with Dr Pfeiffer or anyone else. My papers, such as Medical Association card, pistol permit, driving-licence, have been taken from me because they say I am a stowaway. They refused my request to communicate with

249

Dr Pfeiffer at my own expense; only after I told them that I was willing to pay $156 for a tourist-class ticket, and which money I voluntarily surrendered, was I given the right to become a passenger. They also permitted me then to wire. That I could not do because I had no more money.

How can I get along with only one collar and one shirt and without credit being accorded to me? They told me on the bridge: "I have to treat you that way as your identification papers are probably fictitious and no one knows you personally here. To permit you to communicate with Dr Pfeiffer is out of the question. We do not know who he is or where he lives, or if he exists at all, and that also holds good for the other Germans you have mentioned.

"On the other hand, you cannot communicate with the United States until you re-establish yourself as a passenger."

This is experience No. 1. I will take note of that.

Tell Turrou I will come back in due time.

With heartiest greetings.

IGNATZ

Now what do you make of that? Sometimes, when I read it, it sounds as if Griebl was tricked aboard by promises that all would be glory and sweet cream, and now was sore because, once on board ship, everybody disowned him. Sometimes it sounds as if he is complaining to his wife, as if she had a hand in getting him into this. Sometimes it sounds like a plain fake, meant to throw me off the trail.

In certain parts it is obvious that Griebl was lying. He says he had no money left for messages after paying $156 passage money. But the ship's log says he had $180 on him when he appeared.

I am suspicious, too, because Mrs Griebl and Miss Moog turned Griebl's letters over to us readily. I am no longer in the F.B.I. service, and so have no official interest now, but I would give quite a bit to be able to get hold of Dr Griebl and question him, and try to find out just what that was all about, and just how his flight was managed.

If you want to believe that letter to his wife, there are indications that somebody made promises which were not kept. But why did he risk going on board that ship at all? Was he so vain, so egotistical, so sure he could outsmart everybody in the world that he thought he could escape punishment in both countries, after the way he betrayed both?

Did he think Nazi spy headquarters would never find out how he squealed to us, and betrayed some of its most valuable spies to us in a desperate effort to save his own hide? Did he think he could lie his way out of it there? Did he think he could laugh off the cruel Nazi inquisition, the torturers, the dungeon—and the Nazi headsman?

Dr Griebl was lying when he wrote that the ship's authorities would not let him communicate with Kapitan-Leutnant Pfeiffer. Or maybe the ship's officials had a sudden change of heart. For at Cherbourg, the first stop of the *Bremen*, Griebl handed a message to Johann Kleiber, assistant wireless operator. It was addressed to:

Dr Erich Pfeiffer
c/o *Marine Nachrichten Stelle*,
Bremen, Germany.

And it read:

Arriving on steamship *Bremen* Tuesday without passport—without baggage—tourist cabin 656.

DR GRIEBL

That was not the only message he sent. The man had plenty of gall. At Southampton he handed a message to Karl Gerstung, chief wireless operator of the *Bremen*. It was addressed to:

F.B.I. Chief, New York.

And it read:

Will return in time to testify at trial. Please arrange with American Consul at Berlin for my passport, as I left too hurriedly to get one.

You might think that made us angry. It didn't. We had to laugh. You had to know the man to understand what made him try something like that. He had that insolence and egotism, in a high degree, we found so often in these Nazis.

It was not that he seriously thought it would work—but yet he considered everybody except himself such a fool that he thought he might as well try it. Bruno Richard Hauptmann had some of that almost insane conceit and contempt for the intelligence of every one except himself. It is in line with Griebl's daring to go to Germany though death awaited him if Pfeiffer or other Nazi spy chieftains found out how he squealed on them, believing he could outwit them.

He is now practising medicine in Vienna (at least he was in early autumn, 1938). He had applied for permission to practise medicine in Germany several years previous, when he was in hot water in America for his Nazi propaganda activities. The permission came through suddenly and secretly, by way of the office of his close friend, Dr Hans Borchers, Nazi Consul-General at New York, shortly after the spy case broke.

I wonder how long, now that the Nazi spy chiefs know how he betrayed them, he will remain free and alive?

But let us go back to more pertinent facts.

Pfeiffer met him at Bremerhaven. This was after Captain Ahrens refused to surrender Griebl at Cherbourg. Incidentally, I am not blaming Ahrens. He was between two fires. He had to obey orders.

Pfeiffer made the arrangements well. He and the Nazi Government treated the United States Government with the same kind of scorn and almost insane conceit that Griebl treated the F.B.I. in his telegram asking us to get his passport for him.

At first they instructed the Bremen office of the North German Lloyd to cable the New York office thus:

Advise American authorities Griebl will be taken to Bremer-haven, where proceedings will be instituted against him for boarding ship without permission. If American Government desires Griebl, they should institute extradition proceedings with the German Government.

That was ridiculous. They must have known full well there can be no extradition in espionage cases, because espionage is considered a political offence. Or, rather, all we wanted Griebl for at that time was as a material witness. We couldn't extradite for that—all we asked was they should let us get at Griebl, an American citizen, wanted by the United States Government. If he refused to waive extradition, that would be another matter. But here was the Nazi Government protesting blandly it knew nothing about a spy ring, protecting the master Nazi spy in America against us, refusing to let us get to see him.

They went all the way. At first preparations were made to put Griebl in jail there for entering without a passport. They had to punish him for that, they contended blandly. Afterwards, they would deport him to us, they promised solemnly.

The idea of jailing him for entering without a passport was, of course, ridiculous. That is almost never done where the entrant can prove identity. They didn't put Griebl in jail. The moment the hue and cry died down a bit, and our State Department relaxed pressure, Griebl was, according to official dispatches, "released upon payment of sixty marks' fine."

Nothing more was said of deporting him to the United States. The bluff had worked, and that was that.

And where did Griebl get the sixty marks to pay his fine? Remember his letters said he had no money left?

Apparently as reward for successfully engineering the feat of getting Griebl safely back to Germany, Kapitan-Leutnant Pfeiffer was promoted to full Kapitan in the Nazi Naval Corps. (Kapitan-Leutnant corresponds to the rank of Lieutenant Commander in the United States Navy, and Kapitan to the rank of full Commander.)

CHAPTER XIX

MY request for the films found on Lonkowski nearly three years previously was granted by the military authorities, and finally they arrived from G-2 headquarters, where they had reposed in a file all the time. I turned them over to the F.B.I. photographic expert with instructions to make enlargements from them as big and as clear and as quickly as possible.

When they were ready, I stared at them a long time. I turned them this way and that way and the other. Still they made no sense. I spread them on the floor, and began putting them side by side, and one above the other.

And suddenly, even to my eye, inexpert on aviation matters, the answer became apparent. Put together, they formed blueprints of sections of an aeroplane.

But what 'plane?

I called Voss in and confronted him with them. I watched his reaction intently, for he was a phlegmatic man, well able to mask his feelings. But I could tell the shot did not strike home. He was interested, as a crack aeroplane mechanic would be, but made not the slightest sign of recognition or anything to indicate he had a guilty conscience regarding those blueprint photographs.

Not content, however, I sent them to the Seversky Aircraft Corporation officials. They shook their heads. It wasn't one of their 'planes.

"But what 'plane is it?" the agents persisted.

"It looks like an experimental scout-bomber," they said. "It might be the Curtiss X-2, manufactured for the United States Army by Curtiss-Wright at Buffalo, N.Y."

Something clicked in my memory. "Buffalo. . . ." Senta de Wanger had said that Lonkowski made a trip to Buffalo shortly before he was caught.

It seemed to me there was still another link tucked away in my mind—something picked up which was not clear at the time but which subconsciously I had filed away until something else might make it clear.

But I couldn't get it until, requestioning Voss one day, I flipped through the pages of his diary and saw the name Werner Gudenberg again. Something clicked in my mind. To this day I don't know just what it was that made me connect Gudenberg with Buffalo.

"This Gudenberg," I threw at Voss suddenly. "Who is he?"

"I met him while I was working for the Ireland Aircraft Corporation at Roosevelt Field, in 1928," he said.

Ireland Aircraft . . . that was where Voss had met Lonkowski! Now I was positive Gudenberg was my man. I started an agent at once for Buffalo with a twofold mission: to see if the Curtiss-Wright people recognized the photographs, and to locate Gudenberg.

The agent telephoned a report early.

"Yes, the films are copies of the blueprints of X-SB-C-2, sometimes known as Curtiss X-2, built by Curtiss for the United States Army."

"Fine," I said. "Now what about Gudenberg?"

"Not so good," replied the agent.

"What do you mean?"

"He's gone. He quit in January, 1936. It surprised his superiors, because he was a crack man and in line for big promotions. He gave no reasons and didn't say where he was going."

My heart sank. Had another one escaped? But then I reasoned that he probably was still in the country, since there was no reason for flight as far back as 1936, and that he would be working at his trade in an aeroplane plant. A skilled 'plane worker ought to be well known and easily traced in that limited field.

And so it turned out. We picked up his trail the same day and discovered he was a foreman at the Hall Aluminium Aircraft Company at Bristol, Pa. Agent M'Laughlin and I caught a Philadelphia train immediately and went down to get him.

I was surprised when I saw him. He was such a clean-cut chap, with an open, honest face. He had a jolly, pretty wife, American-born, of whom he seemed extremely fond, and a beautiful boy-child whom he obviously loved deeply. He had a nice little house, well-furnished, which he was buying, and seemed in every way the highest type of American working man, and a real home-loving man.

We talked to him in an upstairs bedroom of his house from 1 P.M. to 7 P.M. He broke easily, and while he told some preposterous lies, they seemed a desperate effort to save himself and his family rather than to protect the Nazi spy ring. He seemed genuinely sorry.

Here is his story:

He was born on November 10, 1899, in Hamburg. His parents and his brother still lived there. He went to the public schools there, and to a trades school, where he learned mechanical drawing and took a general technical course.

In May, 1917, he was drafted into military service. But he was so good a technician that pretty soon he was transferred to the Navy Yard at Cuxhaven, where he did electrical work on torpedo boats until the end of the World War.

From then until 1928 he worked as a coppersmith at Solter Altona, near Hamburg, with his father in the plumbing-trade and in his own shop making brewery equipment. But in 1928, hearing the tales of wealth in the Golden Land, he headed for the United States on the s.s. *Hamburg*.

He arrived in America on October 27, 1928, and within two months he had a job as a mechanic at the Ireland Aircraft Corporation. He was delighted to find working there two men from Germany of approximately his own age, who had come over at almost the same time as he did. The men were Voss and Lonkowski. Voss he had known in Germany, and he was particularly delighted to see that homely but familiar face.

Within a year, at the high wages then prevailing, he had saved enough for a trip home. When he returned to America he worked at various aeroplane factories—Berliner-Joyce, Glenn Martin, Bellanca Aircraft, Keystone Aircraft, and, beginning in August, 1932, Curtiss Airplane and Motor Co., Buffalo.

He was already marked as a crack man in aeroplane work, and he went to Curtiss as a foreman, with thirty men under him.

He lost trace of Lonkowski, he told me, but kept corres ponding with Voss. He heard nothing concerning Lonkowski, he claimed, until suddenly one day in July or August, 1935, Lonkowski drove up to his home, 252 Victoria Boulevard, Buffalo, N.Y.

I believe Gudenberg's version that Lonkowski sort of worked him into the plot before Gudenberg quite realized what was happening. This Lonkowski was an able, quick-witted, highly persuasive chap, trained to such recruiting-work.

After a few beers, during which they waxed quite senti-mental over the Fatherland, Lonkowski dropped a hint that he was a Nazi secret agent. Then he let slip that Otto Voss, Gudenberg's old friend, was giving him a lot of information. He told Gudenberg how safe it was because he, Lonkowski, personally took the information to the German ships docking at New York and turned it over to trusted agents.

He talked of the Fatherland and every German's duty to

it. He got Gudenberg to boasting how many military aero-
nautical secrets he had access to. Then suddenly he cracked
down with a demand that Gudenberg should bring some blueprints home from the plant. The rest he would take care of.
He put it in a light that would make Gudenberg appear an
ingrate and a traitor to Germany if he did not aid.

And so Gudenberg began. He brought home blueprints,
and Lonkowski would come and photograph them. That is,
he said Lonkowski photographed them. I believe Gudenberg
took the photographs himself. The negatives we examined
were mostly under-exposed or over-exposed, and the camera
had not been focused properly. Lonkowski was an able
photographer, while Gudenberg was a rank tyro.

Gudenberg admitted that he gave Lonkowski a lot of verbal
information and drew sketches for him. He denied giving
secrets to anyone else. He admitted Lonkowski promised he
would be paid for his services by Nazi spy headquarters, but
denied he got any money. I'm not sure that he did. His
home and style of living were in keeping with his income,
and he had less than $700 in the bank, when we nabbed him.

He testified with every appearance of frankness before the
Federal Grand Jury. Like myself, the Grand Jury, Mr Hardy,
his assistants, and all others who worked on the case were
impressed with his apparent basic honesty and regret over
what he had done. We trailed him carefully for a while. No
official Nazi sources made any move to aid him, as they did
others in the ring. He did not contact anyone in the spy ring.
He did not try to touch his money in the bank. We took
into consideration the fact that he was buying his home, had
a good job, seemed passionately fond of his wife and child,
and so decided it was safe to let him go back to his home and
job until we wanted him again.

He stood the test. When we sent him word that we
wanted him to testify again before the Grand Jury on May 26,

R* 259

he promptly came up to New York from Bristol, appeared before the Grand Jury right on schedule, and testified readily. We relaxed all vigilance on him.

The next day, May 27, Captain Ahrens, of the *Bremen*, was before the Grand Jury undergoing further grilling on the flight of Dr Griebl. I was sitting in the Grand Jury anteroom, guarding other witnesses and doing some last-minute questioning of them. They were pantryman-*Ortsgruppenführer* Böhnke, Chief Officer Erich Warning, and Chief Wireless Operator Gerstung, of the *Bremen*.

The door opened and an attendant told me that a man who said he was Captain William Drechsel, Superintendent of the Hapag-Lloyd Port in New York, wanted to see me. I was always glad to see Captain Drechsel, but I wondered why he, a busy, dignified man, came running up to the United States Court House to see me rather than use the telephone.

He was a bit breathless when he came in, and there was a cablegram form in his hand.

"I just received this, Mr Turrou," he exclaimed. "It is from Captain Koch, of the *Hamburg*, which sailed last midnight. You said you wanted me to inform you right away of all stowaways."

"Yes," I said, instantly interested.

"This says they found a stowaway on the *Hamburg* this morning. It says his name is——"

Captain Drechsel paused to refresh his memory from the cablegram.

"It says his name is—George Gudenberg!"

I must have jumped three feet. I'm sure my eyes popped.

Mr Hardy, too, in more dignified fashion, hit the ceiling. At first he couldn't believe it. I got Captain Drechsel to radio the *Hamburg*, now 300 miles at sea, for an exact description of the stowaway. It was our Gudenberg all right.

Captain Koch reported that when he found him, Gudenberg had no passport, no luggage, and no money.

I telephoned the Hall Aluminium Aircraft Co. He had not shown up there since he started the day before for New York to testify before the Grand Jury. His wife, the plant superintendent told me, was obviously frantic with fear and worry. When I talked to her afterwards that fear and worry seemed real enough. I doubt she had any idea he was going to flee to Germany. She remained bitter and volunteered to testify at the trial anything she knew about Voss and Lonkowski.

I doubt very much that Gudenberg had any idea of flight when he started for New York to testify. I am convinced that he had no such idea while testifying before the Grand Jury, or when he left the Federal Building that afternoon. I believe Gudenberg was observed by Nazi *Gestapo* men whom we had not discovered. I believe they saw him enter to testify before the Grand Jury and then followed him. I believe these *Gestapo* men then prevailed upon him, by threats or force or other persuasion, or by a combination of methods, to flee. I don't believe Gudenberg went voluntarily and in his right mind—and subsequent events aid that belief.

The next morning Mr Hardy informed the State Department at Washington of the seriousness of the situation and of the conduct of the Nazi Government, and the officials and members of the crews of the German steamship lines, in giving assistance and encouragement in escapes from our jurisdiction.

Drastic action was recommended. Promptly our State Department gave authorization to go as far as deemed necessary to get Gudenberg off the *Hamburg* at Cherbourg, and gave Mr Hardy permission to call U.S. Ambassador Bullitt, at Paris, and Ambassador Kennedy, at London.

On May 28 Mr Hardy got Ambassador Bullitt on the trans-

Atlantic telephone. He asked our Ambassador to use every lawful means to get Gudenberg off the *Hamburg* at Cherbourg.

Even a suave diplomat like Bullitt got hot under the collar when he heard Hardy's story, particularly when Mr Hardy explained the background, including the disappearances of Rossberg and Griebl. Ambassador Bullitt promised to do his best to get Gudenberg off the ship and have him held for us at Cherbourg.

Then the call to Ambassador Kennedy was ready. He took it the same way our representative in France did. He promised to insist on getting Gudenberg off at Southampton if the Nazis by some trick baulked us at Cherbourg.

To make doubly sure, again, Schröder, Ahrenkiel, and Captain Drechsel were summoned before Mr Hardy. He told them in no uncertain terms that unless an immediate stop was put to the practice of aiding and encouraging Nazi spy ring witnesses to flee back to Germany on German ships using our ports, the officials of the German steamship lines would be prosecuted and the American public officially informed that the German steamship lines not only permitted this flaunting and defiance of the United States Government, but even encouraged it.

They were a badly worried group. Schröder and Ahrenkiel pledged their words of honour that they would do absolutely everything they could to put a stop to it. They swore they would impress the seriousness of the situation on the home office in Bremen and would urge with all their authority that Gudenberg be surrendered at either Cherbourg or Southampton.

They kept their word. I took pains to verify that.

They sent lengthy cablegrams, in Hapag-Lloyd code, to the directors of the company at Bremen. They told the German office of the heavy bail in which we were holding officers of the *Bremen*, on which Griebl escaped. They pleaded that unless the German office co-operated and handed Gudenberg over, business here would be ruined. Their attorney sent a lengthy cable of his own, advising co-operation with the United States Government, on legal, moral, and business grounds. He cited terrific loss in business because of the revelations so far as to how the German steamship lines were implicated in this dangerous Nazi spy conspiracy against the United States.

All three reported that they were having trouble with bonding companies whom they approached to put up bond for men we held as witnesses, and that one company flatly refused to write bonds for them because of the way Nazi witnesses were skipping on German boats.

"United States Government has issued warrant for his (Gudenberg's) arrest in Cherbourg," read one of the cables, "and United States Attorney urgently requests our company does not object or interfere as in Griebl case but hands man over to American Consul, maintaining Gudenberg United States citizen and stowaway and company therefore should have no interest whatsoever in carrying him to Germany (stop)."

But it did no good.

The Hitler high command cracked down with orders, and we did not get Gudenberg.

At one port Gudenberg was reported in sick bay, too sick to talk or be taken off.

At the other he was still in the ship's hospital, and when interviewed, said feebly that he didn't want to be taken off, but wanted to go to Germany.

And so, though technically he was a stowaway, the steamship officials insisted on taking him to Germany.

I wonder what made Gudenberg, a husky, healthy, comparatively young man, who looked clear-eyed and absolutely fit when he testified before the Federal Grand Jury on May 28, so very sick so soon after he got on board a Nazi ship?

CHAPTER XX

WE were angered and disturbed by the series of strange flights, and by the Nazi Government's flagrant efforts to baulk our investigation, and some of us were inclined to feel that we had been checkmated. But Mr Hardy did not lose his perspective. He conferred with officials in Washington, then told us:

"The important point is that the American public must be made aware of the existence of this spy plot, and impressed with the dangers. Our Government and citizens must be awakened to the fact that it is imperative that we have an efficient counter-espionage service, to protect us against such vicious spy rings as this. We will go ahead with the case."

On Monday, June 20, 1938, the Federal Grand Jury indicted eighteen persons on charges of conspiring to steal military codes and confidential information concerning the armed forces, ships, and aircraft of the United States. The indictments charged that the conspiracy began on January 2, 1935, a few hours after Chancellor Adolf Hitler, at a New Year's reception in the Presidential Palace in Berlin, called for "honest co-operation" among nations.

Those indicted were:

Kapitan-Leutnant Udo von Bonin, the War Ministry, Berlin.

Kapitan-Leutnant Hermann Menzel, the War Ministry, Berlin.

Kapitan-Leutnant Dr Erich Pfeiffer, the *Marine Nachrichten Stelle*, Bremen.

Ernst Muller, the *Marine Nachrichten Stelle*, Hamburg.

THE NAZI SPY CONSPIRACY IN AMERICA

"Sanders," first name unknown, the *Marine Nachrichten Stelle*, Hamburg. (Later information was that it was an alias for Muller.)

"Schmidt," first name and headquarters unknown.

Herbert Jänichen, Germany.

Theodor Schütz (*alias* Karl Weigand), Germany.

Karl Schluter, Germany.

Karl Eitel, Germany.

Wilhelm Lonkowski (also several aliases), Air Ministry, Berlin.

Dr Ignatz T. Griebl, escaped to Germany.

Werner George Gudenberg, escaped to Germany.

Mrs Jessie Jordan, Scotland, serving four years in a British prison for espionage.

Günther Gustav Rumrich, in jail in America.

Johanna (Jenni) Hofmann, in jail in America.

Erich Glaser, in jail in America.

Otto Herrmann Voss, in jail in America.

Indictment of most of them was, of course, purely a gesture to show how indignant the United States was over the plot. There was naturally no hope of getting Nazi officials such as von Bonin, Menzel, Pfeiffer, and Muller to America for trial. "Sanders," if he existed, "Schmidt," Jänichen, Schütz, Schluter, and Eitel were safe in Germany before we were able to get at them, and most certainly would not risk coming back. Lonkowski had fled nearly three years before, and surely would not surrender himself. Mrs Jordan was already being punished in England, and Griebl and Gudenberg had escaped us. That left us only Rumrich, Miss Hofmann, Glaser, and Voss to place on trial.

There were others concerning whom there was long debate as to whether indictments should be sought against them. But in the cases of some, demonstrable overt acts were hard to prove, and others, while their acts were reprehensible, were technically free of law-violation. It was decided to proceed only against those against whom proof of guilt seemed iron-clad.

The day after the indictments were handed down, I resigned from the F.B.I. My work on this case was done. I was tired. I had given the best years of my life to a service I loved, but now my doctor was warning me ominously. I had worked an average of sixteen and a half hours a day, Sundays and holidays included, for the past three and a half months. And I wanted to give the warning this story exemplified to me to the United States. To be able to do that fully and without restriction, it was necessary to resign.

I expected to be attacked by Nazis and defence counsel in the case, but even my years of experience with defence methods did not prepare me, I must admit, for the type of campaign of vituperation and personal character attacks which promptly began against me, openly led by Henry C. Dix, counsel for Jenni Hofmann.

Trial was delayed while Dix got in touch with Dr Griebl. According to Dix, he accomplished that by writing to the *Gestapo* in Germany. The *Gestapo* knew where he was, and promptly forwarded Dix's letter to him. Griebl was in Vienna, practising medicine. Dix's letter urged Griebl to send him anything derogatory to me that he knew, and contained a list of questions which insinuated I took a bribe from Griebl to let him escape. Griebl, apparently puzzled, wrote back that it was not true: that I had nothing to do with his escape, and that he was sorry he had violated the confidence of the F.B.I. and the United States Attorney's office. He gave a copy to the United States Consul; that's how we knew what was in that letter.

Dix insisted that it was important to the defence that Griebl be examined. Desiring to lean over backward to be fair, the Court appointed a commission consisting of Dix and

Assistant U.S. Attorneys John W. Burke and Lester Dunigan. Dix preceded them to Germany. Burke and Dunigan took F.B.I. Agent J. T. McLaughlin with them when they sailed. The commission examined Griebl in Berlin.

At last, on October 14, before Federal Judge John C. Knox and a jury from which anyone who might be accused of being prejudiced against Nazis was carefully excluded, the case went to trial in the United States Court House at New York.

A more competent Judge for the task hardly could have been chosen. As Chief Assistant United States Attorney, he was in charge of spy prosecutions during the World War. He refers to that as "my dime-novel experiences."

Early struggles made him understanding and sympathetic. Orphaned at ten, he sold newspapers, worked on railways, struggled through college, became a justice of the peace—all before he was twenty-one.

When, in 1918, President Wilson appointed him to the Federal Bench, he became the youngest Federal Judge. He was only thirty-six. A demon for work, he never absents himself from Court. He also finds time to teach at four law schools, and is considered one of the most learned Judges in America. Asked last May if, having served twenty years and being now eligible for pension, he would retire, he replied to newspapermen, "Hell, no ! I wouldn't retire on a bet."

Rumrich pleaded guilty and took the stand to testify against the others. He told his story over a period of three days. Dix hammered at him in vain in cross-examination, finally resorting to insinuations and remarks to the jury that Rumrich was a Communist and had concocted the story with me. Judge Knox was forced to censure him for conduct unbecoming an Officer of the Court, because even in law school it is impressed on fledgling lawyers that under Court rules they must not make speeches to the jury except when

267

summing up, and that at no time may they make statements to the jury unsubstantiated by the evidence.

The examination of Griebl was introduced in evidence. Government counsel did not fight against it, taking the attitude that it would prove itself worthless. Apparently it did, for the jury laughed out loud at several points, and the members of the jury, questioned by newspapermen after the trial was over, said it struck them as "palpably cock-and-bull." In it Griebl accused me of bring a radical, a Jew, and of tipping him off to flee. He said he knew I was a radical because he had heard I was; that I was a Jew because he could always "recognize one by facial landmarks." If I am a radical, I am certainly a most Judas-like one, for it was I who exposed sabotage on the United States dirigible *Akron* by radicals, as Court and F.B.I. records show; and I won high praise and promotion in the F.B.I. for my work on cases involving dangerous radicals. As for Griebl's recognition of me as a Jew "by facial landmarks," I have a Slavic cast of countenance, and just to keep the record clear, I happen *not* to be a Jew, either by birth or faith.

Nowhere in the deposition did Griebl make it clear how I was supposed to have tipped him off to flee. When Dix put repeated, pointed, insinuating questions to him as to whether he gave me a bribe, Griebl refused to answer for quite a while, then finally said I had hinted I could fix it for $5000—the exact sum mentioned by Dix in his questioning. And further, under Dix's persistent grilling, he repudiated much of what he had told me, and which I had read off in his presence to Reed Vetterli, and which was incorporated in his unsigned statement at F.B.I. headquarters.

Agent McLaughlin was sent along with the commission for a dual purpose. He was to act as *aide* to the commission, and also to see if there seemed to be anything in the charges Dix was making about me and saying Griebl would corroborate.

The F.B.I. takes no chances on its men. It wanted to be sure, despite my long record and rating in the service. So McLaughlin made it a point to become friendly with Griebl during the days over which the taking of the 17,000-word deposition dragged, and to chat with him as often as possible. They all stayed at the same hotel in Berlin, and relaxed together. McLaughlin kidded him about the supposed bribe, and they soon reached a stage of frank talk. One morning at breakfast, before Dix, Burke, and Dunigan came down, they had quite a frank talk.

McLaughlin took the witness stand late in the trial and testified concerning that conversation. Griebl told him, McLaughlin declared, that he was lying in the deposition.

"I am in a position where I can do nothing else," McLaughlin quoted him as saying, "I have been indicted in the United States and I have found a refuge in Germany. Of course, I didn't give Turrou $5000, or any other amount. From the contact I had with him during his questioning of me, I think he would have clapped me in jail immediately if I had even suggested a bribe.

"But you can understand that if I did not say that, and did not contradict the things I told the F.B.I., what would happen to me here."

And Griebl, McLaughlin testified, motioned with his hand that his head would be cut off.

Griebl wound up, McLaughlin said, with the statement: "Personally, self-preservation has always been my god."

The trial droned on. Dix accused me of everything under the sun. He said I made up the whole story and framed the defendants, particularly Jenni Hofmann, who, he swore, was innocent. The Government quietly put on more than a dozen F.B.I. agents, and a number of stenographers and attachés who were present during various phases of the questioning of the prisoners, and witnessed the signing of the confessions by the

THE NAZI SPY CONSPIRACY IN AMERICA

defendants. It put on a parade of witnesses, each of whom substantiated some detail of the case.

Dix charged that I had, under another name, tried to commit suicide twenty-four years ago. He charged that I was dismissed as a United States Government attaché and interpreter on a Government service in France right after the War. He put on witnesses to prove those things—and they flatly contradicted him.

Then he charged that the indictments were illegal because United States Attorney Hardy had been in the Grand Jury room while the jury was deliberating on them. Challenged for making a statement like that before the jury without proof, Dix retorted, "All right, I'll prove it." And to prove it, he called as his witness Dr N. L. Lederer, German-born member of the Grand Jury.

But Dr Lederer denied Mr Hardy was in the Grand Jury room. It turned out Dix was mixed up on his dates. Dix, red-faced, said he thought the indictments were voted on Monday, June 20. Actually, they had been voted on Friday, June 17, but not released until Monday. Mr Hardy had been in the Grand Jury room on June 20, as was his right and duty, but had *not* been in the Grand Jury room on the Friday preceding, when the Grand Jury was deliberating in secret.

Dix, as he had had to do before, was forced to apologize to Mr Hardy, the Court, and the jury.

Just before opening his defence, Dix moved for a directed verdict of acquittal of Jenni Hofmann. His argument was novel. It was based on the contention that the crimes alleged by the Government were committed on board a German ship under compulsion by Nazi officials, and that therefore the courts of the United States were without jurisdiction.

The jury had been sent out of the Court-room, and Judge Knox felt free to express himself without fear of influencing it.

"It would be a fine state of affairs, wouldn't it," he demanded, "if Germany could do anything it wanted to over there and we could not do anything about it over here? That's the way some people in this country would like it, but I can't understand the theory under which the German Government can send its ships over here laden down with spies and we cannot act because the German Government told the spies what to do.

"We would be in a bad way indeed if we could not punish anyone who committed acts harmful to us on direct orders from his own Government. It would be a fine state of affairs if that doctrine were enforced. The Germans could come over here with their fingers crossed and say their Government crossed them for them.

"Motion denied."

In his charge to the jury at the conclusion of the trial, Judge Knox again leaned over backward to be fair. He ordered the jury to disregard the nationality of the defendants and to give them "consideration equal to that of American citizens."

He summarized the evidence, as is his duty under American law, without comment, except that in the case of the testimony of Rumrich he pointed out that Rumrich himself admitted that he was often quite a liar. "Examine his testimony with the utmost discrimination," Judge Knox warned the jurors.

On Tuesday, November 29, the jury retired to reach a verdict. It took only a few minutes for the jury to reach a verdict on Otto Herrmann Voss and Miss Johanna Hofmann. The verdict was:

"Guilty."

It took the jury longer in the case of Erich Glaser. It was the next day, after asking that the testimony concerning him be read to it again, that the jury made up its mind on him. But the verdict was again:

"Guilty."

While the jury was out deliberating, Judge Knox relaxed and explained in an interview why he had—in his own phrase—"leaned over backward" in charging the jury. The tall, grey Judge explained that it was because he "wanted other nations to know that America provides a fair, honest, and humane trial for all, regardless of nationality or the offence charged.

"In some countries spies are given a secret trial and shot immediately. A few months later an announcement is made of their death, and that is all we hear about it.

"I am certain foreign countries were represented in this Court-room and knew what was going on daily. I am convinced some of the daily spectators at the trial were spies for those foreign countries. I believe I could point them out. They took notes and watched everything that went on in the Court-room."

Judge Knox's imagination was not playing tricks on him. Trained F.B.I. men spotted those spies, too. There were a couple of them at the Press table, in the guise of foreign correspondents, as well as half a dozen among the spectators. Those among the spectators worked hard, too, poor devils. There were always more people trying to get into the Court-room than the room would hold, and so, except for reporters and attachés and others with special passes, it was a case of only those who came first getting in. The spies would arrive two hours before the opening of Court daily and stand waiting patiently at the head of the line. They didn't even get a chance to eat during the day, or answer the calls of nature. The moment a recess was called, in mid-morning, noon, or mid-afternoon, they would march out with the rest of the spectators and promptly take up places in the corridor near the door so as to be the first to get in again.

"However," continued Judge Knox, "I want the world to know the American way of doing things. Our courts are open, our justice is the best we know how to give."

On Friday, December 2, Rumrich, Miss Hofmann, Voss, and Glaser were brought before him for sentence.

It was a solemn, nervous scene, with the four defendants standing there before him with hanging heads. Miss Hofmann was weeping. The Court-room was jammed.

"Had these defendants been apprehended within the confines of Germany," Judge Knox began, looking sternly at the four spies, "their fate would have been much more fearful. As it is, the agents of a totalitarian state are receiving the mercy of a democracy. There is no sawdust sprinkled in our prison yards."

He described the crime of espionage as one of the most contemptible, and remarked that this was not his first contact with Germany's secret agents.

"I recall quite vividly," he said, "what they did between 1914 and 1918. In fact, the technique shows little improvement over the bungling efforts of Bernstorff and Boy-Ed during the War."

For Miss Hofmann, who stood with bent shoulders, sobbing into her handkerchief, he expressed sympathy.

"She was thrilled to think she served her Government," he said. "If she alone were involved, I would be glad to withhold the sentence and return her to Germany. But her fate must serve as an example for the benefit of stewards and other employees of the Hamburg and North German Lloyd Lines."

Then he sentenced her to serve four years in the Federal Prison for Women at Alderson, W. Va.

In Voss, he said, he saw a man "inspired by a dream of *Deutschland über Alles*."

He sentenced Voss to six years in a Federal penitentiary.

Of Glaser, he pointed out that the jury recommended mercy for him, but that on the other hand he had received requests for a heavy sentence to serve as warning to others in the Army. He decided to let the jury's request for mercy weigh more heavily.

He sentenced Glaser to two years in a Federal penitentiary.

When Judge Knox came to Rumrich, he said he was taking into consideration the fact that Rumrich, pleading guilty and testifying against the others, aided the Government. "For this," said Judge Knox, "I must pay the price."

Then he sentenced Rumrich to two years in a Federal penitentiary.

The sentences were eminently merciful. Each defendant could have been sentenced to twenty years under the law.

Later Judge Knox told the Press: "I am glad that the Government prosecuted this case so that the people of this country might have an appreciation of what is going on within the borders of this country, which is supposed to be at peace with all the other nations of the world.

"I am glad that persons coming to this country on ships, soldiers in our Army, mechanics in our aeroplane factories, will learn that engaging in espionage is dangerous work; that when they are caught they will be punished."

United States Attorney Hardy declared: "The conviction in this case is a condemnation of the German espionage system working in this country, directed by high officials residing in Germany. It serves as a warning to any nation or faction engaged in or contemplating such activities in the United States.

"We have no counter-espionage in this country, unfortunately, and as long as that is so the United States is an open field for foreign spies.

"We have only scratched the surface. We cannot deny that these defendants are obscure. In their obscurity lies their value. The leaders of this ring could not be available in the United States as stewards on ships, mechanics in aeroplane factories, privates in the Air Force.

"Only through men like Voss could information about our military aviation reach Germany. Only through the treachery of a man like Glaser could Kapitan-Leutnant Pfeiffer obtain information about our Air Force. Only through the diligence of a girl like Miss Hofmann could the German Intelligence maintain contact with its far-flung agents."

There is, as I said before, no glamour to spies, and there never was. The spies of fiction exist only in fiction. The real spies are mostly like those in this case. The mystery, the racing drama, the thing called glamour which traditionally is credited to spies, grow only out of the incompleteness of the accounts of other spy cases. If you could get all the facts in other cases, as you have in this, the 'glamorous' spies would turn out to be much like those I have just told you about.

Now this case is over. As Mr Hardy said, we only scratched the surface. It was enough, I hope, to impress the Government and the public with the need for a larger and better equipped G-2, and a first-rate counter-espionage service. There is evidence that for every spy we exposed, dozens more lurk hidden there.

Many puzzling angles remain.

To me one of the most intriguing angles is how Rumrich was able to feel so sure that Nazi Germany wanted spies here.

"What made you think," I asked him, "that the *Völkischer Beobachter* would turn your letter over to Colonel Nicolai and Nazi spy headquarters?"

He looked surprised.

"Sure they would," he said. "I was offering valuable services."

"Don't you realize," I pointed out, "that if such a letter came into an American newspaper office it would be thrown into the waste-paper basket, or hung up as a big joke?"

"I suppose so," he shrugged. "But it's different in Germany."

275

"What made you think the Nazis wanted spies here?"

Again he looked genuinely surprised.

"Sure they wanted spies here!" he exclaimed.

"But how do you know?"

He looked at me as if I were incredibly stupid.

"Why, anybody in the Bunds or in Yorkville knows that!"

"But how—and why?" I persisted.

I got no satisfaction. He seemed willing but unable to explain. It seemed very simple and natural to him. I got the impression—strengthened again and again as I questioned others in this case—that it is an ingrained feeling among Nazis that America is a potential enemy—or victim. That point in Nazi psychology has me stumped. I can't figure it out—unless the Hitler doctrine that they are destined to conquer and rule the world, "without mercy or pity to our foes"—the "*Morgen die ganze Welt*" philosophy—has driven them berserk.

I asked the gentlemanly captain of one of the German liners, after I discovered that many of the captains, like virtually all decent, higher-type Germans, secretly hated and despised the Nazi *régime*.

"How do you explain it, Captain?" I asked him.

"They're madmen, Mr Turrou," he replied sadly. "This is a bitter era for my beloved Germany."

www.ingramcontent.com/pod-product-compliance
Lightning Source LLC
Chambersburg PA
CBHW052031090426

42739CB00010B/1861